Fowl Play

FOWL PLAY

Scott Capurro

HEADLINE

079155093

First published in 1999
by HEADLINE BOOK PUBLISHING

10 9 8 7 6 5 4 3 2 1

ISBN 0 7472 7571 8

Typeset by Palimpsest Book Production Limited,
Polmont, Stirlingshire

Printed and bound in Great Britain by
Clays Ltd, St Ives plc.

HEADLINE BOOK PUBLISHING
A division of Hodder Headline PLC
338 Euston Road
London NW1 3BH

This is for Mark Farrell,
who should have been dead years ago.
And for my grandmother, who, hopefully,
won't have time to read it.

This is Fowl!

When asked to suggest a saucy dish that will most likely satisfy the appetites of both the heartiest eater and the pickiest of nibblers, we almost always recommend that flesh that is winged. But not just any game will do. Some birds are difficult to acquire. Others only appeal to provincial tastes. However, the chicken is a cosmopolite. A favorite dish in many countries. The chicken's popularity perhaps rests in its versatility. Many experienced gourmets from around the globe enjoy adapting this fresh fowl to satiate their adroit, seasoned palates.

Of course, the first step in preparation is finding a bird in prime condition. Whether you procure your chicken in fields far from home, purchase your young domestic at the neighborhood market, or lure the feathered creature out of the nearest coop, you must first consider its potential. This is where any connoisseur worth their salt will begin their relationship with this most pliable of main courses.

PART ONE

About Poultry

When sizing up your chicken, make sure the bird is not past its prime. Look for moist skin, soft legs and feet, and flexible bones. Beware of skin that is hard, bruised or scaly, or that has long hairs sprouting from it.

CHAPTER ONE

Chicken must be plucked

'"Yellow",' he said.

'Huh?'

'That's our code word. "Yellow". When I say that, you stop.'

'Okay. Stop what?'

'Whatever you're doing. That means that the fantasy is over, or that you've gone too far.'

'Fine.'

Later, he moaned, 'Stop.' So I did.

'No, don't stop now. Keep pulling. Only stop when I say "yellow".'

But when I saw tears, I pulled out.

'What are you doing?'

'You look upset.'

'I'm fine. Don't stop!'

'Unless you say "Hello"?'

'No. "YELLOW"!'

'Sorry. "Yellow". Got it.'

CHAPTER TWO

Now, cut off the head

I am just kicking myself for always asking for 'paper'. Christ, look at all these fucking paper bags. Drawers and drawers of these useless brown sacks. Why do I bother saving them? I could never produce enough garbage to fill them. Maybe I've started collecting paper bags, unconsciously, like my grandmother does. Just for the sake of having them. Just to prove that I exist: I shop, therefore I am. Maybe I *am* that crazy.

But I don't shop all the time. I eat out too often. Maybe they're to-go bags. Nope. Wrong. They actually come from Safeway. See? The Safeway logo is stamped all over them. That's where I buy toilet paper and toothpaste. And gin. Stuff like that. And I suppose household goods and gallon-size bottles do require a large sort of carrying bag. But I must cook sometimes, because these stacks of paper sacks had to have been filled with more than just toiletries and booze at some point.

Actually, the only food items I ever have around here are sweet snacks. Treats I buy while filling up my gas tank. Crap that fits in small containers. Cookies. And cup cakes. Those little dark brown cup cakes with cream in the center and a white swirl over the top. Do you know the ones I mean? I really like those. And ice cream. That's another weakness of mine. That's why I'm getting fat.

And that's why I have so many of these annoying little paper bags, too. Stuffed inside the big ones. Like here. Alongside my refrigerator. And in this broom closet, too. Big and little, new and old. Jesus, they're everywhere!

If I really cared about the motherfucking environment, I wouldn't just say 'paper', and then shove all the bags away somewhere. I would fill the little bags with minor bits of garbage, and then put several of those in a big paper bag and throw the whole lot in the garbage chute. Is there a garbage chute in the building? Why don't I know that? I've lived here for eight years. Maybe I could ask a neighbor where the garbage goes. If only I talked to my neighbors. But that's my mother's doing. She told me never to talk to neighbors. They might have wives, and before you know it, you're getting death threats.

Maybe I should just throw all these bags away. Right now! That might clear my head. I could stuff them all inside one another, and toss them down that chute, if it exists. Maybe there is an incinerator at the end of it, and then all the bags would burn! Along with my little problem, which I could shove in with the bags.

Oh, who am I kidding? Apartment buildings don't have incinerators anymore. I mean, what is this? *The Bad Seed*? Landlords don't burn rubbish in the basement. This isn't an *I Love Lucy* episode. Unfortunately. This all makes a lot less sense than anything Lucy ever did.

And anyway, burning the bags or just throwing them away would defeat the purpose of asking for paper bags in the first place, since they're supposed to be reused to store garbage. They're supposed to replace plastic garbage bags. That's called 'recycling'.

Fuck that. I fucking hate recycling, because now I'm fucked. I've got all these paper fucking bags, and nothing that resists grease stains. I'd kill for plastic. Anything plastic and bag-shaped. Handles would be good. Something white and elastic, that could hold weight and wouldn't sag too much. All these brown, recyclable, environmentally correct bags are driving me up the fucking wall. I don't even have plastic wrap. What the fuck is this kitchen coming to?

I need a maid. And a happy childhood. A maid who could obtain both a plastic bag and an airline ticket to Bolivia would be ideal. A mother with orange juice and crackers would be nice. An OJ and vodka would be nice, too. A maternal maid with a cocktail in one hand and a piece of vinyl Samsonite carry-on luggage in the other would be fantastic.

Where's that bowling bag? A bowling bag would work just fine. Who am I kidding? I don't own a bowling bag. I haven't been in a bowling alley in years. I can tell you're not the type who would have bowled. It's way too uncool. That's probably why it's affordable, but bowling always seems like the kind of thing you do when there is nothing else to occupy your time. Bowling is way past masturbation on the things-to-do list. It's past everything. It's past nuclear war. In fact, if I'm bowling, you'll know that someone has dropped the bomb. My skin is peeling away from my body because of radiation poisoning. I've buried my entire family, like Jane Alexander's character was forced to do in that depressing atom-splitting film *Testament*. All the movie theatres have shown their last matinee. And yes, that includes those shitty revival houses that proudly feature stale popcorn, lots of stairs and hand dryers! The next time I want to blowdry my hands, I'll call my therapist. Sounds like a fetish to me. In fact, if I am bowling, then I've already called my therapist. I've called my agent. I've blended my parents' ashes into a pitcher of margaritas. It's too late for a tooth extraction.

Now it's time to knock down some pins!

I think the last film I saw was *Testament*. I can only afford rentals. Where is that gin anyway? Have you seen it? *Testament*, I mean. Not the gin. Actually, have you seen the gin? Oh, here it is, near the video of *Testament* that I rented. Last month. Jesus, the late fees must be huge by now. Renting it will cost me about five times what I would have paid to see it in the theatre. Now I really need a drink. Shall I pop this movie into the VCR? I'll mute the sound. It's nice to have some background visuals. And who needs to hear that bleak dialogue again anyway? It's the most humorless movie ever. I never would've rented it if the notes on the video jacket weren't so alluring. They said this film was about the decay of rich white heterosexual families in Seattle. Or maybe that's what I gleaned from the front cover. Either way, I thought, hell, this looks pretty amusing. I figured the least it would do was make me feel better about my own life.

But how could I compare my problems to a suburban mom who buries all her kids in her garden behind her house after Russia drops the big H? I don't have a back yard. All I felt after that dreary movie was envy for how good Kevin Costner looked in the aftermath of a nuclear explosion. Every hair – and he still had a lot – was in place. It reminded me that I'd never be in a film. Even with a tan, and all pumped up from the gym, the best I've ever looked was 'manicured'.

And film work would help a lot right now. Movie stars can get away with almost anything. And rich people probably have loads of plastic. Plastic bags, plastic tits, plastic hair. Hell, if I were rich, I could fill a Louis Vuitton and drop it off at the airport. Some Filipino security guard would be glad to take care of this as long as they could keep the bag.

But I can't get my hands on the cash to purchase a signature suitcase. That's why I'm in this mess, if you want to know the truth. It all started in that boy bar, the Pilsner. I go out to bars because they're cheap. Well, cheap for me. I'm totally broke, so my best gay friend, Gregg, buys me all my drinks. And pot. And speed. I only use the speed in the morning. Not necessarily the morning in my own time zone. But then that's the beauty of living on a *round* planet – it's always morning somewhere when I do speed.

It's not like I *need* the drug. It just perks me up, like coffee used to. And why is speed so different from caffeine anyway? It's all bad for you, and if I'm going to knowingly use something that's gonna kill me, I'd rather it be glamorous, like an illegal substance. Coffee is so mundane. It's been around for ever, and you can buy it anywhere. But speed is modern and fickle. And romantic. At least, that's the way it feels when I'm packing it up my nose in afternoon traffic on my way to therapy.

Gregg runs the volunteer department for the Stop AIDS program. They're the non-profit group that tries to educate people in the city about safe sex. Like San Franciscans need more information about HIV. Why don't they try educating born-again teenagers in North Dakota? Why hand out condoms in the Castro? I mean, those faggots know the odds. They're gonna swallow come, whether or not Stop AIDS says it's safe.

Gregg and I used to argue about this when we were dating, years ago. 'Dating' – Jesus, I hate that word. Makes it sound like we were teenagers. 'We dated.' It's embarrassing. We actually hung out for a couple of weeks. He lived next door to me when I moved in here. We had sex before I had a chance to unpack. Then he helped me paint my apartment. But by the time we finished, I knew too much about him to have sex with him again. We became kind of intimate kind of fast, so the idea of sucking his cock seemed incestuous.

We're better off as friends, especially because he's so political, and that really bores the shit out of me. Turning sex into a political act just ruins the whole orgasm. He wanted monogomy and respect. Snore. And he got really angry when he found out I'd fucked someone else. And not because I'd cheated. No.

He said he was angry because casual sex is degrading. Uh, yeah, that's why it's fun. How can I enjoy fucking a stranger in a public toilet if they're *proud* of what they're doing. Yech. The turn-on is the shame.

That's why Hasidic Jews are like my biggest fantasy. Whenever I play a comedy club in New York City, I always wander down to the Lower East Side, to a street off Houston. That's where all the Hasids buy their heroin and cruise the dirty bookstores. What could be better than getting a blowjob in an alleyway by a strung-out Jew who's full of self-hatred? Black suits and long, curly sideburns just make me hard. To me, they mean repression. And repressed guys will do just about anything, when given the chance.

I never told Gregg about my Jew fantasies. He would've judged me, told me I was being anti-Semitic, and tried to 'counsel' me, the way he does his volunteers. He drives me crazy. He actually thinks a gay community exists. Can you imagine? Men are men, plain and simple. A male community, yeah, but a gay one? That's pushing it. We all objectify everything, the way men are taught to do. Gay, straight, we all want the same thing. Beer and blowjobs, and keep 'em coming.

One thing all men *don't* want is to be told what to do, and that's why I thought Gregg's idea about condom distribution was all wrong. He thought, and he still thinks, that all bars should display condoms proudly, in a fish tank near the door, so that queens can grab as many as they need. Some bar owners resisted him, refusing to ruin their well-planned décor with anything as vulgar as a bucket of prophylactics, and he had the names of these 'homophobic clubs' printed in the local queer press. I thought that was such bullshit. It's not the bar owner's job to save people's lives. And bars in San Francisco will provide condoms upon request, like in other cities. Often times, though, the condoms wind up on the floor, still in their wrappers, unused, ignored. These faggots get drunk so they can have unsafe sex, not the other way around. Condoms are an annoyance to anyone who doesn't already have them. Distributing them the way Gregg did, and still does, is a waste of time and money.

We don't argue about it anymore. We've agreed to disagree. But sometimes, on the weekend, when I go out with Gregg and listen to him interview boys in bars about their sexual habits, I still cringe when he hands out a few condoms along with his advice. I kind of back away, and hide under a palm, or outside, on the deck. I stand in the cold, facing the foggy night, smoking with the other two or three exiled Californians who still enjoy a cigarette. I try to keep a low profile. The last thing I need right now is for some second assistant director from *The Tonight Show* to see me in a gay bar. I'm just about to get my first chance at a three-minute stand-up spot on that show. And that's just about all any comic needs to make him a star. I don't want to sacrifice my professional future for cock, so when I'm cruising, especially with Gregg, I keep my head down.

The weird thing is, some guys just confuse my quietness with sullenness, and they assume I'm an artist. They figure my 'still waters' must be the result of my struggle as a poet or a painter, so when I'm out, I usually get at least two or three phone numbers from artsy wannabes with names like 'Jonah' or 'Cody'. Unfortunately, we can't drink when doing this volunteer stuff. Well, actually, we're not supposed to, but we do. How can anyone stand a gay bar sober? I have two drinks to Gregg's one, because I'm part Irish. And anyway, the alcohol enhances my artistic pose. My eyelids drape, my slouch becomes pronounced. Gregg claims I appear lost in deliberation, as though I'm wondering how to rhyme this couplet, or what brush stroke to use on that profile. Actually, all I'm usually wondering is: 'Why aren't I on a fucking sitcom yet?' But desperation is never appealing. Instead, I become a remote drunk. The whiskey doubles for my soul.

The great thing about booze is that everyone looks so much better after I've thrown a couple of shooters down my throat. And I look better as well. And I'm a lot nicer when I'm loaded. Alcohol is like MSG. It's easy to use, and it enhances the flavor of everything it touches. However, when I'm drunk, I slur. So I must smoke pot. It's a rule. The pot makes my mind work faster, and my speech sound clearer. At least, that's how it seems to me. Of course, I'm stoned and drunk, so I might be misjudging myself.

But I don't think so, because, by 2 a.m., I always have lots of ribbed-shirted boys to chose from, if that's what I want. And when I'm ripped, that's almost always what I want, because dope makes me so horny. And more likely to drag home an unlikely candidate. Young men that Gregg describes as 'riddled'. They appear overcome by some dreadful disease. Pasty, puny little bodies, topped by huge heads with sunken eyes and pitted skin.

But I think my ego is more at work than the pot when I'm making my choice of a partner. I like to be the pretty one in any relationship. Like Clinton. Which means I've had to endure some scary-looking motherfuckers in my lifetime. I have slept with men who were so ugly I couldn't sleep. Guys who were so homely, they looked like there should've been a foundation named after them. After I fucked them, I wanted to donate something. Like a kidney. And when you're hung over, a pockmarked ginger with yellow teeth – I'm sorry, tooth – is a particularly frightening wake-up call. Bolero at 7 a.m.

So I don't often let anyone stay over. In fact, usually I cannot wait until the current cocksucker in my bathroom wipes up and takes off. Maybe that's because I don't love myself enough. At least that's what Oprah would say. I think it's because I don't love Oprah enough. Either way, I never expect a relationship that starts in a bar to go anywhere. Most queers that go out are creepy.

CHAPTER THREE

If the chicken is young, then store the head for good luck

I first met you in a queer bar. I think it was the Detour. It's my favorite dark, druggie dump. There's that chain link fence running down the center. Something to hold on to. Gay men are so romantic. Most guys just stand around, staring at the ground, hands stuffed in pockets – theirs and other people's – swaying to the same three dance tunes played over and over. The whole atmosphere is kind of like a gay *West Side Story*. Well, gayer. Gayest?

Compared to all that, you seemed so kind and unaffected. Like a puppy. I thought you were the most normal person I'd ever spoken to while out on the scene.

Of course, later I learned what a total lying freak you were.

So when I saw you again, by chance, just a couple of nights ago, over Gregg's shoulder, partially concealed by the pinball machine and the pool table at the Pilsner, my left eyebrow must have sprung up, alarmingly.

I thought, 'What the fuck is Taylor doing here? He has a boyfriend, after all. Why won't he leave me alone?'

Gregg saw me staring. 'He's a wild boy, that one.'

'What do you mean?' I played dumb. I couldn't remember whether or not I'd told Gregg about having met you at the Detour.

'Well, he gets around,' Gregg said, while chewing ice. 'He'll sleep with anything.'

'Have you fucked him?'

'Only once. I kept calling, but he didn't call me back.'

'That's for the best. He's a bit too young.' I realized how mean that sounded, especially since I didn't know your age. And Gregg is only thirty-two. But he's an old thirty-two. He looked hurt, so I added quickly, 'And anyway, I bet he was a boyfriend already.'

'It doesn't matter, Tom. He's a slut, and that boyish act of his bores me.'

I sauntered nearer to you. Gregg watched me, ignoring our other friends. We were with some of the guys from Stop AIDS. They actually irritate the fuck out of me. They're all couples, and it's like pulling teeth to get them to come out for a drink. When they do, all they talk about is their pets – 'our children' – and their vacations with their pets. That's one reason why my eye, and then my body, started wandering toward you. I had to get away from those assimilationists before I puked.

And when we finally spoke, Gregg looked on with a combination of disdain and admiration. He just hated us for wanting each other. Of course, he could only see my face, not yours. I kept smiling, as if things were going really well, because, well, I'm a professional. Never let them see you sweat, you know?

But after our conversation, when I returned to Gregg, I told him the true story.

Well, the true-ish story. As true as I tell most stuff. I mean, hell, I'm a Scorpio. I have to keep some aura of mystery around me.

'What happened?' Gregg asked. 'I saw you tap him on the shoulder.'

'I had to tap twice until he turned around to see who the annoying person was.'

'Oh. That's harsh. Then what did he say?'

'Nothing.'

Gregg rolled his eyes. 'Men are such dorks. And what did you say?'

'I said, "Hey".'

'Clever. And . . .'

'And he just looked at me blankly. Then he said, "How ya' doin'?" Then he turned back to his staring position.'

'And you kept trying?'

'Yeah. Well . . .' I felt myself slipping into one more lie, 'I realized I'd met him before.'

Gregg leaned back on one heel, and crossed his arms. 'Uh huh. Go on.'

'Yeah, well, anyway, I said, "Taylor, it's me. Tom." And he acted like he remembered me.'

'How sweet.'

'Of course, I knew he still had no idea who I was. So I just continued the façade to torture him. I said, "What are you up to, Taylor?" And he goes, "Oh, nothing. How about you . . . ?" And I'm like, ". . . Tom".'

'You had to remind him of your name twice, too. Tap twice. Name twice. At least he's consistently rude.'

'I know. Hot, huh? Then he says, "So, Tom" he says, "What are you doin'?" And I wanted to impress him, right? So I told him I was off to LA in a week to do some TV stuff.'

'That's a lie.'

'Well, Gregg, it might be a lie for now, but who knows? Something may come up by next week. Plus, you know how young guys love that TV stuff. His eyes just lit up. Any mention of even potential film or TV credits make most fags under the age of twenty-five fall to their knees.'

'And he was no exception?'

'Nope.'

'Men are whores.'

'No, Gregg.' I reminded him. 'All men are pigs, and all women are lesbians.'

'Right. So what was the outcome?'

'I'm making him dinner on Saturday night.'

'Tom, you are pathetic. This kid doesn't give a shit about you.'

'Wait until he tastes my pot roast.'

But we never did get to the meal, did we? I mean, how do I serve pot roast to someone wearing a dog collar?

When you showed up last night, dressed like a *Mad Max* extra, I thought, it's so strange what happens to boys in San Francisco. All their parents' wildest nightmares about what might happen to their sons usually does come true. Boys are curious. They'll try everything. Even a jaded, tired old comic, like me.

CHAPTER FOUR

Twist off the neck, close to the body

I've been trying all sorts of new things myself lately. That's what happens when you've got too much time on your hands. I've been cooking. Well, I've made some toast. But even toast gets boring after a while, so I bought a cooking video, to learn how to make more exotic dishes. Turned out it was a dirty film, with these guys coming all over a pizza and some strawberries, and then devouring everything. That's what I get for buying my cooking videos in a porn shop. I guess the fact that the video jacket featured two nude blond chefs should have alerted me. But I thought, well maybe it's Swedish cooking, and you know how the Swedes love to strip. Don't they? Anyway, it's back to toast, but I've started adding toppings. Nothing as wild as my own semen, but I'm a slow learner. And a poor shot.

I've also been going out, at night, alone, without Gregg. I don't tell him. He'd get jealous, the way exes always do. He'd want to know all the details, and then he'd berate me for spending too much of my time chasing around younger guys. At least, they all look younger than me.

That's what happens when you've got too much time on your face.

Sorry if I like a little flesh-to-flesh contact. Excuse me, but fuck this 'Phone sex instead of the bars' crap. That's Gregg's modus operandi. He tells me that phone sex has saved his life. He thinks I'm slutty, in a time when being a slut can be detrimental to your health. Whatever. The way I see it, the point of using condoms is that you can be a tramp without worrying about AIDS. So I usually use condoms. Unless I know the guy, and he seems clean. Christ, the thought of having completely safe sex for the rest of my life totally depresses me.

I think Gregg just hates sex. The couple of times we fucked, we had to be in the dark, with the curtains drawn and all the doors bolted. Anything that would've distracted us from what we were doing, which, at the time, seemed like film-developing, had to be eliminated. God forbid we actually made eye contact while blowing each other. He might've felt over exposed. For some of those faggot politicos, actual sex is just way too scary. They can't eroticize the risk, so they try to minimize the act. That's why those queens at Stop AIDS can be so clinical about sexual contact. It's like any body function to them. It's like pooing, or sneezing. Just one more thing some people do each day.

Well, some people. But not cautious Gregg. Sometimes, I'm almost sure he avoids physical contact because he actually hates his body. He will only take off his clothes in front of someone he can trust. And since the Pope hasn't been in town since 1967, Gregg's dick hasn't had an audience for quite a long time. He won't even shower at the gym. Can you imagine? I have most of my day sex at the gym. Isn't that the point of going to the gym? If you go to a gym, you are either preparing your body for sex, or cruising for bodies to have sex with, or having sex with the bodies you've been cruising. I'm sure I'm correct about this point. Haven't they done studies? Oh God, I sound like my grandmother, Virginia. She's always quoting fictitious findings to support her meager arguments.

'Honey,' she always says, in her most sympathetic of southern drawls, 'it's not that I'm racist. I love the darkies. It's just that they can't drink. They're actually allergic to alcohol. They're missin' a gene, or their DNA is weak. I've seen the studies. In the *Times*, maybe. There were pie charts. I'm sure of it.'

Virginia goes to the gym. And she lifts teensy weensy barbells over her head, so that her triceps don't get flabby. She doesn't want anyone to see loose flesh while she waves goodbye. She wants to be remembered enviously.

Of course, all I'm thinking as I wave goodbye to that racist old bitch is, 'I wish she'd drop those little weights on her skull. Or maybe she should lift them with her head. There's some loose flesh that could use some tightening up.'

And though Gregg shudders whenever I mention Virginia and her 'research', I remind him that both he and my grandmother have one thing in common. They are both looking for Mr Right. And until Gregg finds the male version of Mother Teresa, Mr Right Hand is about all he can stomach.

I feel sorry for Gregg. He's missing out on so much. Falling in love is fine for those guys with the time and patience of an underpaid babysitter, but in the meantime, have some fucking fun. Phone sex? That's for faggots in Oklahoma, who'd have to drive through about thirty postal codes just to get a pathetic grope from a pale hand slid under a toilet-stall door at a truck stop. Actually, that does sound kind of hot. At least, the truck stop part.

But why pay these outrageous San Francisco taxes, unless we take advantage of the hedonistic pleasures that are available twenty-four hours a day? Hell, between here and the Detour, there are at least five places I can go, anytime, and get my dick sucked or my ass licked, free of charge. The gay Mecca is our back yard, so to speak. So, if I've got an itch only a balding diabetic with leering eyes can scratch, I don't pick up the receiver. I just make a disguised visit to only the seediest of gay bars on my own.

In this town, there is a bar to satisfy every craving anyone might have. If I want some black puddin', it's the Pendulum. If I require an Asian diet, if I'm just dying for white rice, then it's the 'N Touch. And when I'm craving some motorcycle cock, then it's gotta be the Hole in the Wall. For all their liberal posturing, the homos in San Francisco don't really mix and match too much. At least, not in the bars. The sex clubs are a free-for-all, but bars are segregated. Which saves a lot of time, don't you think? Lots of my straight friends have to wander from bar to bar, looking for what they want. That kind of shopping is so exhausting, and the truth is, they hardly ever find what they're after.

But we queens, we've worked it all out. We just go straight to the source. It's really what we've been fighting for all these years. 'GWM seeks same for sex, for housing, for a job.' Queers crave any convenient way they can avoid spending time with anyone they don't agree with and don't want to fuck. We spent our first eighteen years celibate and quietly disagreeable. Now, some of us are not wasting any time.

I go to all the bars. Like I said, I'm not choosy, and I have a look vague enough to fit in just about anywhere. Like at the Detour. That's where you go if you've gone everywhere else, and you've still come up empty. That's why it's so badly lit. No one wants to be recognized in the remnants basement. I always make sure I conceal myself when I'm there. I wear a baseball cap pulled way down over my face, and sunglasses. I sip from a bottle of beer I've hidden in the inside pocket of my gray overcoat. I suppose I look a bit like a felon. Like I'm trying to escape from something. Which, when you're in a room full of queer adults, goes virtually unnoticed. I don't know why I bother. Those faggots don't go out to comedy clubs anyway, but even if they did, they wouldn't go to see me. Queers like divas. Or drag. They never go out to the mainstream clubs. Actually, no one I know goes out to mainstream clubs anymore. Most of the comedy clubs have closed, and live comedy is dying. Long live live comedy.

I need another drink if I'm making a toast.

Like I was saying, minority comics can still fill a club. Blacks go out, and Latinos too. Even the Chinese. But white people stay home. I guess they're too afraid of being blamed for everything bad in this shitty country, or maybe they want to avoid getting mugged on their way to the BMWs after the show. Or maybe they're happy to watch all their straight white favorites on TV. Television is crammed with white male comics. I should know. I've been a pal to most of them.

Everytime I turn on the TV I see someone else I've toured with starring on some sitcom. Maybe I should come out. I'd get a lot more attention that way. But no one really wants to work with a faggot. Dyke actresses are okay. Dykes are even hot. But cocksuckers are a bit tragic, and sometimes even dull. People are sick of hearing about AIDS. Go tell it to your fucking support group. AIDS, AIDS, AIDS. Like it's the worst thing that could ever happen to you. Some queers are so fucking AIDS-phobic. It is so self-hating. Especially now that they've basically cured the disease, haven't they? I haven't seen a friend in the obits in ages. These faggots are living for ever, with these cocktails . . . Well, not *these* cocktails, but you know the ones I mean. We don't even garner sympathy anymore. Even queerbashing seems like last decade's news. Maybe that's because *Vanity Fair* is writing about it.

I need a gimmick to get me noticed. Especially at my age. Maybe I should get thrown from a horse. Christopher Reeve works constantly now. Popping his vertebrae was the best career move he could have made. He wasn't looking so cute in those Superman tights anymore, but in a wheelchair, he really commands the screen. He's kind of butch now, like Raymond Burr on *Ironside*. That was a very popular TV show. People love cops and they love the handicapped. And Raymond Burr was a fag, wasn't he? Well, not on *Ironside*, but in real life. Although, that show was set in San Francisco, so maybe his character was a fag, too. A crippled fag. Maybe they should be a new gay sub-group. Faggots on Wheels. They'd need a flag. Every gay sub-group needs its own flag. Maybe a wheelchair falling off a broken rainbow. Or a dove, painted in rainbow colors, with one broken wing. But maybe that's not tasteless enough.

I wish I was a crippled fag. Physically, I mean. Better yet, a black crippled fag. I'd get a grant for that. Hold on. How about if I was a female, quadriplegic faggot from some Third World country. Like Ireland. A crippled black dyke with a brogue. Christ, with those credentials, I could win an Emmy.

I know I should do what my friends have done, move to LA, get a penis enlargement, and wait my turn. I suppose I have as good a chance as any to get on to some mindbendingly awful piece of crap role on a sitcom. But I tried that years ago, when I still appeared fresh and eager, and I hated LA. Still do. It smells, and everyone looks like they're one bench press away from blowing their own head off, or at least the heads of several passers-by.

And anyway, I like performing on the road. I like telling dick jokes in far-away places, like St Louis. And I don't just like working in clubs for the free booze. Or the closeted young comics I get to fuck every so often. Although those are two lovely perks.

I also like writing jokes. It's what I think I'm best at. I did try to write a sitcom once because I thought I'd have more power if I actually had a script of my own when I walked into those stupid meetings in LA with those damaged children who call themselves 'producers'.

I do go down there infrequently. I have to. Show business is more LA-centric than ever. My pathetic agent up here gets me an audition, through some act of God, and I wander down there, with my tail between my shaved legs, to read for some nutty neighbor on a show written by people who obviously don't laugh. Or sometimes someone calls me down for a 'meeting'. They've heard about my work, and they're very enthusiastic. At least, that's how they sound when they're scheduling our appointment.

But something strange happens during my 400-mile flight down, because by the time I arrive for lunch the next day, all those producers want to discuss is themselves! And all their problems sound like themes on *The Ricki Lake Show*: 'My girlfriend is a drug addict' and 'That difficult star is also my mom!' are two standards on that hit parade. I mean, why confide in me? Am I a fat girl holding a portable microphone? Am I wearing a lab coat? Do I look like a fucking therapist? Or are these freaks merely the most annoying people on the planet? So irritating, in fact, that nobody within 400 miles of their office will even talk to them? The last time I was down there, I just went for a piss and never went back to the table. That guy's probably still waiting for me to return, a sea of broken breadsticks before him, each one representing a different ex-wife. Believe it or not, I've got enough of my own pathetic problems. Unless those fucks have a TV show to offer, or a movie role, I'd rather be left alone to live my dreadful single existence in this shitty little studio apartment in San Francisco.

Strangely enough, my sitcom idea did get bought. Nothing to do with LA, of course. Nature of the beast, I guess. You never know when your lucky break might hit. For me, it was in Canada, of all places. Toronto. The most boring city on earth.

Four million people, and you can still hear a faggot fart. These are people who are morally opposed to jaywalking. They stand at the light, poised, waiting for it to change, even if no traffic is coming. That's because they have NOTHING TO FUCKING DO! It was like hanging out with the Mormon Tabernacle fucking Choir.

You know that joke, 'How do you get ten Canadians out of a pool?'

'Please leave the pool.'

Anyway, I met a producer at some comedy festival in Toronto, and I told him about my idea. He was really excited. So excited, in fact, that he gave me some money and I wrote the pilot.

Then the producer went back to LA, and when he sobered up, he dropped my 'project'. He didn't like it anymore. He felt that TV's target audience, which was and is fourteen-year-old boys in the Midwest, didn't want to see a show that focused on an evangelist who ate a different congregation member each week, and then collected their government checks.

'But Jerry,' I whined over the phone to LA, 'you loved *The Last $upper* last week!'

'Yeah, Tom, but that was before I found Christ. Since my epiphany, I've had a change of heart. And anyway, we can't get any advertisers.'

Apparently, the cereal and soap companies didn't find my sitcom 'real enough'. Oh, that's right! Sitcoms are real! How dopey that I forgot how realistic sitcoms are supposed to be! I forgot that we all live our lives in twenty-two-minute blocks. And I love solving all my problems before the next commercial break.

You know what part of my 'real sitcom life' I liked the most? It's the time when I arrived from another planet, and moved in with a skinny girl in Colorado who didn't want to fuck me. I loved wearing those rainbow suspenders.

Or how about the time I lived in New York City with all my 'friends', and we were cute and funny and smart and successful, and 'straight'. In Manhattan? Yeah, like that happens.

Or how about the realistic time I owned a hotel in England, and my wife was a cunt and my bellhop was a Spic. And everytime I tried to improve the place, everything went pear-shaped, since I hired the cheapest men to do the work. Once, some guy put up a wall where a door was due! Can you imagine?

I also love when we go back over previous seasons while looking at a photo album. That's when we laugh at our silly hairstyles and outrageous outfits. And it's really neat when those moments, captured by a Polaroid, come to life! Fade-outs and fade-ins are so fun. I love fade-aways!

But I really enjoy the realistic moments of sorrow and pain when one of the characters in my life gets cancer, which we cure through humor.

Or how about those zany times when we raise money for a charity or a hospital by doing a talent show! Who knew Mom owned a top hat and cane?

Who knew producers were such fuckwits?

Who knew Roseanne had such depth?

Sitcoms aren't real! Real life is barely real! Nothing is real anymore.

Including that producer's excuse. He blamed the advertisers. He blamed his religious convictions. Lies! I know he lied to me. He'll probably steal my idea, and usurp my position as creator. Then he can keep all the money for himself. After all, he needs the cash so he can afford heroin, hookers and hotel rooms. Hobbies in LA are very expensive. When a cleaning lady has to scrape a prostitute's eye off a headboard *and* be quiet about it, you're looking at a big tip.

That's another reason why bars are bad. People lie. And that's if they're interesting. Other people – well, most people, actually – are just plain dull. Sure, everyone has a story, and that story usually belongs to somebody else. That's why, in San Francisco, if you've met three queers, you've met 3,000.

But meeting you was such a relief at first. You seemed so fresh and innocent. So real. Almost too real. I wasn't looking for anything other than high-pitched fun. I'd had a really awful day, and a tough evening. I just wanted to get drunk, play pool, and then maybe fuck somebody senseless. Alcohol, laughs and nasty sex. They're the three major food groups, and spending the day with my family had put me into a feeding frenzy.

CHAPTER FIVE

When twisting, don't tear the neck skin

That first evening I met you, at the Detour, was the night of my grandmother Virginia's ninetieth birthday. I'd taken her to lunch that day. With my sister. By day, I was the dutiful grandson, escorting my oldest living relative to a family steak-house. By night, I was the repenting, lascivious chickenhawk, stalking nubile flesh around a billiard table. It all sounds very *Gods and Monsters*, doesn't it?

You might think I was an idiot, but the first time I saw you I reckoned you weren't gay, because you made eye contact with me the minute I walked into that slut hut. No self-respecting gay man would ever make his intentions so clear. Gay men look at their prey, then look away. Look again, then, when there is almost contact, look away again. No, you caught my gaze and inappropriately held it. I couldn't get away. I didn't want to.

I don't want you to think I felt special because you seemed straight. I know that as far as some of my peers are concerned, popping a straight cherry is like the biggest coup imaginable. They think that fucking a hetero guy is like winning the Super Bowl. The glory continues long after the final score. They high-five their friends, reliving the experience many times, in many ways. But I've usually veered away from straight-acting guys. I don't want to waste my bedtime endlessly repeating 'Too much teeth' through a clenched jaw.

I like my boys experienced, but not jaded; a bit smaller than me; easy to cuddle against after a long, torturous fuck.

And that's why I saddled up against you, my little pool partner. A couple of inches smaller than me, blond, green eyes, and just so sweet. And your jeans were too tight. Just a bit too snug. Cute. So, we spoke, played pool, all within the disapproving glower of my friends. Actually, Jerry and Marty are a couple of men I know from going out. Drinking buddies. They buy me drinks, and I'm their buddy. They're two guys I don't want to fuck, so I suppose we're friends.

I was leaning over the table to make a shot.

'Do you even know his name?' Jerry asked me.

'It's Taylor.'

'As in Liz?' Marty almost shrieked.

'Please. I'm trying to concentrate.'

'Will you two make love?' That was Jerry. Tanned Jerry. He owns a tanning salon. He dyes his hair so black that it's purple. He smiles constantly. He looks like Anne Miller after a week in Cancun. He often says 'make love' with a faux Italian accent when he wants to be ironic.

Marty pushes back his baseball cap. Why can't queers dress their age? 'Yes, Tom. Tell us. Will the caged bird sing tonight?'

'You faggots are both so cynical.'

You were across the world, at the other side of the table, probably wondering why I was taking so long. I took my shot and missed. My testicles shrank.

'If he fourths you,' Marty said, while flipping up the collar of his pink polo shirt, 'we want to know.' 'Fourth' is fourth base. These two always speak in bases, and fourth – rimming – is as intimate as two people can get.

'Do you really think I'd tell you?'

I walked back as you positioned yourself for your shot. I

placed my hand under your nylon jacket – green! I recon-sidered, maybe you were bisexual – and I ran my palm up your back, admiring the indentations created by the muscles on either side of your spine.

I watched your ass. Then I watched you miss your shot. You didn't care. Ahhh, youth.

You were so kind that night at the Detour. Very boy-next-doorish. You have a very marketable look. You would've been great on a sitcom.

Hey, let's do our own sitcom! Let me snort the rest of this.

This is just how they do it in LA. Someone comes up with an idea, or just a setting, then they all 'workshop' the story. They improvise. Only, we already know the story. We were there! This will be incredible. Maybe I should record it. We might come up with something amazing. Something charming and funny. Full of pathos. Something I could sell to some independent film company. Two guys meet this way, they wind up here. If only I could find my tape recorder. And a tape. And some batteries. Well, I'll have to remember it.

Okay, so, let's say we are sitting here, in my kitchen, the way we sort of are now. Only, we have a photo of ourselves. Yeah, it's a few years later from when we first met, and we are looking at a photo of us, in a bar. It's one of those photos women in scantily clad outfits take of a straight couple smiling way too much while on a date. You know, the photo they try to sell to the guy as he and his pal are leaving. The kind he has to buy, so he doesn't look cheap. Well, let's say someone took a photo of us on our first night together at the Detour. And we reminisce. Fade out: Fade in . . .

We are near the pool table. You're putting powder on your palms when I return from chatting with the previously mentioned queens.

You touch your own nipple casually when you ask, 'You know those dudes?'

'Just from seeing them here.'

'You come to this place to connect?'

Connect? Jesus, that word is even before my time!

'Are you in a relationship?' It's none of my business, I know, but your haircut just begs the question. It's practically feathered.

'No!'

We stand there, looking at our shiny balls. Then you tell me you lied.

'I have been in a relationship for five years. I don't know why I told you that.'

'What's her name?'

'What do you mean "her" name? I'm straight! I mean, I'm not straight. I'm gay!'

I try to calm you down by saying that it doesn't matter. 'Look, I think men's sexuality is very fragile. It's impossible to define.' Then I lie again. 'In fact, I feel uncomfortable anywhere on the Kinsey Scale.'

I pause, realizing you have no idea what the fuck I'm going on about, so I add, 'I can see you feel the same. So why not come home with me?' I sound needy instead of commanding. I have to remind myself I am in the company of a potentially violent first-timer, which of course turns me off, but then your smile is so wide that I want to lick your full red lips and I am once again aroused. I'm frightened, yet I have an erection. The story of my life.

You ask me what I'm currently reading. I lie one more time, telling you something vaguely French, then I ask you to come home with me. Again. You flinch. I'm lost. I make a desperate play. That fifty-four-yard field goal attempt, also known as the 'intellectual approach'.

'We can read to each other.'

'That sounds okay.' You're still flinching. I pray that's a habit, and not a comment. Then you add, 'But I always regret it when I do this.'

I have absolutely no desire to find out what that cryptic remark means.

Back at my 'pad' – your word, not mine – we simmer through a courtly hour of reading aloud our favorite selections from *The Catcher in the Rye*.

Then you ask, 'Do you have any rubbers?'

Rubbers?! What decade did you just crawl out from under? This is gonna be like fucking my Spanish teacher's aid in high school. And for that I was almost expelled. If you say, 'Yeah, come on my nuts!' I'll call the police.

CHAPTER SIX

Reach in at the base of the neck, and see what you can find

After I met you, I thought about calling my uncle, Carl. He'd make a great sitcom character. He's a cop, and he's cross-eyed. We could get a lot of comedy mileage out of that. Instead of preventing car accidents, he causes them, that sort of thing. Anyway, I hoped he could ask around about you. He knows a lot of people. Well, he sees more people than he knows, if he's not wearing his glasses.

I know you've lied to me. And I'm not stupid. You must have known that some day I'd figure you out. You have to take some responsibility for things that happen. You told me all sorts of things about yourself. You were a pianist one moment, then you were a lawyer the next. You acted straight, but you sucked cock like a priest. And you had those fake names. Things you called 'nicknames'. I call them lies.

I really hate being lied to. I try to warn people about that when I first meet them. But I've dated so many men that sometimes I forget who I've told. And I don't like repeating myself. Makes me feel old. And sometimes I forget to tell people that I hate repeating myself for fear that I've already mentioned it.

Maybe I should have a list of the men I'm dating, and put a check next to their names each time I tell them something important.

'Don't lie to me.' Check.

'Don't make me remind you to *not* lie to me. I hate repeating myself.' Check.

'I'll use a condom the next time.' Check, mate.

But to create such a list, I'd have to know the names of all the guys I fuck. I'm sorry, all the guys I 'date'.

No, what I should do is make up a list of things I like and things I don't like. On a 5x7 card. Something I could offer my date at the beginning of the evening, a convenient inventory he could keep in his breast pocket and refer to from time to time. Perhaps I might also include a few of my favorite songs, and the funniest stories about me. A list like that would save so much time and energy. I wouldn't have to traipse through my past every time I wanted to get laid. Reheating this award-winning joke or that somber moment over and over again gets exhausting, bores the waiter, and stars Robin Williams.

Hey, maybe my potential paramour could give me a little postcard about himself. Once we've been seated at our table, we could exchange cards, which we'd read after we've ordered our first drinks. Sort of a quick compatibility conference. The date might end before the soup arrives, but at least I haven't wasted an evening with someone whose favorite film is *Steel Magnolias*.

And if some of his own stories are funny, I could add them to my act. He wouldn't mind, because he wouldn't know. If he were funny, I'd never see him again. *I'm* the funny one in any relationship. Another benefit of my plan is that, after reading the little card I've supplied, my date wouldn't be shocked when I dump him for having a cock that is 2 inches shorter than he'd promised, since number 1 on that list of things I cannot stand is lies.

Number 1, I would write, in big, bold red letters: **Don't ever lie to me. EVER!**

Number 2, don't get mad when I lie. It's just a result of my damaged childhood.

In the third category, I might list my favorite films, maybe a couple of impressive book titles, and then a selection of what I consider to be the best television shows of all time. And if I hear 'Who the fuck are Starsky and Hutch?' come out of his mouth, the date is over, pretty neck or no pretty neck. (I like smooth, white necks.)

Maybe that should be mentioned in the fourth category on the list, entitled 'turn-ons'. These would also include youth and potential cures for cancer. That cancer reference would win me the humanitarian blowjob.

Of course, number 5 would have to be 'turn-offs'. This category would be updated frequently, depending on the currently fashionable but completely unnecessary and forever unfortunate hair that gay men are growing somewhere on their faces. But for now 'turn-offs' would definitely be freeways at five – because I don't want to sound too clever, that would be intimidating – Hitler-style mustaches, and turn-on/turn-off lists.

Numbers 6 through 10 will be all my favorite stories and anecdotes about me. My zaniest and most clever moments, briefly sketched, always ending in a wry, ironic twist that emphasizes my humility. Stories that feature my ability to simultaneously laugh and cry in the face of danger. Saving lives with humor, that sort of *Patch Adams* thing. And at least one story that might include a domestic setting, and perhaps a puppy, or a senior citizen, or anything rather docile and urine-smelling that has helped me deeply explore the banality of life without love offered and love received.

I suppose this much information might require something larger than a 5x7 index card. Unless I could write really small, like my first lover. John practically wrote in Sanskrit. His shopping lists, Christmas cards, even suicide notes, were almost impossible to read by anyone other than the little man who wrote them. He sent me letters, which I found charming and about as readable as graffiti scribbled anxiously in Latin by someone with a gun to his head and lots of apologies to make. So, I sent them to a priest to be translated. And he sent them to the FBI. I should have known John's missives were full of paranoid delusions and threats of violence. I was too blinded by young love to see how crazy all those tiny words looked, squeezed on to a piece of parchment paper. Like someone with way too many thoughts to fit within mere margins – someone like, I dunno, a fucking psycho – who needed to write from edge to edge in teeny letters to make his point. A point that he could have made in five words: 'I love you. NOW DIE!' And yet I stayed with him and I paid for his lithium. Until he left me for someone else. I'm nothing if not pathetic.

Maybe I should include that story on the index card as well. Under the Failed Relationships category. I guess that should be numbers 11 through . . . infinity. Oh, this will take more than just one card. Maybe two. Maybe 2,000. Maybe I should put it on microfiche, but the only people with the equipment to read fiche are spies and librarians. Spies are hot, but generally closeted. Like Tom Cruise's character in '*Mission: Impossible*. Otherwise, they'd be security risks. And librarians? I guess they're okay, if you like hairy backs and ears. And those are the females.

But I don't have time to make a list right now. My hands are too sweaty to write anything anyway. And you and I are past that point. This isn't our first date. This isn't a date at all. This started out as a date, but it's become more of a happening. Like Barbara Streisand in Central Park, except without the costume changes and the death threats.

I wonder what in this room illuminates something about my character. What, I wonder, among all this crap might garner me some empathy? Let's make this my turn to share. We can do our own little version of *The Prince of Tides*. You play Barbra. Look concerned. I'll arrange your nails. Good. Now, where shall I start?

CHAPTER SEVEN

If the liver is yellow, throw it away

Let's begin with my family. That photo, on the wall, is my grandmother and all her brothers. In the 1920s, I think. Look how frightened and timid they all look. They're a sea of harelips and disproportionate ears. Well, that's what happens when cousins love each other just a bit too much. Thank God for mustaches and plastic surgery. Too bad they had to get old, although they still look presentable. If they'd just never talk, you might think my kin were almost normal.

I grew up with a Southern family that didn't live in the South. Instead, the Pettidoigts lived in a dream world of honeysuckle and streetcars named Desire. In a Californian suburb. Truth is, they're still just misplaced hicks. Trashier than tinsel, and even less sincere.

And they seem to live for ever, even though they've been removed from their natural habitat. How do they do it? They should be studied by scientists, dissected, poked at with prodding instruments, or perhaps pulled apart by wolves, since that's the only way they are going to die.

For instance, my grandmother, Virginia, is older than clay. I think she turned ninety purely out of spite. She's still got a few lives to ruin. Her great-grandchildren can't stay happy for ever!

Oh yeah, and she's got buckets of cash. Isn't that unfair? How do evil millionaires subsist for so long? She has outlived all her peers. And, like most leeching relatives, we are all terrified she'll outlive us. Instead of dying, she'll probably do a backflip out of her Edwardian mansion and morph into acid rain, destroying the crops in some small village in China, since, as she puts it, 'The Chinese are ruining San Francisco.'

She was raised by white trash boneheads. She'll of course tell you differently. She'll camouflage her past with a genteel Southern accent, which, though charming, is a complete affectation. This seems harmless, until she mentions all those 'African-American euphemisms' – that's hard to say after eight cocktails – handed down to her from previous generations: Nigger, of course, for all-purpose use, and 'darkie', 'nappy head' and 'jiggaboo' for family functions. And of course, her favorite term for a black child is 'piccaninny'. This she uses in mixed company because she considers it a compliment. Which is why I got the shit beat out of me in kindergarten. I thought black people liked being called 'niggers'. And Lord all mighty, they get especially mad when you say it with a Southern accent.

Virginia is named after the Southern state that is slightly affluent, at least by Confederate standards. She claims her family were French aristocracy who escaped France during the Revolution and settled in Chesapeake Bay. But I know the truth. With my family, the truth can be bought with just a few brown cocktails and a bit of handholding.

Virginia's stock were German immigrants named Schreider, who were chased out of Heidelberg for printing fake coins, and, claiming religious persecution, talked their way into the US in the 1880s. They changed their name to Fowler, and forged some Yankee cash, so they could buy a flourmill in some shithole called Copperhill, West Virginia. They named the town and the mill after themselves. However, Fowler Flour went out of business when the chunk of an appendage was found baked into someone's biscuits. An extremity count among the townsfolk ensued, led by the local doctor/blacksmith. Eventually all fingers pointed to Frederick Fowler, my great-granddaddy, who ran the plant with an iron fist. Literally. His digits had been sliced off his right hand in a nightmarish hoe accident during harvest season. Many fragments of bone and tissue had been recovered, and then disposed of in a Christian manner. The local residents assumed the matter had been laid to rest. Little did anyone know such a trauma would resurface so distastefully. In shame, Frederick Fowler sold the mill, buried his misplaced finger, and got a job on the railroad.

He fucked his way across seven states until he wound up in Oakland, California, destitute and devalued. He wired his wife, and she dragged her four sons across the country to join her homeless hubby. She cleaned for dough, while Freddie drank and wandered the streets of Oakland looking for whores and free booze.

The last child they had together was Virginia, my grandmother, named after their beloved home. Well, West Virginia was their home, but West was a bit too butch as a first name, even for my female relatives. Heidelberg might have been their home originally, but Germans were even less popular in those days, so Virginia it was. And at that time, around the time of the Great Earthquake and the orgy that followed, there were a lot of French people hanging around the Bay Area. Just like today. In San Francisco alone, 5 per cent of the population is French-speaking. Tourists think it's the bay they're smelling. Wrong.

Anyway, I suppose my great-grandmother thought, in memory of the small finger lost, let's change our last name, too. And let's give people a reason to think we're all French. Other than the disastrous condition of our nails and teeth, that is.

And so Virginia Olivia Pettidoigts was created!

Who knows where 'Olivia' came from. Probably my great-grandmother's favorite dog. Southerners often name their kids after their favorite pets. Tells you a bit about their priorities, doesn't it?

Unlike the state, Virginia was diminutive. Her family hoped she would grow into the grandness of her appellation. When she remained a short bitch, something had to change. The state wasn't gonna shrink, so a nickname was required. Unfortunately, Cunt already belonged to several other family members, so a search began. The family scoured books they could understand – comics, atlases, the Farmer's Almanac – looking for a quirky name that might describe an overly bleached beauty who insisted on wearing short shorts while shopping for laxatives.

Then, as luck would have it, my cousin Ginger was born with a slight speech impediment. She pronounced the word 'grandma' as 'ama'.

Upon hearing this, Virginia said of her first grandchild, 'We never had a retard in the family before.'

In Sanskrit, the word 'ama' means toxic waste. I've always wondered how my cousin knew that at eight months.

CHAPTER EIGHT

Feel for the gizzard,
and pull it out, slowly

Just hours before I met you, at her birthday lunch Ama
was going on and on about how 'that nigger would've
never gotten off if it weren't for that chink judge and dirty
Jew lawyer.'

Thank God for the OJ trial. It gave Virginia the chance to
use three racist terms in one sentence. Pretty grand accomplish-
ment, don't you think? With that kind of talent, she'd pass just
about any pop quiz a Mormon university English professor
could throw her way.

'Ama, we don't use words like nigger and chink. Dirty Jew
is fine . . .' I was trying to find some common ground, '. . . but
nigger and chink aren't.'

'What do you mean, honey?'

'Well, we just don't call people by those derogatory terms.'

'There's nothin' derogatory about nigger. Our niggers loved
bein' niggers. They loved their work. They loved pickin' cotton
because that's what they were built for. Their arms were longer
and their hands were bigger. Now don't look at me like that.
I'm not bein' racist. They've done studies.'

The 'studies' she often refers to are the observations her
brother, Taz, makes while commenting on his twenty years of
work as chief of homicide for the Oakland police department.
My family is loaded with crime fighters. My dimwitted Uncle

Carl, my narrow-minded Great-Uncle Taz. Maybe that's why I don't have much respect for the law.

Taz, short for 'Tazwell', is more hateful than Virginia. And he's even smaller! He's 4 feet of golfing horror. A little, white-haired, squinty-eyed ball of red skin and gritted teeth. He's like a tumor with a pension. Don't try imagining that. You'll pop a vessel. Suffice it to say that letting Taz work alongside the black community in Oakland during the 1960s was like letting Eva Braun run the Holocaust Museum.

While quoting his 'studies', Taz's voice can barely be heard over the wailing of Sammy Davis, Jr, ('A classy nigger. He's okay.') and the tinkling of ice in his chocolate-brown Manhattans at Christmas. Fortunately, he's memorized several statistics, and he'll repeat his findings at any time. On the phone. In the car. Over a loudspeaker. The stats change when he needs them to, but mostly, his synopsis of the struggle for racial equality in America sounds something like this: 'Hell, we got nothin' to worry about. From what I used to see from my office window . . . (another gulp of his unending cocktail) . . . them niggers are all killin' each other!'

Thank you, Jane Goodall.

Actually, I've cut way back on my visits to Virginia's side of the family. And the next time I see any of them, I hope it's at their funerals.

But I have to see Virginia. We all do. My brother wants a speedboat, my sister has a mortgage, and I want to fuck lots of boys in Thailand. And Ama is the cash cow. The moneylender. The gold purse. She holds our future.

So, we trade off on birthday lunch duty each year. This year was my sister's turn, but she couldn't manage it alone. And when she offered me 5 per cent of her first year's inheritance after Virginia's death, I gave in and came along. I guess I'm just an old softy.

Ama eats like a horse, by the way. And she looks great. Doesn't look a day over eighty. I guess that's because she eats well and exercises regularly. At the same time apparently, because sucking the blood out of a baby's neck is a lot of hard work. She's Satan. She's satanic. She would be Dorian Gray if she could read.

And the jewelry! The diamonds practically pour off those prunes she calls fingers! With every gesture, Ama features glistening rings she offers to one granddaughter, then when that gal disappoints her, she offers them to another. What a lovely, backstabbing, ponytail-pulling momentum that sets up among eight ladies already one lap dance away from being guests on *The Jerry Springer Show*. Subject: We tried to kill the old bitch . . . *BUT SHE JUST WOULDN'T DIE!!!*

She has had all the diamond rings from all her five dead husbands seared into one huge sugar loaf of a diamond to wear on her wedding-ring finger. It's so big she had to sprout an extra knuckle to support it. Luckily she's a demon, and she can get away with that.

Two of the diamonds are from my grandfather. One marriage, two diamonds. Not a bad deal. She married him twice, because she didn't kill him the first time. He got away and joined a Mother Earth cult in Utah, but she found him, in a wool smock, digging beetroot with his hands. So much for the glamour of being a Druid. Anyway, he begged for his life, begged her to leave him in peace with his goddess.

'But honey,' she hissed, 'You know I need a driver.'

They found him dead from a massive stroke two years later. He'd collapsed while talking on the phone to Ama. She'd called him from a black-jack table in Reno, Nevada, drunk, to remind him of his inadequacy. I think the last word he heard was 'micropenis'. Neighbors found him, dead, face down on the kitchen floor, with the receiver in one hand, and a tearstain on his right cheek.

Okay, that last 'tear' detail might not be correct, but I'm using it to illustrate a point.

SHE'S EVIL!

My sister spent most of the birthday lunch staring at her mobile phone, hoping her kids might call and tell her they've been kidnapped, so she could escape. Lisa didn't eat. She picked at everything, including her skin. She'd have picked on her husband, if he wasn't off scoring pot somewhere.

I can't eat anything without the food burning my asshole on its way out. Even yogurt hurts. Bananas might as well be Jalapeno peppers. Whenever I go to poop, it feels like someone is shoving the food back into me. Sometimes I check the toilet in mid-movement, to make sure no one is down there, pushing up. After all, I live in San Francisco. You never know. I suppose the problem is that I have the intestines and the rectum of a . . . well, of an old fag who's eaten and drunk too much.

Yet Virginia ate meat, drank wine, ordered dessert. My sister and I just watched her, waiting for her to choke on that chicken bone we slipped into her cognac.

And we're not the only family members who feel that way. At every family function, everyone keeps looking at his or her watch.

'Tick tock tick tock, Ama. Don't you have to be somewhere soon?'

Our eyes look upward, innocently.

'Don't you have friends waiting for you?'

She stares at us like we're nuts. Have we forgotten that she's never had friends?

We try a different tactic.

'Hey Ama, BOO!'

Blank stare.

'So, Ama, how's that cough? Are those liver spots or lesions?'

We all hear her death bus honking its extra-loud horn. Why the fuck doesn't she get on it? We'll pay the fare!

Maybe we'll push her in front of a bus. All of us will do it. My cousins, my brother and sister, and I. We'll all push her, again and again and again, until she's nothing but a mangled heap in front of the motor coach. And we'll all take responsibility for her murder, in case there is an inquiry. Like in *Murder on the Orient Express*. And when the police find out how evil Ama was, they'd let us off the hook, and share in our wealth.

Because when that old cunt dies – AND SHE WILL – there will be lots of cash to spread around. I'll get $4,000 a month for the rest of my life. I won't have to eke out a living by telling girlfriend and dick jokes. I'll be at home, watching porn films with actors in them that look sort of like Brad Pitt. Hell, with money like that, I can probably afford porn films starring Brad Pitt.

We all gotta start somewhere.

'So, then, what do we say?'

'What?' During the conversation's lull, I fantasized about rimming Brad Pitt on national television, while my grandmother watched, with the rest of the studio audience and Jay Leno, the host, looking on with mocked horror.

'Where is Lisa?' I asked Ama.

'She just disappeared.'

She was probably in the bathroom, throwing up the olives she ate in the bar while waiting for Virginia to torture the hostess into giving us 'our usual booth'.

'Honey, tell me, what should I say instead of "nigger" and "chink"?'

'How about African-American and Asian-American.'

'Oh honey, that's too many words. I'm too old. I don't have time to sit around learning new words, faggot.'

Check, please.

While we waited for her '67 Impala to be excavated from a huge cement structure near the mall that entombs TGI Friday's, I wondered how Virginia endures being alone. Who does she yell at in that big old house, once she's caged all the servants for the night? Like I said, all five husbands are deceased. I don't think she'll remarry, because five is as high as she can count while holding a cocktail. She can't have a pet. They smell, and create dirt. The one parakeet she did have wound up with an old woman's hand wrapped around its little yellow torso forcing it down a toilet bowl. Virginia thought the bird was dying, because it was losing feathers. She was being humane by ending its life before the true pain of molting set in. After that, I always prayed to God that I didn't lose my hair. I was afraid I might wake up with Ama's old but determined claw on the back of my neck, while I choked on a toilet bowl full of chlorinated liquid. I just didn't want the last thing I saw on earth to be poop-stained porcelain.

All she has left to keep her company, after nine decades of living, are several outfits individually wrapped in plastic. I wonder if, while alone, she recollects her proudest moments, her highest achievements, her crowning glories. Well, that must take about three seconds. What next? Vanity! Did I mention my grandmother is a model? All 5' 4" of her. Well, 5' 6", when she's standing atop a dead husband. Apparently, senior citizens don't have those silly height requirements that models seventy years their junior have to abide by. She struts up and down the runway in front of other rich old ladies, sporting outfits that only she can really get away with, all the while raising money to feed starving children in Africa. The money winds up buying matches and petrol for her Daughters of the American Revolution crossburning ceremonies, but at least Virginia's heart, or a facsimile thereof, is in the right place.

CHAPTER NINE

Ignore the tendons, and cut off those little feet

Before she drove off, Ama offered me a clove for my breath.

'In case of an accident,' she said. Because you know how annoyed those paramedics would've been if they smelled onions on my breath while scraping my brains off the dashboard.

Virginia always carries three things. Cloves, for the breath. Talcum, for the shoes. And musk, for the scent. But it ain't for her. No, even her farts smell like flowers. She takes pills so that everything about her, even her excrement, leaves an everlastingly fresh aroma, like a rose garden in spring that busily follows her wherever she goes.

The problem lies in the male population. See, to Virginia, men smell curious. Especially me. To my grandmother, I have a distinctly unpleasant odor. Always have. She determined that, when I was young, something went wrong, and so I'm queer and I emit a peculiar pungency. That's Southern logic for you. You just can't fight it.

Ama has even suggested that maybe something odd happened in my mother's womb. While pregnant with me, my mother walked around, barefoot. 'You walk around like that,' Virginia warned her, 'without shoes, and honey, you're just asking for trouble.'

And trouble popped out, all cross-eyed and stinky, in the shape of me.

I gnawed on my clove as I waved goodbye. Then I looked at my watch. Shit! I've got to stop wearing my watch on my drinking wrist. Fuck, now I smell like a beggar, which I will be soon if I don't stop wasting booze like this.

So I looked at this cheap Timex. I just wanted to know how much time I'd wasted with that sarcophagus. It seemed like days had passed, but only one hour had trickled by: 2 p.m. I wanted to kill myself, but I didn't like what I was wearing.

Especially this watch. The crystal is chipped, and the band is held together with tape. Not even good tape. Masking tape. The kind we used to use in school. Who wears watches like this? Homeless people. And why do homeless people wear watches anyway? Where do they have to fucking go? I have a home, and a job, sort of, and I only look at my watch maybe twice a day. Well, I look once, then, when I'm telling a story that includes the watch, I look again, and spill booze. I must look like hell. Like a boozy loser.

I had a nice watch once. It belonged to my grandfather. I borrowed it one day, and then I forgot to give it back. And strangely enough, he never asked for it. I guess that's because he was dead.

No matter how hysterical my grandmother became at Christmas that year when she saw the watch on my wrist, I still don't think he would have minded me taking it off his wrist after the service. He didn't resist. I think he'd always wanted me to have it, but then he got cancer, and that sort of took a lot of his time, and maybe he forgot about promising the watch to me when I was seven. But I hadn't forgotten. Listen, he was frugal. He would've hated just burying that watch and giving it to the worms. What a waste. I got the antique cleaned, showed it off and, when Virginia saw it, she barely remembered which husband it belonged to. She vaguely recognized it, and what I should've done was lied. But I was drunk, Taz was throwing out statistics about the number of single black mothers who buy mink coats with their government check money, and my sister was barfing up the fruitcake I'd spent all afternoon waiting in line for at the Italian bakery that only took cash. I was annoyed, and I felt defiant. I wanted to assert myself, so I told Virginia it had belonged to Soupy, my grandfather, and she threw a brush at me. It shattered into several pieces when it connected with my crown. I ran off with my inherited timepiece, leaving behind my date to pick up the pieces of the brush, and thank my family for a lovely Christmas dinner.

Happy Holidays, from the Pettidoigts.

That was a mild Christmas. I was the only one injured. Usually, one of Virginia's brothers would fall and hit his head on the side of the coffee table. Always the same table, a big glass number in the middle of the living room, conveniently facing the walnut liquor mini-bar. After their eighteenth trip to the bar, I guess that shag carpeting got slippery, and bam! Down they'd go, Taz or Johnny or Bobs, or sometimes all three. One after another. And they'd lie there, on top of one another, just a pile of white trash.

My grandmother, drunk as the rest, yet relying on her lipstick and hostess duties to help her maintain some of her dignity, would find me trying to coerce my cousin Kyle into disrobing in the upstairs bedroom. She'd move toward me, slowly, while Kyle scrambled to button up his Levis, and she'd place both her bony hands on my little boy shoulders.

'Honey, your Great-Uncle Taz is dead. He was a good man, but he's gone now.' She'd pull me into her, and press my head against her bosom. Yikes. She'd hold me there so long, the pattern from her Wonderbra leaving a crease on my cheek.

Then she'd release me and say, 'Let's go downstairs and wrap him up in something.'

By the time we got down there, Taz would be sitting up, holding an ice pack to his forehead. I'd call an ambulance, while Virginia yelled at Taz for getting blood on her shag.

Then we'd open our gifts.

The only thing I ever wanted was that watch. Once I got it, I was never going to give it up. Funny how it wound up on the wrist of a stripper from Portland. When I put a dollar in his Speedo, he leaned down from the horseshoe shaped bar he was prancing around on, and whispered into my ear, 'Nice watch.' A few minutes later I was peeing into his mouth while he lay back on my bed in my hotel room. He kept making me pee. I mean, I didn't necessarily want to piss, but he kept demanding my urine. He lapped it up like it was baby's milk. Lap, lap, lap. While he spit it out, I had to drink more water, so that I'd have more fluid to piss. It was a neverending cycle.

Finally I told him I was dehydrated, and he had to leave. He asked for cab fare, because the strip club in Portland only paid at the end of the week. I was broke, and he started breaking things, so I gave him the watch and sent him on his way. A lovely Bulova. It was a gift from my grandfather's parents on his twenty-first birthday in 1932. A 14-carat gold casing, with thin etching all around the rim of the case, and a ruby at the 12. That stripping hooker probably sold it for less than he gets blowing someone.

And I replaced that art deco masterpiece with this watch I bought over the counter at Woolworth's. For about the price of a blowjob in Portland. So in a way, this is worth as much as my grandfather's watch. At least to a hooker. But to anyone in the know, this thing is an embarrassment. It enhances this drunken, fucked-up look I'm so actively sporting lately. My new watch is the finishing touch to a look that has taken me years of pain and disappointment to perfect.

Maybe, with a better watch, I could turn back time, and start refining a more impressive appearance. A fashionable new watch, something clever and chic, something so hard to read that it's practically useless, might lend the sort of *bon vivance* that attracts, say, wealthy gay producers. David Geffen might notice my expensive Movada when we both reach for the same peach in the produce department at Safeway, and before you know it, I'm sleeping my way to the middle. I'm swallowing gallons of Geffen, while I'm *finally* starring on my own sitcom. I'm on the cover of *People*, I'm the only guest on *Oprah* for a whole fucking week, and I'm inhaling huge piles of heroin with the cast from *Friends*. The watch could do all that for me. It could be the beginning of my comeback.

But before my big comeback happens, I've got to get famous. Then I can fall apart on camera. And *then* I make my comeback. And somewhere in there I have to get my face lifted. That's how Cher did it, and she's still recording hit singles.

I looked up from my watch, and I burped up the teriyaki chicken that 'Brianna' at TGI Friday's was sure I'd 'adore!'. I glanced across the parking lot. A busboy was holding back my sister's hair while she barfed all over the side of her white Mustang convertible. She tipped him. She seemed to be throwing up more now than ever before. I wondered if she was pregnant. But by whom? Her husband, Dennis, only has one testicle. Actually, he has one real one, and one fake one that is made of metal. Well, a lightweight metal. I hope, for his sake. He had ball cancer when he was a kid, and he's been shooting one-sided blanks ever since. She adopted her kids from a Korean family. That went over big with Virginia. She calls my sister's house 'the last chopper out of Saigon'.

As I waved goodbye to Lisa, I wondered how Dennis ever gets through customs at the airport.

Then, I thought, with any luck, Virginia would fall asleep at the wheel of her Impala, and soon my drug store Timex would be a Rolex. 2.04 p.m. So early in the day for so much hatred.

I usually save that feeling of total disgust for my audience.

CHAPTER TEN

Now, using tweezers, remove all pinfeathers, one by one, and expose the flesh

At the show that night, I punished the patrons, real bad. I figured, if I have to feel like shit, then we all have to feel like shit. So the first thing I did was get l-o-a-d-e-d, loaded. I just can't stand to perform sober. Neither can most of my pals. The staff at those clubs are used to pushing us guys on to stage. It's become part of my act. The audiences in the smaller towns love that sloppy drunken stuff.

I prefer to drink alone, like the female headliners. Women comics – all three of them – are considered unsavory alcoholics if they drink. I envy them. We boys are expected to slam a few with the club owner. It's tradition! Unfortunately, every club owner I've ever met is a mindless fuck. But if I didn't drink with the club owner, he'd think something was wrong with me. Which means he'd watch my set. Fuck that. I'd rather he stay in the office, and assume things are going fine. That way, if the show goes badly, I can tell him the opening act was bad, or it was the audience's fault.

I learned to drink from the first headliner I ever worked with. She was big and sassy. She wasn't very funny, but then women aren't funny. They're just so dirty and self-referential. Like queer comics. They just haven't found their niche yet.

But I liked her. One night, when she drove me home,

she warned me not to expect too much from the spectators.

'Tomorrow night,' she told me, as she pulled in front of my
apartment, 'look out at them during your set. Really look at
them. They'll just be staring at you, with their mouths hanging
open. Gawking. They aren't there to laugh. They're on a date,
or with their buddies from the office. Or they won the tickets.
But Tom, they are not comedy lovers. Ninety-nine per cent of
them don't get it. They never have, and they never will.'

The next night, after I introduced some new jokes I'd
worked on real hard – I actually used to rehearse – I sneaked a
peak before I introduced the next act. And there they were. The
gawking throng. Just like she said. Their eyes seemed glazed
over, like they'd just witnessed an execution. In fact, I felt like
they'd rather I died, so they could have told a funny story about
public humiliation at coffee break the next day. I wondered
if these fucking losers were the kind of people I wanted to
entertain. Suddenly the banality of my work overwhelmed
me, and I thought, 'Are these inbred pond scum the kind of
fuckwads I want to impress?'

It's like when you're an adult, and you realize your life means
nothing and everyone has been lying to you about everything
all along.

And that's when the drinking started.

It's pointless to stop now. The booze adds an edge to my
work. When I have to be lifted up from a green-room couch five
minutes before I'm supposed to be on stage, I work a bit harder.
Makes the other acts nervous, like they have to try harder too,
but that's only fair. When I was first starting out, I had to scrape
my own bevy of headliners off the naugahide. I had to extend the
set I was being paid $25 to do so that Mr About-To-Be-A-Has-
Been could barf the rest of his 'flu' into the cushions before he
made his grand entrance. Now it's my turn.

After I informed the audience that I was drunk, I ordered a shot of tequila to be delivered while I was on stage. Then I did the incest stuff. This bit I do about my grandmother wanting to sleep with me spoon style. It really sets the mood for the evening.

'That old bitch isn't dying fast enough. She's like that Queen Mother cunt. If we take away her tiara, she'd drop into a pile of shit, which is what she is. Help me kill her! I have drink tickets.'

The ticket-holders gasped, as they always do. Some left the club, and they probably demanded back their money. And the more they resisted, the more I pushed.

When I'm on stage, I don't feel like I've done my job until I've walked at least twenty of those fucks, and searched through at least one woman's purse while she's in the ladies' room.

Maybe that's why I don't have my own sitcom yet.

Actually, why romanticize it? The reason I'm not on TV is because people talk. Especially in this business. Gossip, gossip, gossip. And even though they pretend to not care that I'm queer, and even though most of the people that run Hollywood are fags and dykes, they just don't believe a homo could play anything other than a homo. Even though faggots have been playing straights for ever.

I'm not gonna try to figure out why I'm queer, whose fault it is, if fault is due, and how I could've maybe changed it all. I mean, yes, I was close to my mom as a kid, and yes, I was an overachiever as well. All the hall-marks of a major dicksmoker, brought on perhaps by overbearing women controlling every motherfucking move I ever fucking made. But why harp on the past? What's done is done. And my cock isn't the most interesting thing about me, anyway.

Which reminds me, I just saw a totally fascinating episode of *Oprah* yesterday where all her guests were suffering from an eating disorder that takes over during sleep. Apparently the snoozers get up and go walking around the house like mummies until they reach the kitchen, where they eat treats. Like cookies rolled in butter. Or cold pizza dipped in mayonnaise. All that stuff you consider consuming when you're stoned, but don't because you have some small amount of self-esteem left somewhere. Or because you have a history of colon cancer in your family. Or more importantly, because you have a photo shoot in the morning, so there won't be any time to scrub the vomit off the porcelain before your cleaning lady arrives at ten, and that bitch gossips.

The kicker is that each guest on *Oprah* was filmed by their husband or their wife! A camera jiggling from the laughing body of an evil spouse recorded these defenseless noshers, standing near the fridge, their eyes shut, looking almost dead, shoveling in food. Oprah then showed the film back to the couples, and the sleep eaters acted all innocent. Like they didn't remember doing it at all. And I could sense Oprah's audience, even Oprah herself, almost not believing that all this was possible. In fact, Oprah looked like she was ready to prosecute those closeted eaters, which was understandable. We all know about Oprah's eating patterns. Binge and purge, binge and purge. She's a bit touchy on the subject. Maybe she was annoyed with herself for not having eaten in *her* sleep. Eight perfectly good eating hours – wasted! She'll probably develop the disorder just so she can gain the book and movie rights.

But I felt sorry for those sleepwalking snackers. I know how helpless they must've felt. I've been a sleepwalker my whole walking life. When I tell most people that, they laugh. They don't really understand what walking in your sleep is all about. Even my friends think it's a goofy disorder, like something you might have seen on *Frasier*. Except funny. And a lot of people think sleepwalking can be cured with home remedies, like placing lemons near the bed, or wearing warmer socks during the day.

But sleepwalking can't be cured, because nobody knows why it happens. That's what makes it so scary. Well, that, and the fact that walking in your sleep makes you completely vulnerable. See, when you sleepwalk, you are totally unconscious. It's not like you're having an out-of-body experience. Its not like you're drunk or high, and you can kind of see what you're doing, but you can't really control yourself. You are actually asleep; with all these odd dreams in your head that have nothing to do with what you are actually doing, which in my case was pretty outrageous. At least, once.

Usually, when I sleepwalked – sleptwalked? – I'd wind up in my sister's room, telling her I had to talk to her, but my eyes would be closed, and she'd just walk me back to my room. Sometimes, if she was feeling frisky, she'd do something real fun. Like the time when I was 12 and she tied my hands and feet together and poured red food dye in my hair.

When I woke up, I thought I was paralyzed, because I couldn't move. I verbally chastised myself for having criticized my own limbs. My arms and legs were so long and thin that I felt freakish. Now I prayed for the use of my appendages, no matter their length, just one more time.

'Perhaps,' I said, quietly, my eyes turned upward as I spoke to the heavens, like Jennifer Jones in *The Song of Bernadette*, 'God would grant me one more walk in the park, picking daisies and ignoring small children. What a joy it would be to feel the sun on my skin as I show off my new manicure when offering a simple wave to a passer-by.'

That was all I asked from the universe. That was all I, a long, skinny, frightened, frail, probably dying, crippled child wanted. If only I could have used one hand, or even just one finger, I'd have dialled the Make-A-Wish Foundation. I'd seen on television that they're the bleeding hearts who arrange and fund the last wish of a dying child. All I would have begged for was a handshake with an astronaut before all my nerves went permanently numb.

And when I turned my head – thank God I could move my neck! – clearing away my tears, I suspected my head had been bludgeoned, because red liquid – blood! – was dripping into my eyeballs. Perhaps I'd been left for dead, like Barbara Eden in, well, in any of her made-for-TV movies. Maybe the house had been robbed, and all my family members were murdered. Perhaps I was the only one alive. I'd have to start afresh, with the help of local donations, and the Salvation Army, to build a new life for myself.

'As the Lord is my witness,' I cried out, 'I'll never touch myself again!'

Like I had a choice.

Then, I heard giggling, and by the time I rolled off the bed and caught sight of my sister standing near my open bedroom door with some of her blond and braided friends, I realized I'd been sleepwalking.

'Only faggots cry.' She whispered in my ear, as she united me. 'Jesus Christ, it's only a bit of rope. You'd think I'd tortured you.'

'Yeah, well, next time you need Mom's signature on something from school, don't ask me.'

'I don't care about school anymore. Kristen and Marta' – the scary Hitler Youth twins who were also my sister's best gal pals – 'have decided to become stewies, and I'm going to, too.'

Stewies was a contemporary term for 'stewardesses'.

'Lisa,' I told her, wiping the food dye from around the corners of my mouth, 'let me tell you something. You have to be cute to be a stewardess. Haven't you ever seen a Sandy Duncan movie?'

'I AM CUTE!'

'Yeah, right.'

'SHE IS CUTE!!' chimed in one of the twins.

'Don't bray, Marta.'

'Well,' claimed my sister, proudly, 'the boys at school think I'm cute.'

'They're 14. They'll tell anyone anything for a handjob.' And if anybody knew that fact, it would've been me. 'And anyway, even cute won't cut it. You need tits.'

'Sandy Duncan doesn't have tits.'

'Yeah, well, that's Hollywood, baby.' Where did I learn to talk like that? Probably from Mom's boyfriend at the time, Sammy Scazaflapha. After Dad left, Mom only dated guys with foreign-sounding names and foreign cars. Dad's middle-class mentality had bored her stiff. She wanted a guy with facial hair, who could pronounce the things he sautéed. Sammy owned a body lotion store called Bodica Erotica, and to gain entrance you had to stroke the torso of a well-sanded body sculpture that stood near the entrance. He was a real fuckwit, but I admired him because he wore leather trousers, like a movie star. But he hit my mom. Like a movie star.

'In the real world,' I continued, throatily, while rubbing the rope marks on my ankles, 'you need big knockers to fly the friendly skies. And with those fat shoulders, any tits you're able to sprout are gonna look small.'

'I am not fat. The twins say I'm just big-boned. Right, girls?'

'Yah!'

'Lisa, dinosaurs are big-boned. You're fat.'

Sometimes, when I was even younger, I'd wake up in the morning and all the Halloween candy I had managed to ration, so it would last from one Halloween to the next to spite my mother's drunken burglary attempts, would no longer be organized by size and color. I was told later I'd entered the living room after midnight, hands full of M&Ms and Mars Bars, which I wanted to trade for whatever drugs my mom's Sammy was stashing away in the glove compartment of his convertible. As puritanical a straight-A student as I was while awake, apparently, in my sleep I became a drug-crazed fiend.

'Come on, Man.' In those days, we capitalized the word 'man'. Even in conversation. 'I just need a bit of snow to get me through the night.'

'Daunting words from a nine-year-old,' my mother would say, as she ushered me off toward my bedroom. 'He's got to stop watching *The Streets of San Francisco*.'

My behavior, though alarming when described to any elementary school therapist I've ever met at a party, became amusing family stories during boring holidays. My mother was not bothered. She knew I wouldn't leave the house while sleepwalking. I had nowhere to go.

'And,' as Virginia observed, 'if he does escape, you can always follow his scent.'

CHAPTER ELEVEN

Make a lovingly shallow incision through the skin, from the neck, down

But, soon after Lisa untied me, our house was suddenly filled with the stress and tension of a new arrival, and my sleepwalking went from amusing to downright disturbing.

Penny, a cousin of my mother, and her husband and kids were visiting from Guam. That seemed so glamorous and exotic to me. I was so young. Only now do I know what a dump the army base on Guam really is.

And Penny had been a model. I wish I had a photo of her and my mom together. They were so pretty when they were teenagers. Penny was a high society type, who did all that runway-with-attitude bullshit. When I met her, even after she'd had all her kids, she looked like Grace Kelly. All her neurosis was just wrapped up in the French twist on her head. She carried around her own espresso maker. I admired her.

My mom was nervous about Penny being at our house. Apparently they'd competed for men when they were teenagers. Obviously Penny had won. Her husband was an officer who wore a really impressive uniform, and she travelled all over the world. My Dad worked in a liquor store. And he had left my mom for an asthmatic cocktail waitress. Yet my mother was determined to seem proud to be single, with three kids and a rented ranch-style home in the hippie suburbs of San

Francisco, and she maybe could've gotten away with it. After all she looked good in hip-huggers, which in 1971 was a cause for celebration.

Yeah, Mom could've maybe pulled it off, if not for Virginia's disappointed gaze. My grandmother was there, her left eyebrow up – that's *real* bad – watching my mother's every bell-bottomed move, even criticizing Mom for the messy garage and the dirty hand towels in the guest bathroom.

'Penny has learned to speak French.' Virginia said over blended drinks. 'Carol,' she'd continue, 'do you even know where France is?'

It was a regular family reunion, complete with all the scary little trimmings. Cousins who acted like they liked each other, around little kids who knew better, all of which was overseen by an old, conniving bitch with too much eye makeup who actually still looked good in pedal pushers. The men were invisible. Interchangeable. Certainly, not memorable. Funny how some things never change.

Anyway, everyone was anxious. And when my mother is nervous, the kitchen becomes a dangerous place. Penny arrived in the morning, so Mom had planned an elaborate brunch. Unfortunately things among the pots and pans had not gone well. I think the eggs were dropped. Or thrown. Suffice to say that what started out as Eggs Benedict and fresh fruit, with croissants and homemade jam, turned into a bowl of cereal and an orange. Served by a woman with ten bandaged fingers and one less Cuisinart.

And, during this, our first meal together, when I caught my mother staring at my brother, Rob, with pure rage in her eyes, as though she might kill him for leaving his dirty underwear in my cereal bowl again, I decided to hide all blunt instruments. Perhaps my mother was comparing us unfavorably to Penny's children, as much as I was comparing my mom to Penny. And though I knew that somehow a Higher Power had made a mistake when He/She placed me in this family, I saw my current circumstances as unchangeable.

Maybe Mom had thought she had options. She was still young. She could, of course, have started over. Which would have meant getting rid of her three children. Perhaps she was planning to end our lives quickly, painlessly, with poison in our TV dinners. Arsenic in our oatmeal. She might have planned to bury my body deepest in the backyard, otherwise my scent would have permeated the neighborhood. And how long, she might have wondered, would it be before any of the neighbors noticed her little ones missing? They all have their own families, their own children to punish and perhaps, later, destroy. By Halloween, Mrs Crumpet next door might wonder why Tom hadn't come over to demand more than his fair share of bite-sized Butterfinger bars. But Halloween was months away. By then, Mom could have skipped town. And become pregnant. A baby would've wiped her slate clean, and in all the fuss of restarting her family, miles and miles from this one-pony town, with perhaps a new identity, she'd forget that we three ever even existed. People's attention spans are so short.

As I sat at that table, watching my brother lift his bowl with both hands and drink the milk at the bottom of his corn flakes, I realized that I couldn't even remember who won last year's Academy Award for Best Actress. And that award was a lot more important than three little punks with no discernible skills.

It might have been at that blundered meal that Rob, Lisa and I all became aware of our suddenly tenuous positions in our mother's future plans because, for the first time since my father left, we tried to remain on our best behavior. Lisa helped Mom clear away the plates and throw away the orange peel.

Rob closed the bathroom door when he peed. He even lifted the seat.

I became conversational, but I had an agenda. I privately coveted the idea that Penny would somehow deem it necessary to adopt me. My mother might resist, but she could easily be disposed of. I was sure Penny's husband had high-ranking connections at the Pentagon. I dreamt of flying away with Penny's family. Soon, I thought, she'll ignore her own children, and see that she and I were meant to spend our lives together. Paris! Rome! Wherever our fantasies allowed!

But then my grandmother appeared with her armory.

'Tom, take this clove! And put some powder in your shoes! Oh, Penny, he smells so odd. Not like your children.'

Penny looked down on me and smiled. 'He's a boy.' She noticed! 'All boys have that smell.'

I was in love with Penny.

CHAPTER TWELVE

Now remove the heart, and discard it

Finally, Penny's first day came to an end, and, exhausted from being so fucking nice to each other, we all happily headed off for bed. Penny took my sister's room, which was next to my own. My sister wanted to sleep in my bed, near my Halloween candy. As I've mentioned, during lunar hours, both the candy and I were vulnerable to attack. That night the house was filled with even more enemies, some unfamiliar, like Penny's brats, and some, all too common, like a chubby sibling who had often found solace in a peanut butter cup. So I sent her to the living room, to drool on the couch.

I then closed my bedroom door. This was something I had never done, because I was always afraid of walking into it while I slept, thus breaking my nose and spoiling my plans for a future in daytime television. But I took the risk, for the sake of my candy.

I also wanted to be alone with my Penny thoughts.

What happened next isn't even a blur, because I was asleep the whole time. I can only relay the story as told to me. Apparently, I was in a greeting-while-sleeping sort of mood, because not far into the night, around midnight, I was already up, and moving toward my sister's room, where Penny slept peacefully, like a corpse, next to her husband, what's-his-name.

Years later, I pictured them in bed together, she with her hands and forearms folded gently across her chest and him wearing nothing but his officer's hat, smiling kindly as he dreamed of bombing some Third World dungpit to smithereens.

I walked into Penny's chamber and strolled right over to her cosmetics bag, which was neatly situated to the left of her bed, right near her head. I lifted the lid to the bag, and I guess I wasn't trying to be quiet, because Penny woke up. She said, 'Tom, what are you doing?'

I responded by whipping out my twelve-year-old penis and filling her overnight bag with urine. That's right, I peed right into it. I didn't try to impress her with my swordfighting abilities. I didn't even spell out my name with my own yellow Magic Marker of fluid. Nope. I just peed all over Penny's foundations and her travel-size canister of hair spray. Apparently the piss just kept on coming. Long enough for Penny's husband to be woken up, so he could tip back his hat, clear his eyes and say, 'Now, see here young man, this just won't do.'

I think Mom had allowed us two Cokes at dinner, since we were eating out. Might as well get that free refill. Who knew it would end up all over Penny's lipstick tray? When I finally finished, I put my penis back, and smiled.

'Shut up,' I whispered, and walked right back to bed.

I guess I'd been looking for the bathroom, and took a right instead of a left. A rather fatal deviation, although Penny was a good sport. She didn't say a word to anyone.

Well, not until the morning, when everyone had a good laugh. She showed Mom the recipes for Grilled Mahi Mahi and French Onion Soup she had brought with her. In her cosmetics bag. Those recipes were yellow, dripping pieces of wet paper now. They looked like instructions some sad lady had cried over. Which is exactly what they would've been, if my mother had attempted to follow them, wet or dry. Penny held them up, showing everybody at the breakfast table.

Everybody laughed.

Virginia said, 'I told you, Carol. I told you there'd be trouble with him.'

That's when I knew I'd never get to Guam.

Finally Penny left. Well, after she hit on my father. Apparently she and Dad had been pals when my parents were dating, and Penny was 'just dying' to see my father again. I couldn't imagine what it felt like to crave my father's company, and so I figured Penny was lying and just wanted to show off her ugly, spoiled kids to a new audience. When Mom called Dad, hoping he'd turn down her dinner invitation, he offered to take us all out.

Somehow, we wound up at the Nave Lanes, a bowling alley near the freeway. Well, it was a nice bowling alley, with glow-in-the-dark balls and twenty-four-hour food service. It was hard to find a restaurant that was kid-friendly, I guess.

Actually, it was hard to find anyone kid-friendly at our table. My siblings and I waited for our burgers, fidgeting, trying to cripple Penny's kids by kicking them mercilessly, while the adults were all over each other. Well, certain adults. All of us, including Penny's husband, saw Penny put her hand on my Dad's leg.

'Penny,' my mother said, while snapping her fingers to get the cocktail waiter's attention, 'Ted is in love with that Greek whore he's married to. I told you that.'

That's when Virginia's eyebrow took its normal lowbrow position again, and she stopped picking on my mother.

And I stopped sleepwalking. I think. Actually, no one is around to tell me. Lately I've been thinking about purchasing a video camera, and filming myself in bed at night, just to see if I still walk in my sleep. It might of course be cheaper to get a boyfriend, and let him tell me in the morning what I've done the night before. But to get a boyfriend I'd have to start up with the cloves and foot powder again. And that is something I'm not willing to do.

I should warn people about that on my 5x7 card.

CHAPTER THIRTEEN

Cleanse the inside with running water

You didn't complain about any sleepwalking, and you never mentioned a distasteful odor. You seemed to like that I smelled like gin and vermouth. And I liked that you didn't know who I was. I know you just thought I was some drunken 'daddy' type. Made you carnivorous about my cock. You could not get enough. I remember thinking, when we first slept together, how weird it is with you 'straight' guys. You boys just cannot wait to get down on it. Of course, *now* I know you're queer as crystal, but those real straight men – that security guard from that comedy club in Atlanta, even my electrician – they suck it like its made of candy. And you know, my dick is nothing to write home about. I guess I'm about average. Not that average is bad. Average is fine. If you've ever been with someone who's below average, you'll know how above-average average can be.

And I can shoot pretty far. That's sort of my specialty act. I can put an eye out, especially if I'm stoned. Which is why I usually get stoned before I go out to a bar.

In fact, that first night we met, I was ripped. I was such a mess after being nice to that old cunt all afternoon that I didn't even bother rolling a joint after my set, like I usually do. I just ingested a bud of pot with a Diet Coke at the mini-mart near the freeway. I never would have been brave enough to drag home a guy like you from a place like the Detour unless I was completely smashed. So this is all Virginia's fault, right? Maybe she'll loan us her car. Mine couldn't last through a long drive.

I usually don't tell people when I'm high anymore. Used to be you could pick up a hitchhiker, get him stoned, take him to a party, jump in the hot tub and bang! You've got an orgy. But nowadays everyone is so uptight about his or her own space being violated. And the only fags who admit to smoking pot are those queens who need it for medicinal purposes, because they're griddled. That's a term I use. Remember how AIDS was called GRID in the early '80s? Of course you don't, you're too young to remember that. Well, doctors first used the letters 'GRID' to identify the virus. It meant 'Gay-Related Immune Deficiency'. I think. Doesn't matter. Anyway, instead of saying that some faggots look 'riddled with AIDS', I abbreviated, and came up with 'griddled'. Do you know the look I mean? It's those cocksuckers that look like they've shot up one too many hits of steroids. Their skin is bright pink, and their cheeks are really sunken in. They have absolutely NO body fat. They look like gay action figures. Well, gayer action figures. And if there's lots of griddled faggots in one bar, I might say to Gregg, 'Boy, they're really griddling cakes in here tonight.'

Gregg gets very worked up when I say that, but he really needs to get a sense of humor about AIDS. I'm probably one handshake away from being griddled myself. Most guys I know are.

And when I'm taking up a cot at my local hospice, I need to know Gregg will be there, by my side, cracking some tasteless jokes while he passes me my flat Sprite with a paper straw.

These fags go on and on about safe sex, how important condoms are, blah, blah, blah. I told these queens at the Detour the other night to shut the fuck up about it. There's that group of sober, HIV negative Asian bottoms that hang out near the pool table. They're young, they all look like teenage girls, and think they'll live for ever as long as they put some rubber on every cock they meet. Stupid fucks. Just one rip, and they are history.

And what if they're lucky enough to drag home a cute white boy? That's all any of them want. They fuck each other, but they would kill for a real man. Are you telling me that if they had, who?, any male cast member from *Party of Five* in their beds, and they couldn't find a condom, that they wouldn't somehow rationalize some skin-to-skin contact? Who hasn't just sat right down on some hot stud's cock when there were no condoms nearby? I've woken up with shit on my dick more times than I care to mention. A person can't always follow these tedious, arbitrary guidelines about what you should and shouldn't do in bed. I need another drink. Everyone likes to break rules. Everyone likes to take risks. It's just human nature.

Which is for the best, anyway. Look, I know that by the time I'm fifty, I'll want to be released from this mortal coil. Why would anyone want to grow old and pathetic? I don't want to wind up like those old men I see on the bus, with bushes of hair sprouting out of every nook and cranny. Still, I'm too weak to commit suicide. What will I do? Skydive, and pray for the worst? Live on a Scottish diet for a while? That will kill anybody.

Or, I could just get fucked by a guy with purple lesions all over his body. I'll resist any medication, while I collect my government check and my church cheese. When I'm down to 7 T-cells, I'll name them. Dumpy, Sleepy, Grumpy, etc. I'll whistle while they work, then when they stop working, I'll gasp my last stale, griddled breath.

Let's face it, life just ain't no fun no more. Booze is barely tolerated. Pot is a no-no, unless I'm griddled. Our society isn't just clamping down on faggots. Things are getting worse for anyone with even half a brain who wants something more from life than a sports utility vehicle and three strokes.

That's why, when you saw my eyes under the street lamp on the way to the car, I didn't tell you I was high. I told you they were red because I'd been crying in therapy that morning. Which wasn't a total lie! I did have therapy that morning, before I went to lunch with that shriveled old twat.

CHAPTER FOURTEEN

Stand the chicken up, and, facing it, grab the neck bone, wrapping it with twine

Truth is, I've never actually cried in therapy, which has always disappointed me. I really want to cry, so I can see what all the hullabaloo is about. My friends go on and on about their therapy, how they cry every week, what a release it is. I have no idea what they mean. It's like being out of town during an earthquake. I feel so left out.

Sometimes I get stoned on the way to therapy, then I lie to my therapist and tell him my eyes are red because I was crying in the car on the way there. I just cannot bear therapy sober. My therapist thinks I am such a loser. He doesn't think I'm funny. He's never bothered to see my show. When we first started together, last year, he asked my to tell him some jokes in therapy. Excuse me! Who's paying who here? So I did this stuff about having a fourteen-year-old girlfriend, how I like to pee on her in the shower, because women like that. And she likes to tie my shoes because she just learned how. It's pretty funny stuff, but my therapist just stared at me, like I had shit rubbed all over my face. I'd never told him I was closeted in my act. I didn't want him to judge me. Now I know he thinks I'm just some gay-friendly straight guy who gets his kicks cruising lesbians at the Gay and Lesbian Therapy Center. Which isn't true. Although the vulva posters in the lobby are a definite draw.

What's odd is that after all these years of hiding it in my act, now I have to prove to my therapist each week that I'm gay. Which is why I think I embellish my sexual encounters. I just reenact some porn film I've seen.

'Well, Doctor, I was by the pool, and the pool boy came over and started massaging my shoulders. Then he asked me if I'd ever been fucked up the ass, and I said, "uh, I don't know about that."'

I can't even swim! What if my doctor and I rent the same porn films? Then he'll know I'm plagiarizing. I'll have to suck his cock to prove I'm gay, and that's just crossing way too many boundaries.

Have you ever been in therapy? Don't bother. Every week something irritates me and makes me more anxious than I was before I got there. Last week, I arrived early, because I'd actually woken up in my car, and was parked only a few doors down from my therapist's office. So I got stoned, and, once I crawled into his waiting room, started reading an article in *National Geographic* about the pain and torment the Tibetan monks suffer at the hands of the Chinese Army. When my therapist came out from his office to get me, I was annoyed because I was hungry, and because I was in the middle of this really great article. I didn't want to stop reading about the Tibetan monks so that I could deal with my mother's emotional absence during my childhood. I mean, several Tibetans had been burned alive in their own temples! Who cared if my mother didn't make my lunch every day? Those two tragedies hardly compared. And I *needed* to read about the Tibetan monks, because, like everyone else, I find pleasure in the pain of others.

In other words, therapy started on a sour note. We both sat in silence, with the clock ticking over my head. Then I remembered that I wanted the judge to think I was at least trying to get better, so I talked about my week, which consisted of one failed attempt at success after another.

That's when my doc did his usual 'reality check'. Asked me about my feelings. Apparently I'm good at facts, bad at feelings. I reminded David not to use hack terms like 'reality check'. After all, this was not a parody of a therapy session. We were actually doing this, so the more he stayed away from '80s self-help-book pitted-skin-guru talk, the more likely I was going to return the next week.

Then we discussed my hostility. I eyed the clock, just because I know it annoys him when I do that, and I paid by check.

I wonder why the fuck the judge ordered me to do this, when all I did was punch an audience member in the nose. Why couldn't I have just cleaned garbage off the road? Or paid a fine? After all, it was self-defense. The guy in that club was coming at me with a gun. At least, that's how it appeared to me. In court, he said he was just taking his hand out of his pocket to shake my hand, but he was a surfer. Those people are capable of anything.

I suppose the pot does make me a bit paranoid. At least, that was my defence in court. Which is why I usually want any trick I've dragged home out once the sex is over. I don't want them stealing from me. And I've got sheets to wash, and wallpaper to replace. Then there's the neighbors to calm. I'm usually dialling a yellow cab as I'm coming.

But I let you stay that first time we had sex because, well, I wanted to have sex with you again. And I wanted something positive to tell my therapist. I thought I'd impress him with the way I was 'changing'. That I'm a better person, who's learned to share his body in a caring way, and who doesn't need court-appointed help.

That sounds manipulative in so many ways, doesn't it?

Fucking you, fucking the system. I sound so revolutionary, when all I really am is disgruntled. I guess I don't believe in therapy. I've never benefitted from it. I mean, two decades of therapy, off and on, and look at me. Bitter, lonely and smelling of drink. My family, myself – we all had such higher hopes for me. I was such a smug, indifferent child, and most people who are cunts as children end up taking over the world. Look at Bill Gates. He's been patronizing for forty-two years!

The young Hitler apparently had a very nasty sense of humor. He wound up doing very nicely for himself. Doesn't he run a successful Argentinian beef restaurant in Los Angeles?

But me? I've been actively offending people with the same confrontational adjectives and dirty dick jokes I've been telling for eons. But do I occupy most of Europe? No. I patiently perfect my craft, while my peers pass me by.

I hear they're going to rename Holland 'BillGatesLand'.

When do I get to party with Barbra Streisand and her husband, what's-his-name? What is his name? Pussywhip? Yeah, that's it. Anyway, when do I get to party with the main pussy and her little whip? I wonder if Barbra likes Argentinian beef? She's probably chowing down on one of those chargrilled burgers right now, bemoaning the treatment of ethnic Albanians while she tries to wrangle a few million out of anyone who will listen to the plot line of her next movie about . . . her.

CHAPTER FIFTEEN

Cross the twine over the ankles, and pull tightly

Maybe my biggest problem is that I started therapy too late. I needed help at a very early age. It was clear, to most of those around me, that, as a teenager, I was unsteady. And I wasn't managing my awkwardness very well.

Actually, in those days, 'geek' was the nicest thing anyone could have called me. Kids were cruel to me. Much more cruel than they usually were. Actually, they were nice until they hit puberty. Then they turned thirteen, and suddenly, anything different was circumspect. And boy, was I different.

When I was thirteen, my mother transferred my sister and brother and me from San Francisco to a wealthy suburban enclave about a half-hour north of the city. The town of Novato proudly featured an outdoor Olympic-size swimming pool at the YMCA, but the school system sucked. All the kids could dive off really high boards, but getting them to read was like pulling molars.

I had been a decent enough student at my urban school, but in the sticks I was a genius. And kids don't like geniuses. And nobody likes a fourteen-year-old smartass, which is what I quickly became. What choice did I have? I was 5 feet 11 inches, and I weighed 130 pounds. Ouch. I was thin to the point of being brittle. And I had feathered hair, which was fashionable in the big city but a bit too flamboyant for children who skipped stones between classes.

Oh, and I had big, buck teeth covered with braces. Big braces with headgear. I was living in the decade of headgear. The 1970s! And since you weren't even born until, what, 1976? Great, well, baby, let me describe headgear to you. It was a big metal bar that was meant to correct a kid's overbite by using the head for leverage and pulling the teeth back into the skull. The headgear attached to the side of the braces, and went around the back of the head. I felt like a little loser in a stainless steel helmet. If my dentist had his way, the metal would have continued down my back then tied in a hard alloy bow around my waist. Sadistic bastard. I swear he was trained at Dachau.

Everytime I went to see him, he added all sorts of pulleys and hinges to complete the lovely corrective picture. Rubber bands that attached to the braces assisted the metal's friction, so that, with every gesture of the mouth, the teeth were continually moving back into their correct position. The slow torture never ceased. A kid with headgear never gets a break from the pain. And I had this contraption in my mouth for seven years.

Maybe now you can see why I never had a moment's peace in the suburbs.

All the cool kids in Frisco had headgear, but unfortunately the rich kids in my new school in the sticks had been born with perfect dental structures. Those mutants popped out of the womb with a white picket fence from dimple to perfectly symmetrical dimple. Like used cars, my new classmates' flaws were internal. Clearly, they could not be trusted.

I became the school leper, the two-headed monster, the Jew in Hitler's Germany. I knew then how Jesus must have felt. Every group needs a pariah, and I was it. And while I sank into my own bench at lunch time, reading science fiction novels and combing my hair forward, these kids developed, more quickly than my teeth, into something more and more perfect. Where as I wore a big blue parka, hiding my body from the hot sun, my classmates proudly wore shorts and spent their breaks doing pull-ups and glaring at me. Maybe that's because I looked like a serial killer long before anyone knew what a serial killer was. I nervously rearranged my hair, like the doctor on the original *Lost in Space*. I often found dissected creatures left over from science class stuffed in my parka pocket.

I still think children raised in the suburbs should be euthanized.

They were jealous, my mom told me.

'Honey, they're just full of sour grapes. They wish they knew all the state capitals and could add. They wish they were more like you.'

And so, after school, while boys my age dragged me into the bathroom and pinned me up against the wall, throwing wet paper towels at my face, I thought to myself, maybe someone should tell these guys that being me isn't all that glamorous.

They'd whisper 'faggot' into my ear while my hand was raised to answer a question. Others would call me 'girlie boy' and slap my ass as I passed in the hallway. These are all things that, as an adult, I waited anxiously for my sloppy tricks to do. But as a kid, it all seemed really sinister. The twins were particularly evil.

Now, admittedly, twins have every reason to be angry with somebody. They know they're genetic misfits. Some weird fucking chromosome malfunctioned, and they wound up with the same DNA. Or something. It's vulgar. It's creepy. They're a circus act. Especially if they're ugly.

Brian and Brett, the evil twins, were freckled and ginger. And their last name was Gross. Sad, and yet proof that if there is a God he does have a sense of irony, but why take their misfortune out on me? I didn't make them freaks. Why didn't they pick on their parents? If they'd gone nuts, and blown their parents away, and then prayed for the Lord's mercy, any court in the land would have let them off the hook. Instead, they used their powerful football-strengthened knees to pin me down on the lawn during gym class. While one freak tickled me, the other would hang a long wad of spit over my face for about a minute, sucking it up into his mouth, then letting it drop until it was a half inch from my nose. Then they'd let me do their homework.

Perhaps I solicited some of these punishments with my attitude. My brain was all I had to protect me, so I used it like a shield. Whenever another kid made fun of me, I had a clever retort that included calculus and sometimes even a Dorothy Parker axiom. My classmates would just stare at me, mouths agape, as if I'd shit in my pants.

Nobody knew how to respond to me, except my closeted history teacher, Mr Tampton. You can probably imagine what the kids called him behind his back. He adored me. He lived with his mother, and he looked like Roy Scheider after a really bad binge. We'd sit in the library after school and talk for hours about various wars. He'd been in the military, and was dismissed for mysterious reasons. Now, of course, I know what those reasons probably were. If I'd known at the time, I would have smoked his flagpole.

I knew I was queer. Most queers know at a really early age. For me, it was three. I was in love with our babysitter, Gary Achret.

Oh, my God. I'm feeling another tangent coming on.

Gary was thin and balding and asthmatic. But he was all mine, and I doted on him with the kind of fierce love most children usually save for sick kitties. After her divorce my mother needed a babysitter to watch the three of us while she worked all day. Eventually Gary became like a part of the family, and we used to take him with us when we went out of town on the weekends.

The Alvarado Inn wasn't the snappiest resort in the Bay Area, but it had a big bar with big bartenders, and that was all Mom needed for a party. My mother would go out at night and slam a few down, while Gary would stay with us kids in our hotel room. He didn't really have the oxygen intake that your average partygoer needs to get through the night, so we'd all watch scary movies. I was always craving to see Gary naked, so I contrived these silly games so that Lisa, Rob and I would wind up in the bathroom while Gary innocently showered. Lisa would always fling open the shower door, and yummy! There stood Gary, naked and wet and shrivelled. My sister was unimpressed, and my brother was already watching TV, but I just ogled. I stared at my future.

That's why, when I was thirteen, almost a decade later, I couldn't happily handle the horseplay other kids tossed my way. I was defensive when kids called me 'fag', because I knew I was a fag. I couldn't laugh it off. If I had, the hazing would've ended. Instead, I sprayed verbal venom. I was a nasty fag-in-waiting. And that's why Mr Tampton gave me this advice: 'Learn to like sucking my dick.'

Kidding. He never said that. He didn't have to. Kidding. We never did anything. I didn't have sex for years. How could I have sucked cock with all that piercing metal in my mouth? It would've been like fucking a set of steak knives.

What Mr Tampton did say was: 'Save the drama for the stage, Sarah Bernhardt.'

I think he's dead now.

The torture and loneliness went on for the entire school year, until, one day, while riding home on my orange five-speed with a banana seat and frilly plastic fringe hanging from the handlebars, a short, stocky Jewish boy I had a secret crush on named Audi Kippler stuck a stick through the spokes of my front wheel. My bike stopped suddenly, but I kept going, right over my handlebars.

The doctors said I was lucky I was wearing my headgear. Otherwise, my entire head would have gone through that tree. As it was, I hit an oak face first going about 30 miles an hour, but the metal bar that attached to my braces lessened the impact. I had to have what teeth were left in my mouth rewired, along with my jaw. The teeth the ambulance driver found on the road were made into a paperweight by retarded artists down the hall from my hospital room.

The only good thing that came out of the whole experience was I became more familiar with Audi. He was gregarious, and he was a Carpenters fan. He was good at tennis, and his parents and his counsellor made him visit me in the hospital. We actually struck up a friendship, probably because I was drugged and wired shut, so I seemed nice. I fell in love with Audi, of course, and soon I forgot all about Ira, the ambulance driver who had held my teeth all the way to the emergency room.

CHAPTER SIXTEEN

Cross twine over wings, pull tight, and secure all vulnerable parts

I realized, while recovering in the hospital, bandaged and bruised, that some things in my life had to change. I was up to my neck brace in self-hatred and hormones, and if I ever wanted to stick my penis in anything other than a greased-up Coke bottle, then I had to get out from behind my books and live a little. Like Audi. He was so confident. He'd involved himself with the Novato amateur dramatics club. Perhaps I could tag along, make new friends, and see Audi in tights.

I decided to take Mr Tampton's advice, literally.

It was a decision that many queens before me had contemplated, because, in the suburbs, the fastest short cut to Fagville is through the local theatre community. And in Novato, small-time theatre was loaded with closeted husbands and eager stagehands. Where do you think the term 'drama queen' came from? At least, that's what a couple of women I heard talking on the bus one day were saying.

'If there are any hetero actors left at my community theatre,' the shorter lady said to the taller lady, 'I can't find them. And believe me honey, I have looked. What else is there to do during auditions? But I was so disappointed. All those guys have made one too many entrances, if you get my drift.'

Oh, I got it all right.

Local theatre actors in my town were very eccentric. A lot of them had tried, and failed, to be thriving thespians in San Francisco but instead wound up as ex-hippies with televisions in their kitchens, living the lives they'd hoped to avoid. Station wagons. Fast food. Pre-fab condos. And lots of excuses as to why they weren't expressing their inner feelings. In their defense, however, some did create sort of a thriving theatrical experience for themselves.

Novato became the home of the Renaissance Fair, which drew thousands of onlookers every August. For next to no money, local actors happily shoved their pale thighs into tights or squeezed into a pseudo-Victorian ball gown left over from the local college's production of *Scrooge*. Victorian, Renaissance, it didn't matter. They just needed to look old and English. After all, seeing a fat girl stumbling through dirt and 90-degree heat in thick, maroon velveteen, with a huge plastic drumstick in one hand, and a small clown's head on a stick in the other, was easily worth the price of admission. Several accents were thrown about, none of which were accurate or even slightly British, but they were earnest, dear souls. For three brief weekends, these players believed they were townsfolk from the seventeenth century. Or the sixteenth. When did Shakespeare live? Whatever. Anyway, the women working at the fair didn't shave their armpits, which for Americans, who believe that hairy armpits on women are tantamount a crime to child molestation, was a huge sacrifice. I only mention it to emphasize their sincerity.

And three times a day, an actress with a partially-shaved hairline and no eyebrows, dressed vaguely as Queen Elizabeth, was carried through the crowd, while minstrels danced behind her, playing mandolins and drums. At 2 p.m., and then again at 4 and 6, that poor woman, whoever she was, had to pull on that sweaty red wig, tug up her puffy sleeves, and be ogled at by frightened crying children who probably thought she was a flying clown. Or just a high-maintenance queen who desperately craved the adoration of her dusty, overextended subjects.

Actually, the latter could've described most of the male employees of the Renaissance Fair. They acted up a storm, sucking in as much stomach flesh and approval as they could. The females competed with the faggots in volume. And at every performance of a twenty-minute bastardized version of *A Midsummer Night's Dream*, the actors lucky enough to land the roles of the four young lovers minced and quipped about in something beyond mere 'high camp'. They acted in tones so high-pitched, so ear-splitting, that beer mugs shattered, sending glass shards for yards. Mirrors, crystal balls, glass eyes: all fell victim to the outrageously piercing pitch resonating through that walnut grove three times daily.

The straight male actors, who as always had less to do and thus had more time on their hands, behaved as though they were on vacation. They peed in nearby apple groves, then drank more booze — sorry, mead — and fucked each other's spouses behind the ale stand. They fancied themselves living the lives of gypsies, without all the matted hair and political persecution.

And in the true tradition of theatrical flamboyancy, several of the actors made their own costumes so that they could wear them all year long, keeping the spirit of the Renaissance alive long after the spattering of applause from the heat-exhausted, nauseous crowds died out. These mates and wenches could be heard far beyond Christmas, trumpeting their entrances into the local McDonald's with terms like, 'Hey ho, me Lord, your servant has arrived!' or 'Aye, me Lady, I bid you welcome.'

If an actor in Novato wasn't strange, and didn't own at least one leather codpiece, theatrical folk there grew suspicious. They felt infiltrated by unnecessary normalcy.

Unfortunately, I fit right in. I was a total freak. I had just turned sixteen, and almost overnight, I had sprouted to 6 feet, 2 inches, yet my weight had barely changed. I was no more than 140 pounds. My headgear was still there, big and shiny, as was my hair. I was embraced into their world with open, albeit tattooed and sometimes a bit too hairy, arms.

I'd missed the Renaissance so I auditioned for the local college's fall production of *Brigadoon*. I didn't know the show. I didn't care about musicals. It didn't matter to me what kind of show it was. It could've been a musical about something as boring and lifeless as chess. I wouldn't have minded.

I JUST WANTED TO SUCK COCK!

To prepare for my audition, I borrowed the Broadway cast recording of *Brigadoon* from my local library and read the liner notes.

> Brigadoon is a musical extravaganza about a small Scottish Highlands town from the sixteenth century that reappears once every century to recreate love and laughter and clogging. Then, after only twenty-four hours of such joy, the town fades back into the mist, only to reappear again, in a hundred years.

Forces a tear to your eye, doesn't it? Pulls hard on the ol' heartstrings. I personally found the show a bit whiney, almost morose, but I had to audition it. I was determined to impress Audi.

Also, have I mentioned I wanted to suck cock?

However, it seemed as though hundreds of would-be stars showed up for the audition. The college auditorium was a whirl of legwarmers and rainbow suspenders. I wore white slacks and a 'dance: ten, looks: three' T-shirt my mother loaned me for the audition. I sang twelve bars of 'Friendship' and moped home.

The next day I found out I'd been cast as a Scottish High-lands townsperson from the sixteenth century. With braces and headgear. I was so thin that a kilt could not be found to fit me, so I wore a Catholic schoolgirl's uniform, complete with knee-high socks and a rakishly tilted beret. And that's no problem at all when you're sixteen, dealing with your sexuality while your mother is dealing cocaine.

I felt so ridiculous, so miscast. But now looking back on that experience, I realize I was perfectly cast. Because me, in braces and a Catholic schoolgirl's skirt, really is something you only want to see once every hundred years.

I was shy, and so accustomed to hiding away from people that I avoided eye contact with just about every actor in the company. And of course by trying to draw attention away from myself I became the central character in all the theatrical gossip swirling around me.

Especially when a married man named Howie hit on me in the dressing room. He stood behind me in front of a full-length mirror and, as we prepared for the final performance, ran his calloused hand up my skirt. I almost threw up. Not only because Howie was so repulsive, but also because I was so nervous. Oh, and because I was in love with Audi. I sucked Howie's dick anyway. I was sixteen. I had sperm backed all the way up to my tweezed eyebrows.

Unfortunately, my first blowjob was not very good. A bit metallic. So Howie countered. Sweet of him, don't you think? But when I ran my fingers through Howie's hair, I went to lift my hand, and yikes! His hair was still on it! He wore a toupee. When I shook it off, it landed back on his head. I tried to rearrange it, but it just looked like a bad haircut. Afterward, while he was wiping the sperm out of his rug, he said, 'That was great. Most guys don't caress me that much.'

'I wasn't caressing, Howie. I was restyling.'

Brigadoon was my first, and last, show at that theatre.

Audi was not impressed by my work in and out of the dressing room. The rumor about my tryst with a married man at the local college had somehow swept its way through our high school drama department like wild fire. I guess people had nothing better to do in the suburbs than worry about paedophiles.

By then, I'd become a Sir Francis Drake High Drama Club member, and I practiced scenes with Audi. I confided in him that I hoped the rumors wouldn't ruin my chance to play Nicholas Nickleby at next year's Renaissance Fair. I know, Victorian. Audi said he didn't take the blowjob story seriously, and neither would anyone else. He merely shrugged it off as idle gossip.

'Ignore them. They're stupid.'

I'm sure he used a much bigger word than 'stupid', but I'm too drunk right now to remember it. Audi was so mature. He reminded me of an uncle. Not any of my uncles. They're all morons and thieves. But I mean, the way an uncle should be. I trusted him. I even followed him to college, in southern California. Hell, that's why I went to study acting at UC Irvine, just to be near him. But Audi just got more into drugs and into his girlfriend. He ended up quitting theatre in the middle of our freshman year, and going underground, hiding from drug dealers and the FBI. I think he lives around the corner from here, with a young Mexican guy, under an assumed name. I think it's Meister. I saw him on the street, and I followed him, but I didn't recognize the name on the mailbox. Mr Meister. He's still the same. He still cracks me up.

Oddly enough, I almost didn't recognize him. He's really fat now. And he's missing a bunch of teeth. Maybe that's karma. He's also bald. I know it's been twenty years and people change, but when I was in love with him, he was so pale, so eager, so muscly and vital. Now he carries a paper under his arm and lopes from one coffee shop to another. He wears dark glasses and a hat. His Latino friend drives him places in an old convertible Toyota, and they smoke a lot of pot. Maybe he's in the witness protection program. Maybe he's fingering mobsters. Maybe he's fingering the Latino. I wonder if he knows that I became addicted to performing, and now I'm a comic. Among other things.

CHAPTER SEVENTEEN

Now weigh the bird

College was where I started on my contemplative path toward self-examination. Not because I thought I really needed therapy. True, when Audi disappeared, I felt like I'd lost the greatest love of my life. But after a weekend, I was over it. I was eighteen. The elasticity of youth is infamous. The fact is I started therapy for probably the wrong reason. It was offered free of charge to all students. And I liked bargains.

Little did I know that I desperately required some sort of balance. Somewhere between my exemplary work as a high school senior and my freshman year in college, I changed. I became a slacker, which in 1981 was labelled, merely, a stoner.

In high school, I'd been the kind of student who sat in the backseat of my mother's Pinto, writing extra credit reports on the decay of the Latin American economy during the Nixon administration. We were on our way to the movies, and I didn't want to waste time chatting with my family. For God's sake, graphs had to be drawn!

But the summer before my freshman term in college, I got my braces off. Several years of anxiousness were suddenly brushed away, and for the first time I was sporting a winning smile. I was so proud of my pearly whites, in fact, that I went to a party. A cast party for a show I wasn't even in, and I didn't bring my homework along. I was there to meet and greet, metal-free and lookin' fine.

I arrived wearing dill-colored Yves St Laurent slacks and a yellow polo shirt. Times were easier when yuppie clothes were in fashion. When I stumbled upon a group of actors smoking pot around a rectangular table, I asked, 'Hey, what are you guys doin'?' Well, the only thing that can elicit any sort of excitement from a room full of potheads is a drug novice, and within about twenty minutes, I was smoking some of the best weed that any teenager's artificially sunlit closet could offer.

It wasn't good pot. But it didn't matter. For the first time in my life, I felt relaxed. I was with some guys I barely knew, but they all seemed like the nicest people I'd ever met. I experienced the kind of euphoria anyone might feel who suddenly realizes that, hey, maybe the whole world *isn't* against me. I thought, maybe it doesn't matter if I'm attracted to Audi. Maybe it doesn't matter if I'm attracted to men other than Audi. Lots of guys like other guys. I looked around the table, and wondered, are some of these guys into me? Like Billy, the boy who gave me this joint. I liked the idea of using the word 'joint' casually, when referring to something other than my knee or shoulder or wrist. I wanted big shoulders and stiff wrists. I wanted curly blond hair. I wanted to be on MTV. I said, 'Thanks for the joint, Billy.' And he smiled. 'Anytime, dude.' I needed to be the kind of person who could use the word 'dude' as an identifier. Suddenly selling drugs seemed like a viable career option for me. I thought, maybe I can get away with wearing sandals all year long. Maybe I can get away with trimming my own fringe. Maybe I can get away with putting my hand on Billy's crotch.

And all hell sort of broke loose. I discovered that when I got stoned, I got hornier. And so did Billy. And so did lots of boys who claimed to be straight.

My metamorphosis from an uptight gay yuppie fuck to an uptight gay yuppie fuck with a new diversion was complete.

I had a pot plant and a hard-on all the way through university. Nothing was safe around me when I was high. I smoked so much pot one weekend, I humped a dorm chair. The fabric seemed nice. I would've fucked a blowhole if a whale moved into my dorm. Well, a male whale.

So, therapy seemed perfect for me. Who likes talking about themselves more than a horny, doped-up drama student with lots of people to blame and loads of dorm mates to impersonate?

In class, when I decided to show up, late, I was a 'difficult' actor. I would go for the laughs in every scene. I always found a reason to drop my pants, no matter how serious the material. Cancer plays, Holocaust plays, incest plays. It didn't matter. To me, everything was a musical! I'd pull chairs out from other actors while we were rehearsing Chekhov, just to see the shocked looks on their faces. I was probably laughing more than the students in attendance, but that's because I was stoned. I took a Tennessee Williams workshop, just so I could play Blanche in black face.

'I's always depended on d' kindness uh dems strangers, Masser.'

My instructor, a black woman, had to be pulled off me by five leading men.

I wonder if I have a photo of that?

None of the student directors would cast me in any of the shows. I was obviously unable to recognize the depth of expression necessary to confront the truly creative soul. After all, the university was only one hour from Hollywood, so I was competing with some 'very serious actors'. The head of my department, Bob Cohen, pulled me into his office one day and informed me, wearily, that my days in his drama department were at best, numbered.

'Some of these kids have futures,' he told me, while brushing the remnants of a tuna fish sandwich out of his goatee. 'This department is getting lots of attention from some big showbiz types. Why, just the other day Edward Albee stopped by and said hello. In this very office.' Yeah, Bob, and he also hit on just about every tall, skinny actor within a twenty-mile radius. Everybody knew that Albee was just a shaggy lump who hung out at the college to rim thin guys and restage some of the compost he called his 'one-acts'.

'So, we don't have time for your mamsy-pamsy kiddie play.' Once again, Bob was doing his best John Wayne impersonation, mingling some sort of 'real man' gibberish with prudent advice. On the first day of class, Professor Cohen would always tell his room full of beginning actors to 'look up into the rafters, and cry'. When some, like me, looked on, skeptically, at the pasty girls in wrap-around skirts tearing up, Bob snarled, 'Do some of you babies need a slap on the ass? Let's see some tears, or someone's gonna be sweeping up dressing rooms all semester long.'

Eventually most of the faculty refused to work with me, so therapy became my acting class. Each week, I would perform an hour-long monologue for a bright-faced grad student. Every three months, the doctors-in-training would rotate and I'd get a raw victim, who would pick up his or her pad, smile wryly and ask, 'Well, Tom, why the glum look? Do you wanna let me know what's gettin' you down?'

That sort of forced friendliness was all the reason I needed to emotionally manipulate my would-be physicians. So young, so fresh, and so easy to destroy. And so impacted by my past. I told them everything, from the pain I'd suffered with my abusive father, to my abandonment by my drug-addicted mother. Like most good fiction, much of my storytelling was mired in fact.

I'd end pretty much every session by saying, 'And that's how I wound up in that kiddy porn ring, Doctor!'

I guess I pretty much garnished whatever my 5x7 card was at the time. The shrink wannabes would laugh and cry and take their notes home with them. I hoped my first voyeurs wrote expletives like 'heart-wrenching!' or 'painfully exhilarating!'

As the sessions went on, I wanted my next eager caretakers to realize I'd grown through self-knowledge, scribbling 'ironically kind' or 'bravely self-deprecating'. Near the end of our time together, I thought perhaps my last remaining emotional casualties would reach the 'He's a kick!' stage. Unfortunately, I never had a chance to see my 'reviews'. My run ended when I had to graduate.

CHAPTER EIGHTEEN

Fill the cavity with fat

After college, while doing my starving actor bit in LA, I heard that a lot of film deals were being cut in analysts' waiting rooms. My actor's union paid for weekly sessions, and since I had plenty of time on my hands, I found a reputable therapy center in Beverly Hills. It was like a mall of therapy, where several different therapists rented offices but shared one receptionist and one waiting room. I was hoping to meet some lonely, vulnerable producer or Valium-chewing director whom I could seduce near the coffee urn. Boy or girl, it wouldn't have mattered. When you're desperate, you're more than willing to make concessions.

Obviously, my initial goal was to impress. It was designer this and shoplifted that. If I wanted to be a celebrity I had to dress the part. I just copied what the models wore in those glossy magazines. Almost verbatim.

I started preparation early, so I could arrive an hour *before* therapy – can you imagine? – blow-dried and spruced. I was tweezed and spritzed and trimmed and plucked. All hard edges were sanded down to a smooth, shiny finish. It took hours. Once complete, I walked steadily from my apartment to my car, calmly but with direction, while my arms stretched straight out beside me, so as not to wrinkle or damage anything on my person. I must have looked like Sissy Spacek in her final moments in *Carrie*. I couldn't roll the car windows down, because my hair would've been mussed by the wind. Instead, I drove to therapy in a sort of trance, concentrating on not perspiring.

By the time I arrived at the clinic, I was of course drenched in sweat. I always had to rush to the men's room and dry off with paper towels. Which of course smeared my bronzer. And creased my rayon. Being beautiful is a lot of hard work. Naomi Campbell is to be pitied, not envied.

The waiting room had fluffy, comforting sofas that could seat two, cozily. It was there I sat, or, rather, perched, ankles crossed, hands folded, waiting for the first prey wearing anything Armani and dangling a Mercedes car key.

Thank God I'm too old to worry about all that shit now. Let the younger generation mix and match. I've basically become colorblind. I must have misplaced the gay fashion gene. If it were up to me, I'd work and sleep in jeans and a T-shirt. Easy access. So I guess I've never considered myself a clothes horse. Actually, I'm not even sure what that term means, although for years, that is how my mother described her cousin Penny. Before I met Penny, I was sure she looked like Mr Ed in a bonnet. Now, I know that 'clothes horse' doesn't refer to anything equine. Well, I think it doesn't. To be honest, I'm not sure what 'clothes horse' means. And neither does my mother, by the way. In fact, since leaving home, I've realized my mother doesn't know a lot of things that, as a child, I assumed she had a complete grasp of.

I wonder if my messy relationship with my mother influenced my choice to become a performer? You'd think after my years of therapy, I'd know the answer to that. But it's hard to honestly admit that yes, I had a fucked-up childhood. Thing is, all performers I know had brutal upbringings. Some of my favorite comics were beaten silly as kids. Right after church. First they saw God, then they saw stars. Then they became stars.

I guess my parents' ignoring me was harmful enough to make me disturbing, but not excruciating enough to make me brilliant. I wish my mom and dad had beaten me. Just a bit. Here and there, a few bruises, or maybe just a broken arm. I mean, yeah, my siblings knocked me around a bit, but that's not as wonderfully agonizing as when your dad and all his friends rent a motel room and gang-bang you. I read in *Time* magazine that that's how some famous painter got started. My dad was such a pussy he couldn't raise a hand to vote, and my mother was too busy drinking jug wine and listening to the *Lady Sings the Blues* soundtrack through huge black leatherette headphones to ever become violent.

And a hard slap was what I needed in LA. Especially while roosting in that reception area. I kept falling asleep, I was so bored. They didn't serve cocktails. Not even a beer, for Christ's sake. No wonder all those patients were so miserable. All they had to drink was coffee. How could I hit on people in a waiting room with a Styrofoam cup in my hand? It's hard to look cool when you're drinking out of something flammable.

In fact, I have a very frightening, furrowed look in my eyes when I'm drinking coffee. Because coffee makes me sober, and when I'm sober, I'm slightly detached, but also very intense. Which I think are the two characteristics of a stalker. My leering gaze must have been what caused several Italian suits to scamper off to the toilet. And lock the door. And then escape through the window above the sink.

When not in therapy, I auditioned. I'd wangled a rather dubious agent by winning an acting competition in my last semester at college. I'd played a white trash geek in a comedy one-act, and guess what, the crowd went wild. I knew then that if I couldn't get laughs by impersonating myself, I should get out of the business.

After the presentation of the award, a small, bleached, consumptive lesbian named Nina approached me. She placed her pervious hand on my shoulder, pulled my ear toward her puckered mouth, and whispered, 'You're gonna be a big fucking star one day.'

Then she coughed. A lot.

Then she offered me her card. I was afraid that if I touched it I'd burst into a ball of flames. Or be asked to trade in my soul. Or at the very least, contract polio. When none of the above happened, I called her at her office in Beverly Hills.

She asked if I was ready to be a big fucking star.

'How would that feel?' For once, I wasn't being a smart ass. I really wanted to know.

'Like you would do anything – *anything!* – for a part.'

Oh God, I thought, here it comes. She's gonna make a pass at me. It's the old casting couch routine, and we're not even in the same room. I'm going to have to have phone sex with this old woman. I'm going to have to fake an orgasm, while this dried-up old troll fingers herself under her desk. And it's not even lunchtime yet.

I was terrified. I'd never fucked a woman before. I couldn't figure out what I would say to her. I wondered: Are tight holes good on girls, too?

I probably would've tried that tired old line I used on girls in high school.

'I don't want to penetrate you. I respect you too much.'

Even over the phone, that would've sounded cheesy. Luckily, Nina stopped me before I could even utter a word, and she said, 'Now don't get all silent on me. I just need to know if you're willing to audition for any sort of role. I won't ask you to cut off your legs at the knees, and then dance around on your stumps. Unless dancing on your stumps was part of a dream sequence or something. They're doing some weird shit on cable nowadays. But it pays well. It's just that I don't want you to get squeamish on me. Or particular.'

'Oh, don't worry, Nina. I'll audition for anything.'

'Even a queer?' She played this one like it was her trump card. Months later, while in her office to drop off some photos, I heard her ask this same question over the phone to some other aspiring actor. Clearly, in her mind, the question as to whether or not some guy would lower himself into cocksucking ooze just so he could be in front of a camera, no matter how demeaning the material, really separated the losers from the seriously ambitious actors. 'Ever since Bruce Jenner won that gold medal in the Olympics a few years back, queers have been very popular on television.'

'Oh, yeah, Nina. I can play a queer. At least, I can try.'

She coughed. 'Are you sure? Do you even know how gay men act?'

I promised her I'd bone up on them.

'Good for you, kid.'

I asked her if she would need anything from me.

'Sure will. You'll need to send me a résumé. Something that looks flash. Just list a bunch of plays, and type in that you played the leads. Casting people don't care. They don't expect you to be honest. You're in college. They just want you to be young. And you'll need photos. And I don't mean your high school graduation photos. You'll need actual headshots. Got a pen?'

She sent me to one of her photographers. Sir Richie took photos in a studio full of western paraphernalia. Dark wooden walls, adorned with wagon wheels and spurs hanging off hooks. Upon arrival, I thought, 'He must be a cowboy!'

But when I caught a glimpse of him, striding toward me,

shirtless, wearing nothing more than black leather chaps tucked into steel-toed black army boots, I thought, 'Maybe I *don't* know how gay men act.'

He held out his hand for me to shake. His palm felt cold and limp. The pink of his face seemed painted on, he looked almost blistered, and his eyebrows were gray and severely arched. I realized they were drawn on to his forehead, like little ash-colored mountains atop pools of cloudy corneas. It was then that I realized he was basically a vampire. He looked me up, and down. He asked me to turn around. As I did I felt his hand brush against my bottom. It was like auditioning for one of Albee's one-acts, especially when he told me to take off my clothes.

I told him, basically, that I was not that kind of girl.

'Oh, don't get all prissy with me, dear. Nina said she wanted innocence, and what could be more fragile than you, unclothed? You're so thin. And frail. I'm doing this for your own good, so drop your drawers!'

Once disrobed, I felt self-conscious.

'Yeah,' Sir Richie slurred, as he whirled around me, snapping photos. 'You feel afraid, don't you? Show me that fear. Give me some Bambi, baby. Come on, you're Red Riding Hood, and I'm the Big Bad Wolf!'

He should've paid me. Especially since I'm sure he and some friends have jacked off all over those glossies. In one of the photos he dressed me up in a baseball cap and jersey, like a cheerleader at a night game. I'm looking over my shoulder, with a surprised-to-be-sodomized look on my face. Very fetching.

When Nina showed me the photos, about a week later, I felt sick. I looked kind of like Ann-Margret on speed. Well, on more speed. Why was there so much airbrushing? Sparkling bits of florescence appeared to be bouncing off my profile. If I had any more light in my face, I would've been on fire. I looked like a flaming Christmas tree.

Nina liked the photos. 'They work.'

'I look like Sir Richie.'

'I thought they were Sir Richie. We represent him, too.'

CHAPTER NINETEEN

Sprinkle the insides with pepper

N ina sent me to a different photographer, who took photos that actually looked like me. I was relieved, until I actually went on auditions.

I sat in a lot of artificially lit rooms, scattered with a smattering of tall, skinny guys who looked like me, waiting to stand in front of a camera and yell, 'Skippy peanut butter hits the mark!' or 'Got any milk?' And that was a good day.

The bad days happened when I was dressed in a Santa outfit in the middle of July, and I was breakdancing. At that point, I had no idea what the product was that we were trying to advertise. Like a prisoner, I just did what I was told. Everyone did. We all rolled around in red felt, choking on our fake fuzzy beards.

We all wanted to 'make it'. But I wasn't quite sure what that meant. Photos in *People* magazine suggested that 'making it' had something to do with beating up photographers and fucking pop stars. But I wasn't aggressive, nor was I attracted to Madonna. I mean, I wasn't that gay.

I wasn't gay at all, actually. Well, not in auditions. I instead read for the kind of characters an audience could trust. The kind of young men who were too busy tripping over things or repairing their broken Buddy Holly glasses with cellophane tape to have orgasms. We were too zany! The excitement of

ejaculation would've killed us! We would have at least broken
a limb, slipping in our own semen.

Nina's assistant would send me short scripts that required
me to be 'out there' and 'totally over the top (OTT)'. Adjectives
like these, even when abbreviated, threatened every edge of
my ironic being, yet I bit the bullet. What else could I do?
To whom could I protest? I had no power. I was an actor.
An out-of-work actor, with no money and no career options.
Some of the actors I met were actually straight, so they paid
their rent by doing things like carpentry and plumbing. But I
was gay, so I'd gone to college, where I'd majored in the arts.
I was completely unskilled labor. As were the other gay actors
I eventually befriended. And some of them were from Ohio.
Poor bastards. They dressed in clothes I would have rejected
at birth. Big-belled jeans, with wide-striped rugby shirts. They
lacquered their hair. They looked like catalogue models from
the '70s. While I paced the hallway, trying to concoct just
the right amount of angst required to sell potato chips, they
patiently waited for their turn to audition, arms akimbo, smiling
as if they'd just discovered they had teeth. Even out of the Santa
costumes, they seemed ridiculous.

Once, I was so desperate at an audition, so lonely and
forlorn, that I even befriended a clown. Really, he was actually
a clown. In 'real' life. Meaning, he paid his bills by juggling
his balls. He was tall and really skinny and redheaded. He
had freckles. He looked like the illegitimate child of Ronald
McDonald. And when he got the part as Ronald – a very
sought after, lucrative role, he assured me – he took me out
to lunch. And he hit on me. During dessert. I almost barfed my
cheesecake. And he would not take no for an answer. Those
clowns. They sure are pushy.

We actors were an army of damaged children. We schmoozed
each other. We licked the asses of anyone who looked as

though they had anything remotely to do with our futures. We filled out our audition forms meticulously, as if anyone running the audition even cared about our hobbies, or our past accomplishments, or any of our hopes and dreams and fears.

At my first audition I tried to be unique. Since we all looked alike, I figured my best way to stand out among all those actors was to come up with something 'gushy' and OTT to share with the producers. On my audition form, I cleverly scribbled 'wind dance' as my hobby. Then I, like the other 'actors', was handed a number to hold under my chin while introducing myself to the camera. I suppose if the producers and casting agents had their way, they would have tattooed us, dressed us all in striped suits, and then separated themselves from us with metal bars.

They didn't need to, though. We were already their bitches.

Upon interrogation, I told the balding, red-faced, chain-smoking, speed-injecting commercial producer who used to direct snuff films that my wind-dancing techniques had won me a scholarship to university, where I studied Rustling Breezes 101. Blank stares, all around. Pins dropped. Lots and lots of pins. One by fucking one. I stood there, pale and frightened, gripping my number with white knuckles, waiting for an executioner to take his best shot.

Several lackeys' eyes rolled, and many papers were shuffled.

I was asked if I could be reached at the phone number on my form.

'Depends on who's asking!' Wink, wink.

That's me, the producer's bitch, being funny again. The eyes that hadn't rolled yet did so. Someone coughed. It was my soul.

The remaining papers shuffled.

I was asked to read my one line of script.

'Yeah!'

That was it. That was the script.

'Thank you for coming in today, number 27.'

And I scampered out, hands folded and head bowed, like a Japanese bride.

I realized that doing well at these auditions had nothing at all to do with being different. Producers told my agent they wanted someone singular, and they complained about the lack of 'real people' among the acting community. However, they called me in because I looked like someone else. I was an Anthony Michael Hall type, or, sadly enough, a young Barry Manilow. They didn't care about my down-to-earth qualities. They wanted me to be a recognizable copy.

So, I was. When asked about my hobbies, I answered, 'I grow my own herbs.' That had been Ally Sheedy's answer to the same inane question while auditioning for *The Breakfast Club*. I read about that in *Variety*.

I saw some of the same actors at every audition. We started resenting each other, because really there seemed to be so little work. Only one chance in a million that we would be discovered. And we all wanted to be unearthed. Me, the clown, everybody. We all wanted the chance to play the repair guy on some half-witted yet successful sitcom who eventually played the second banana in an Eddie Murphy movie. Before we knew it, although it had taken years and years, we were hosting the Golden Globe Awards, marvelling at our own overnight success. Then we'd hit rock bottom and find ourselves beating up a transsexual hitch-hiker we'd picked up on Sunset Boulevard. Eventually we'd write a book, do push-ups on the Oscars and end our career blaming everyone else for our diabetic seizures. We'd know it was all over when the queers canonized us, or when we got loaded and came out of the closet on late-night radio, or both.

That was around the time when I started receiving correspondence from Edward Albee. He probably got my address in LA from the alumni office at my university, and he wrote me from his home on the eastern seaboard. His letters were both whimsical and melancholy, like his plays, and I used to read them over the phone to my best friend back in San Francisco, Trish. She and I had gone to high school together. She knew the drama crowd, and she was the first person I did cocaine with.

'Pot's for babies,' she told me, while picking at the cold sore on her lip with a needle she sterilized with the heat from her car lighter. 'If you want to drive around in this Fiat, you've got to do coke. Nobody gets in my car who doesn't snort and listen to Jimmy Buffet, in that order.'

That was Trish during her tube top/puca shell days, when I was home from college for the summer. We kept each other humble, and alert. We still do. And we still love making fun of people who are just like us.

But when I read her the Albee letters – that's what she and I called them, as if we were researching some canon of important writing – we weren't laughing. He wasn't like us. He was a famous playwright, and it scared both she and I that he was so attentive to me.

'I'm sitting by the sea, thinking of you . . .' is the way one letter began.

'Why is he thinking about you?' Trish asked, while polishing off a pint of Häagen-Dazs. 'Doesn't he have better things to think about?'

'I guess not. Maybe he's tired of being famous. I mean, he says here, "Memories of the time I first saw you come in waves. Strolling, you seemed distracted. The olive trees in the courtyard near the theatre were casting purple shadows. I wonder, what are you doing in July? Care to share a beach?"'

'Did he ever hit on you at college?'

'I'm not sure. I auditioned for him once. He acted like I wasn't there.'

'Well, he's hitting on you now. Tom, tell me the truth. Did you sleep with him?'

'No. He had a mustache.'

'Yikes.'

'I know. Can you imagine? Oh, also, he was TWICE MY FUCKING AGE!'

'So what? You should write him back.'

'And say what?'

'Oh, the usual. That you'd like to meet him when he comes out to LA, that you'd love to get his ideas on a screenplay you're writing, blah, blah, blah . . .'

'But, Trish, I'm not writing a screenplay.'

'You are such a dullard. What difference does that make? It's just a way to get into his pants.'

'But he's not my type.'

'Tom, in your business, nobody has a type. Showbiz people don't have sex for pleasure. It's about power and control. I read all about it in the *National Enquirer*. I mean, why else did Jayne Mansfield have a career? Because she was talented? No! It's because she slept her way through a windshield. So start sucking, baby. Momma needs a new pair of Reeboks.'

I never wrote him. I mean, bad plays aside, he was still a literary icon. And what do you write to a Pulitzer-Prize-winning playwright? 'Hi, it was nice to meet you, too. You're cool. Is Liz Taylor really an idiot, or what? Call me!'

I kind of hoped he'd just send me a film script, or the names of some famous people I could contact, or some money, just for being me. Instead, he wrote a few more letters, and even a poem.

'Playing poker with a loaded gun, and shyly caressing an angry nun . . .'

Then he stopped writing. To me. Unfortunately, he continued writing poems. And plays. I suppose he moved on to a more amenable skinny actor. I half-wittedly let my first real chance to become famous pass me by.

CHAPTER TWENTY

Never salt the interior

And this is what I talked about every Tuesday afternoon in Beverly Hills. My fear of success. And Kyle, my therapist from Malibu, understood, because he was an ex-Levi's model. He'd already made it. He'd posed, on his haunches, in magazines and on posters all over America. Retail queens had spotted his blond profile in malls. He'd taken off his shirt on *The Tonight Show*. Then Kyle bought his beach home, his BMW, and retired, only to become a really fuckable therapist. So he knew my pain. He felt my core. He'd been there.

I dressed up for every session. I put on tight designer jeans I'd bought on my student loan while still at university. I unbuttoned my stolen Calvin Klein dress shirt down to my one chest hair, and I posed. Not just for the lobby, and any potentially available sugar daddies/mommies. I found myself posing for my therapist, as well. And let me tell you something, posing each week on a leather sofa is not the easiest thing to do. One slides. Slowly. I'd start the session sitting upright, with my right hand on my knee, while my other hand progressed, gingerly, finger by spidery finger, toward his. Of course, since I was sitting on polished carcass, I'd wind up slouched, with my knees up near my forehead, and not in a good way. By the end of the session, I appeared curled up, as though I'd been born without a spine. Which, metaphorically, might have been an accurate diagnosis.

But why did I bother? If only I'd known better. One of the bits of knowledge any functioning adult stumbles upon is that, in the 'sexy' department, less is more. I've seen myself in photos, when posing, sober. I have always looked my most retarded when trying hard to look 'hot'. My lazy eye leans toward my nose. My jaw goes slack, like I'm choking on my own tongue. I look intellectually challenged, not alluring. I'm kind of cute when I'm smiling and joking, but I couldn't joke with Kyle. I wanted him. I wanted to be him. This was serious business.

I know it's common for a patient to fall in love with his therapist. But how many patients have an ex-model giving them sympathetic advice? Not many, I'd bet. Not unless the patient was a minor character on an episode of *Charlie's Angels*. Kyle was gorgeous, and my boyfriend was out of work and losing his hair. Not that bald men are bad. There are some guys who find bald men very attractive. I don't, but some guys do.

But no matter what I did, no matter how many times I talked about suicide attempts, Kyle would not get closer to me. I really thought the suicide stories would work on him, too. My experience has always been that therapists really go for that stuff. You can talk and talk for hours, but until you're talking razor to the wrist they just sort of yawn and nod their heads methodically. But, I tell you, the minute you mention a bag full of pills, or a head-on collision fantasy, the notepad is up and they're scribbling away. I know they're excited because they think they may get to use some of that crap they learned in therapy school. 'Here's my chance to quote somebody.'

They're thrilled, because they might save a life! If they can just find the right quote, they might keep me from blowing my own head off.

And then at least somebody would feel good after that hour.

But my handsome therapist wasn't really worried about my

head. Nope. He wasn't a Freudian. Jung was his Daddy, so Kyle kind of talked about my dreams a lot. Boring. Unless we can talk about my wet dreams. I've got an idea. Why don't you slouch down for a change, while I fuck your face? What if you fuck my face with all these office blinds shut? Okay, you can leave them open. Hey gorgeous, can I ask you something? Do I smell funny? Why don't you rape me?

Why won't anyone ever love me for who I really am?

Blah, blah, blah.

After a few months of this shit, I was so sick of the sound of my own voice that I used to bring my answering machine to therapy and play him back all the messages my family left for me:

'Honey, it's your mother. I don't care what it is you're doing right now, I want you to stop doing it. I just saw a special on AIDS on public television, and I really don't know what I would do if . . . (tears) . . . if you ever got si . . . (tears) . . . I would just have to die my . . . (tears) . . .' etc.

Or:

'Hi Honey, this is Virginia, your grandmother. Remember me? Well, give me a call because your grandmother loves you. And I've found you an apartment near me. In San Francisco, where you belong. Who knows how long I'll last, and I want my entire family, no matter how disappointed they've made me, around me when I take my last breath. Now, when you call the landlady, be nice, don't be yourself. I told her you were gay. Your momma told me, now I tell everyone because I'm so goddam proud . . . (tinkle of cocktail ice, gulp, gulp, gulp) . . . So give Grandma a call because she loves you . . . Remember when you were little. I used to carry you around the house. You'd wrap those long arms and legs around me and I'd carry you all over. You were what, fifteen, sixteen then . . . (gulp, gulp, gulp) . . .' Click. And so on.

And the ex-model would look at me, almost dewy-eyed, and tell me he felt my pain.

'Now feel my dick!' I wanted to cry out. 'Grab me and lick me internally!'

Since I was gay, and out of work, the only way I was gonna get laid in LA was to find a wife. After all, my married male friends blew each other in the gym sauna more often than I could shake my dick at. Of course, they were all actors, so they were expected to be bisexual. I wore a gold wedding band, hoping I could join their club, but no one wanted to shake my moneymaker, either in therapy or in my therapist's waiting room. San Francisco is a much kinder market for alternative-looking guys.

Like my current therapist, David. Thank God I don't have any amorous feelings for him. How could I? He wears matching outfits. Not just colors that tastefully blend together. Nope. David wears button-down shirts with corduroy slacks and socks that perfectly match. He is a slave to the Gap. It drives me nuts! He is such a control freak. I just cannot bear his constant attempt at symmetry with his appearance. The beard is always the same length, perfect on both sides. The *wire-rimmed* glasses never have a smudge, and there's that outfit again. Blue cable-knit sweater thrown over his shoulders. Light blue oxford shirt, navy blue cotton trousers, punished with a very hot iron, so that the pleats line up perfectly. And ARGYLES! Just the fact that they still make argyles makes me think our culture has not progressed at all in the last thirty years. If there is one thing I'd like to count on, it is that I will never have to wear anything argyle ever again.

But who knows? What if I do kill myself, and my mother has the undertaker dress me in argyle socks? Or worse yet, an argyle sweater! That would be reason enough for a cremation.

Of course, if I were to kill myself, I'd have to kill David first. Kill him, burn all the argyles within a 100-mile radius, then blow my own head off. When we're found in a corpse pile, the press might think it was a lovers' suicide, when in reality I just attempted, even at our last moment together, to hide his outfit with my body.

I didn't fucking tell you the worst part! Last week, David brought me a flyer for some queer comedy club. He figures I should go there, and see what this 'gay comedy explosion' is all about. Maybe he's coming around to believing that I am gay. Or maybe he's trying to cure my homophobia.

The saddest part is, I'd already been! I mean, if there is money to be made, what the hell. But Jesus, this 'club' was so pathetic. They only served beer and wine. How did they make any profit? And you can't smoke! I thought, what do people do for two hours? Oh, yeah, they watched this shitty, half-witted comedy show. Really, it sucked. It's in the Castro, of course. Awful, just embarrassing. For one thing, dykes are not funny. Period. They are unfunny. Anti-funny. And fags are so dirty. They go on and on about their cocks. It's disgusting. Maybe it's only pathetic if you're in show business, like moi, and you know those freaks will never get anywhere with their 'acts'. It doesn't matter. They'll be dead soon anyway.

Maybe I should bring you to therapy, and let my therapist take a look. He might be able to tell me why you run so hot and cold. Like that first night we spent together. It was so good, and I felt so connected with you. Then, after holding me for hours, you scrambled out of bed at 7 a.m. and said, 'I've gotta boogie.'

'Boogie?' I have got to get you a Nerd – Hip Queer dictionary. Or maybe not.

And before I could lick you, you were off, leaving only your jacket and your phone number. Two clues to your true identity. I felt like Perry Mason. Well, a naked, vulnerable Perry Mason. Raymond Burr, naked. Yikes. Now there's something I can think about next time I'm trying not to come.

CHAPTER TWENTY-ONE

Pat the outside dry

'Why can't you just meet a nice guy in a normal situation?'
Ever since Trish joined the Psychic Friends' Network,
she has been a lot more opinionated.

'What do you mean, "normal"?'

'Tom, you know what I mean. A social situation that doesn't
include a bar.'

Such pointed remarks remind me that, though she lives in
San Francisco and does volunteer work, Trish is, after all, just
a middle-class white girl from the suburbs who spent eight years
in Catholic school.

'Well, my only other choice is an AA meeting, and I don't
really do well in group things.'

'Are you going to call him?'

'I don't know. Should I?'

'Well, if you are, you'd better do it today.'

'The day after? Why?'

'Because Tom, *The Rules* states that you should never accept
a date for the weekend that is offered after Wednesday.'

'What's today?'

'Wednesday.'

'My youth is flying by.'

'By the way, how old is Trevor.'

'Taylor.'

'Whatever.'

'I'm not sure, Trish. But he's on solids.'

'That's a switch.'

'Excuse me, how old is your Michael?'

'Twenty-six. But it's different with straight people.'

'I know. That's why I'm gay.'

'Or at least that's your excuse this week.'

'Man, what is up with you? An uneven blood flow?'

'No, I just hate penises today. Michael and I are invited to another wedding this weekend. He's the last one in his group to be unmarried.'

'Have you two talked about marriage?'

'Sort of.'

'What does that mean?'

'Well, I mentioned during a Hallmark commercial that I wanted to have children.'

'Good. Very manipulative. And?'

'He said, "That would be fun".'

'He said "fun"?'

'Yeah. Fun.'

'He's twenty-six.'

'I know. God damn this fucking biological clock!'

'Are you at work?'

'Yes, Tom. Some of us actually have to *work* for a living.' I can hear her fingers do the rabbit-ear sign around the word 'work'.

'Well, have a coffee break and calm down. Maybe new shoes would help.'

'Michael only wears old high tops.'

'I mean for you!'

'What do you think I am, twenty-six?!' Click.

You left your number in big numerals. Was that good? Did that mean you really wanted me to give you a call? Trish said it meant you weren't very bright, and that's why you wrote like a child. What fucking difference does it make? I mean, let's face it, after the way you fucked me, I would've hunted you down, knocked you on the head and dragged you home, phone number or no phone number.

'See, Trish,' I told her, when I called her right back, 'usually, I'm on top.'

'Whatever, Tom'

'I am! Of course, I've played the woman before, but usually with guys who are bigger than me. Someone who can overpower me is usually the man I roll over for. So, I had every intention of fucking him last night, but that was certainly not the way it worked out. He grabbed me . . .'

'Do I need to hear this?'

'After the stuff you've told me? Please. Anyway, he grabbed me and he flipped me over, quickly, forcefully, like the page of a good book he was anxiously reading, and he devoured my plot, if you know what I mean.'

'I think I have the general idea.'

'He was all over me, and before I knew what was happening, I felt his hard cock caressing the crack of my ass. I couldn't speak, because he had a handful of my sweaty hair, and he was pushing my face into the mattress. I would have screamed "No!" without meaning it, if I'd had the chance. Instead, I just bit what I could of the pillow as he spat on my hole and shoved his dick right up inside of me.'

'I'm at work.'

'Sorry, Trish. I'll whisper. He kept moaning this embarrassing porn speak. You know I live in fear of porn bravado. All that "You like it like that, don't ya" crap really leaves me cold.'

'You probably can't see past the elegance of the prose.'

'Right. But the way Taylor did it, "Yeah, I'm fucking you, yeah, I'm fucking you, yeah, yeah . . ." it sounded like he really liked me.'

'What a lovely picture you've painted for me. Gotta go.'

'And his voice, so sweet and soft, juxtaposed – big college drama word – against his hard thrusting, drove me NUTS!'

'Really, Tom, I have to hang up now.'

'In fact, I came without touching myself. And then I did something else I've never done. I let him continue to fuck me. Usually, after I come, I have to yank out whatever is inside of me. It's just way too painful, you know what I mean? Am I sharing too much?'

'My telephone is melting.'

'But with Taylor, pumping me like I was a Dutch hooker, I maintained an erection, so I let him go on and on.'

'Call me later, and we'll . . .'

'After he came, he held me for what seemed like hours. Then, he pulled out, we both rolled over, and before he fell off to sleep, he did something really nice. He kissed both my eyelids, which were of course closed. I opened my eyes once while kissing someone, and when I saw them staring back at me, I was so freaked out that I almost leaped out of the porno booth.'

Click.

I stared at your number for hours. Hours I usually spend more productively, jerking off in front of my computer screen, wondering if I should call you. I'm never clear on the amount of time that I'm supposed to stay cool and distant. I wanted to see you soon, so, by Trish's calculations, I should have called you immediately. But I also didn't want to seem like a pathetic loser. I thought, fuck *The Rules*. That's for straight women. They need rules to feel secure.

But being a faggot means there are no rules, right? Men hate following rules, and that's why I think we are just more romantic than women. Chicks like to talk first, and fuck later. Or so I hear. With guys, it's the other way around. The less talking, the more mystery, the better the sex.

How long should I have waited? A few days? A week? I decided to wait until I could discuss it with my therapist. I kept the number, written on a yellow piece of paper, folded up and in my wallet, protected by a condom on one side, and a small photo of Princess Diana on the other.

A few days later, I panicked, worrying that maybe I'd waited too long, and you wouldn't remember me when I called. I threw the piece of yellow paper away. Or, I thought I had. Because the next day, that same piece of paper magically reappeared near my phone. Again, I tossed it, but when I opened up a book, there your phone number stood, as a bookmark. I just could not get rid of those fucking seven digits. They followed me around my room, like the eyes in a creepy oil painting.

And when I turned the piece of paper around, so the numbers faced my dining table, I swear that the paper felt warm. And moist. Like it had been in someone's pocket. Or in someone's hand. I hadn't touched the paper for hours, maybe days, but it was damp and warm and it stuck to my palm. I started to feel like I was the star in some scary film like *Seven*. You know that movie. It's with Brad Pitt. He plays a cop who chases down this obsessive psycho, who is determined to avenge all the seven deadly sins. Except, this time, the seven particulars I was obsessing over were seven largely written numbers, which had taken over my life and made me call you back.

I pondered that maybe you were evil. That made me want to call you even more. I thought, why can't I just talk about Taylor in therapy, fantasize about him while watching my grandmother suffocate, and eventually let the whole experience go. But clearly, part of me didn't want to let it go, and anyway I had your coat, and it was July. In San Francisco? You might have frozen to death. Look, I was just going to leave a casual message, no details, no eagerness. When we talked, I planned to let you know that I wanted to see you again, that even if you were involved with someone we could still get together, hang out, blah, blah, blah.

Can you tell I spend too much time alone?

PART TWO

Chicken At Its Best

Be sure to baby your bird. Cleanse the inside if necessary, and then rub it with a warm, soft cloth. At this point in the preparation, timing is everything. Heat it up too early, and your tender morsel may be dry and cold when it's feeding time. Leave the chicken alone for too long, and it becomes hard and flaky.

The shape, flavor and scent of your fowl depend on your care.

CHAPTER ONE

Let the roasting begin!
Preheat to 450 degrees

I'm not going to whine about how difficult my life has been. I've had every advantage: a good education, a family as supportive as any evil, satanic, Southern Baptist family can be, and then there is my classic bone structure. How hard can a person's life be when he is white, middle-class and living in San Francisco?

Pretty hard, when that person is also seeking some passionate yet sane and definitely discreet companionship. I still have to be careful. If I'm seen somewhere like the Detour, by anyone from NBC, I can kiss my first network comedy spot goodbye. Unfortunately, it's impossible for me to meet men anywhere else. I'm not athletic, and I'm not dying, so I'm not invited to social functions in my community. I'm like a '70s fag, before all the fads started. I guess I'm a dinosaur. I'm the very previous generation. I'm denim on denim. I'm Andy Gibb. I'm Dr Pepper. I'm sort of Midwestern.

Maybe I should've moved to Kansas a long time ago. This whole town is too much for me. San Francisco is like a candy store for queers. Anything a boy can want is walking toward him twenty-four hours a day. A better, bigger, brawnier form is always waiting, Calistoga in hand, around the next corner. But sometimes I don't want sweets. Sometimes I want something bitter. I want to date someone. I think. No, I do. I do want to go out with someone for a while. I'm not talking monogamy. But I wouldn't mind being asked for a repeat performance. I'd like to be brought back on to stage. But why should someone cute go out with me, when most guys my age can lure a sober young victim with homes, hot tubs, hot boyfriends. What do I have to tempt someone?

My mind, I suppose. I'm a brilliant wit. But let's fact it, there is no time for jokes while prowling for cock. Giggling spoils that sexy mood everyone is trying so desperately to set. Funny is not sexy. Funny is too vociferous to be sexy. Stupid is sexy. The stupider someone is, the more butch they appear to be. And if you fall in love with a retard, then find out they are actually smart and have been fooling you the whole time with their stupid act, then everybody wins!

But when guys find out I'm a comic, they freak. They think I'll work them into some part of my material. Some queen asking the question 'Am I gonna wind up in your act?' is the quickest way to get rid of me. Why would I talk about faggots on stage?

I'd rather talk about real things, things that most people can relate to. Crazy families, relationship problems. How different men and women are: 'Women and toilet paper. What is that all about?' Now *that's* funny.

My act has momentum. I don't need to utilize my minority status to get laughs. Making jokes about rainbow flags and queer bars would be so hack, and would lull my audience into a deep sleep. Straight people don't give a shit about that queer stuff.

So, if I'm making fun of queens in a gay bar, saying stuff off the top of my head, stuff that I would never use on stage, there's nothing I hate more than for some gay guy to tell me, 'Hey, Mr Funny Man, you don't have to perform for me. You're not on stage now.'

That statement makes my penis invert. I get a de-erection.

An inrection. I mean, why is it my fault that I just happen to be funny always. It's just a part of me, like my hair and eye color. It's not my fucking problem if most losers can't tell a punchline to save their lives. Not that a good joke will save anyone's life, so forget about it.

The problem is, when I start joke-telling, I never stop. One joke feeds another, just like one martini feeds another, and suddenly I've written seven or eight one-liners about your weakest moments, your most vulnerable points. It's addictive. It's relentless. And don't even try to reply, because I'm the funny one. That's my job, and nobody does it better than me.

Sometimes, when prodded, I say I'm an actor. That lie usually works. Especially if the bar's about to close. At that point, nobody really cares about anything, except sex. The stranger might ask what I've acted in lately, I say nothing, and we go home and fuck.

Actually, it's not a total lie. I do have a degree in acting. It hangs in the hallway somewhere. I'm very proud of that document. It lets any potential employer know that, yes, I am qualified to wait tables and answer phones. Why did I even bother going to university? I should have just stayed home, folding napkins and sharpening pencils.

Imagine how clean this place would be if I could fold a napkin into the shape of a swan. Like Joe Orton used to do. I want my place to look like his apartment. All eclectic and intellectual, with artsy murals and leather-bound books. And organized, in that really anal-retentive, insular, British sort of way. My place looks too straight. Almost serial-killer straight. I save periodicals for potential comedy material, but I realized in college that stacks of newspapers and magazines also make good furniture. I own two pairs of jeans. I don't frame photos. I can't even find my photos. There are no vacation shots taped to the fridge. And you can forget about drapery. Why bother, when sheets hide sunlight just as well? It almost looks as though this apartment is uninhabited. When you've lived alone for a long time, you sort of stop dressing up the place, and yourself.

But it makes guys anxious. I can see it in their eyes when they cross my threshold. Suspicion. They wonder what's wrong with me? Why don't I have pictures of cats hanging above my bed? Why don't I have a bed? Where are my plants and wicker chairs and fabric swatches for that poorly-upholstered-but-marvelously-retro '70s sofa I bought at a garage sale? Where are my throw rugs? Where are my friends? Why should anyone get involved with me, when I'm obviously not good enough for anyone else?

Even as I'm hanging his coat on a hanger, as though I hang clothes all the time, and, really, neatness is my middle name, I feel insecure. After all, Mr Such and Such could turn to me at any moment and say, 'I can't stay. I'm sorry. You seem like an okay guy, and thanks for hanging up my jacket, that's sweet, but this place looks like every psycho's apartment in just about every *X-Files* episode I've ever watched.'

I quickly consider tidying up the place. The problem is, I don't own anything worth tidying, so I just rearrange my two gray bath towels. The damp towel that was on the floor near the front door gets thrown over the radiator, and the other towel is moved from the top of the refrigerator and wrapped with a rakish twist around the fridge door handle. It might be quicker to just toss them both into the bathroom, but then they'd never be used. I shower at my gym. For reasons already stated.

And while whatever slab of beef I've dragged home scouts around my flat for any vestige of humanity or any suggestion that there might be someone on earth who cares about me, I decide that maybe next time I should save the scratch-and-sniff postcard my brother Rob sends me each Christmas from that whorehouse in Cabo San Lucas. I could tape it to the wall near my phone. Then I might remember to call my mother on Christmas Day. And, since my phone is near the front door, all newcomers would, upon arrival, see that someone cares enough to send me a photo of a girl whose crotch looks like velvet and smells like tuna. I wonder if Rob thinks that a brown girl wearing a Santa hat and smelling of fish will change me from gay to straight. Or maybe he's gay, and this is his funny little way of telling me. Either way, my mailman must think I'm an old pervert.

Anyway, while I scramble around my flat, checking for used condoms in the toilet and trying, with as much masculinity and tact as possible, to distract my soon-to-be sex partner from the dreariness that surrounds him, I feel like someone who's seeking employment, after being out of work for an extended period of time.

I keep waiting for my new visitor to suddenly whip around, produce a clipboard, with a pen attached, and say, 'I see on your résumé that the last time you had a boyfriend, you were wearing a mood ring.'

'That's correct, but I'd like to make clear that the ring was on my finger!'

CHAPTER TWO

Massage the sides with butter

I've got to tell you about one other guy, who was part of the
Santería cult. They worship Satan. Who knew? I met him
in a candle shop. Where else? I was there because the electric
company had turned off my power, and he was there because
he was trying to bring the Prince of Darkness back from hell.
Of course, that's not what he told me. He said he was an actor,
and he needed candles for rehearsal. Lies! And he seemed so
nice. He had lots of friends, and he drove a compact car. But
don't devil-worshipers always seem nice at first? I should've
known better. After all, I've seen *Rosemary's Baby*. All of Mia
Farrow's neighbors seemed so kind. What I learned from that
movie, and from my entire childhood, is that it's when you start
trusting people that the shit really hits the fan.

Of course *Rosemary's Baby* took place in the 1960s. In fact
so did my childhood. And until last year, when I met Ekhart
– he was the devil-worshiper – I had no idea that people still
sacrificed lambs and made lamps out of carcasses and ate the
flesh of other human beings. I thought computers had taken the
place of Beelzebub. I shouldn't have let my subscription to *USA
Today* lapse. I guess I'd really lost touch with current culture. Of
course, there's nothing 'current' about craving a virgin. People
have been doing that for thousands of years.

Anyway, Eckhart and I were on our third date. I rarely make
it to the third date, but he'd withheld sex, and that makes me

crazy, in an emotionally crippled sort of way. I developed a craving for the guy. I would not rest, or leave, until I was sated. Eckhart kept saying he wouldn't get into bed with me for religious reasons, so I figured he was a Mormon or something, which made my lust for him greater. Mormons have even more self-hatred than Catholics.

And even though I coveted him, ponytail and all, I knew that the third date was the scariest. Whether you're dating a Satan-worshiper or a secretary, the third date is usually the 'getting to know you' date. You have to talk. To each other. Because, by then, you've had two meals together and you've seen at least two movies. It would be creepy to spend more time with a veritable stranger.

Of course, sometimes people share too much. What started as a third date with Eckhart became more of an initiation process.

'Tom,' he said trepedaciously, as he handed that strange bottle of thick, bright red wine to the waiter, 'I know we haven't known each other long, but I have to tell you some things about myself.'

I thought, this would be a great time for that 5x7 card idea I've been considering. 'Go ahead, baby. I'm here for you.'

'Well, I'm in therapy.'

'Who isn't!?'

'I go three times a week. I'm an outpatient.'

'Some need more help than others.' I was being magnanimous. Horniness will do that to me.

'Anything else, Eckie?'

'Yes. I'm medicated.'

'Well, who isn't?'

'I take the largest dose of Prozac that a human can tolerate.'

'All right. Just drive carefully. Does this wine taste salty to you?'

'Well, Tom, it should. Horses tend to turn out some pretty sweaty-tasting blood.'

Luckily, I'd gotten stoned, alone, earlier that evening, so the idea of drinking horses' blood didn't nag at me. I did, however, suddenly crave both a sugar cube, and the definitive definition for 'clothes horse'.

'Horse-blood wine,' I said, holding it up to the light, as if I knew what a good harvest of blood from a horse would look like. 'How exotic.' Then, I took on my best, snotty, Addison Dewitt accent from *All About Eve*, which is something I often do when I'm unsure of what is coming next. 'How does one procure such a beverage?'

'You hang the horse upside down and slit its throat.'

'Clever. How did you know that?'

'Well, Tom, the answer to that question sort of leads into the last thing I need to tell you. I make horse-blood wine.'

'Fascinating. Why?'

'I'm a warlock.'

Gulp. 'I can work with that!'

And I tried! We went on more dates, I bought black jeans. I wanted to be his bitch. But when he realized how many men I'd slept with, he decided I wasn't virginal enough for him. And I thought 666 would be his lucky number!

Oh, fuck him. I'm glad he dumped me. What if I had let him tattoo me? He said that all the warlocks' bitches had to have the devil on their backs. With horns and hooves, and a tail. Oh yeah, the whole 9 yards. People from the dark side don't mince. Thank God I didn't let him poke me with his tattoo wand! Then my chances of being buried in a Jewish cemetery would've gone right out the window. But I suppose that being Catholic the first half of my life and worshiping Satan the second might have barred me from being buried in a kosher plot, whether I was tattooed or not. But I do like keeping my options open.

I'm glad I didn't marry him. Oh yeah, he would have required a ceremony before sucking my cock. As if sucking my cock isn't ceremony enough. Then we would have lived together for the rest of eternity, which is I guess how most marriages feel anyway. And ours probably would've wound up like most marriages: After giving him the best years of his life, setting up a home where he and I could worship Mephistopheles in peace, he would have met some cute sacrificial type and escaped into the woods. All I'd have left to remember him by would've been a stupid tattoo.

And of course, his god, which was actually a shrine made of a birdcage and several colored light bulbs. That thing terrified me. It seemed so portable. Like a knick-knack. His cult just had too many chachkas. His lamp was his god; his tattoo was his god. Even his toaster had some sort of godlike qualities. God was in everything. And that was too stressful.

I think the most frightening religions are those that travel well. Those guys that can set up a tent and scream at you about your sins and then heal you with their hands scare the crap out of me. They could show up anytime, anywhere. Like a rash.

Speaking of infections, can you imagine a Catholic priest making an out call? They don't go anywhere without their robes, their rings and at least one choirboy. Leaving the church is like an exodus. Do you ever see a priest at a picnic? Or buying shoes? No way. They order out. And they're famous for buying all their clothes from catalogues. Well, there's another reason for that, but the point is, priests like being entombed. Catholicism is sort of stationary. But that's what I prefer. Because, with the Catholics, you know that in church you have to be good. Then you can be bad everywhere else.

But Eckhart had to constantly honor his god. Sometimes, it was embarrassing. We'd be in Safeway, at sunset, and he'd have to make a sacrifice. And most Safeways don't carry an entire lamb, complete with the heart. So then he'd have to find a substitute. And let me tell you, cats run fast. How many winded evenings did I spend with Eckhart chasing greasy tabbies down alleyways? Even the homeless people thought we were freaks.

I just think that worshiping is best left in one place. Otherwise, I could be in the back of a bar, late, getting my dick sucked by some guy who hates his parents, and suddenly Elmer Gantry could spring up from under the pool table and start howling at me about salvation. Actually, I have met a couple of priests in back rooms, but they weren't out to save souls. They did spend most of the time on their knees, however.

Jesus, I'm done for. Not only have I been blown by priests in queer bars, I've almost slept with a warlock. I'm burning my votive candle at both ends.

And doesn't the Catholic Church claim that I'll be cursed somehow for fraternizing with Satan's minions? I'll probably wake up one day with a baby growing out of my neck with a head the shape and size of a plum!

And what would I tell my friends and family and the media?

'I don't care if it is a plum. It's still my baby, and I love . . . it.'

They'd ask the identity of the father.

'Oh, he was just a guy. With odd hobbies. He was so kind to me. He always gave me the white meat . . . of course, most of his victims were white.'

I'd sound like those dopey neighbors of serial killers. Those morons who get their faces in front of cameras and blather on and on about how nice the captured psycho was. 'He seemed so friendly. Sure, we heard the chainsaws, and saw the blood, but we thought, gosh, maybe he's building shelves.'

CHAPTER THREE

Lubricate the rack

M y therapist says it's that desperation for approval and attention that has driven me into the direst of relationships. And guess who is to blame for that? That's right, you win the washer-dryer combo. The blame goes to Virginia, who is more depraved than any of Lucifer's wrong-doers.

I grew up proud of my intimate relationship with that cow, but it wasn't until I met my first boyfriend, Mark, that I realized how totally fucked up my relationship with her was.

College was where I found Mark. That's him, in the photo taped to the wall. He's the one wearing the strapless ball gown. He sent me that years ago. After we broke up. When all his hair fell out. And he started dressing like a girl, which is what he might become, if the state of California will give him disability money so he can get his dick cut off.

We met in a scenic design class at university. I'd show up late, every day, messy and unprepared. And tired. I'd usually been up all night, gluing toothpicks together. And there was Mark, sitting upright and cross-legged, with his current project placed proudly and neatly before him.

Everyone loved Mark. He had lots of floppy blond hair, and he went to Hawaii each summer. Remember that I was living in southern California. It didn't take much to impress people down there. He was everything I wasn't. He was agile and sincere.

And brave. He hated his family. Outwardly, I mean. He

never put up with their bullshit. When they got him on the phone, he would just hold the receiver away from his head, roll back his eyes and yell out, 'Lies!' 'Liar!' 'Lying!' Click.

But they weren't rich. He had nothing at stake.

We did, however, have other things in common. The youngest of three, his Irish mother had divorced his Italian dad when he was two. Mark's father was emotionally absent, and, like my dad, a womanizer and substance-abuser from way back. Our surnames even followed each other in the student registry at University. We first met standing in line to pick up our student loans. Of course, years later we realized that was where the similarities sort of ended, because Mark used his check to buy books and food, and I went with my loan to Buddy's and played pool while drunk as, well, while drunk as I am right now. Thank God for Reaganomics.

Mark and I couldn't avoid one another. Since we were both studying acting, it was inevitable that we would also bump into each other almost every day. All the drama classes were held in a cluster of rooms off the beaten path of the university. I suppose the campus planners felt it best for everybody that we artistic types be segregated from the future movers and shakers. Even so, Mark and I never talked. He was one of the 'serious actors' Dr Cohen had told me about, which meant he was rehearsing the role of Toby in a fabulous, flashy, big-budget production of *Sweeney Todd*, while I was sweeping out rehearsal rooms.

But finally, the day came when I landed a role. Cohen had to cast me. I needed a grade in some sort of production, and so I was offered the part of a retard in a rather obscure Sam Shepard play scheduled to perform in a trailer. One night, Mark was outside, smoking between numbers, chatting with graduate students. He was poised near the workshop where the expensive scenery for his lavish production was being designed, when I and the rest of the cast stumbled by, in character, rehearsing al fresco, since a rehearsal space was not available for our little show. He saw me carrying what looked like a dead squirrel by the tail. It was actually a prop I'd made at home, an airplane that a little retard might own, only I'd tried to make it look really good, but since we've all got a bit of the 'tard in us, my plane actually looked like it was made by someone of very special needs. After all, I was 6 feet, 2 inches, weighing in at 145 pounds, and wearing a shirt that had the words 'Single and looking to mingle' stenciled on it. It wasn't until we were eventually cast in the same show – at Mark's request, he knew the director – that Mark told me that, when he first noticed me, rehearsing, that he'd wanted to see me with my clothes off only to see if my stomach was really that flat. I saw that as an insult at the time. I didn't want to be thought of as skinny. Now, many years later, I'm in workshops to overcome my need for a flat stomach. I'm avoiding ice cream and seeing a physician who will suck the fat right out of my belly. Everything I hated as a child, I not only envy, but also hunger for: skinniness, cigarette breath and men under the age of twenty-five.

It was Mark who suggested that I might want to delve deeper in therapy about my family. He said I was derivative. I bought myself this little dictionary – I still carry it around, years later – and I looked up the word 'derivative'. I'll look it up right now. I'll read it to you. My little Oxford says:

Derivative: a. or n. Something obtained from a source.

I thought the word kind of described any human. I mean, we all derive from something. But Mark said my feelings, my actual motivations, derived from my family. He said that whatever my family thought was normal, I thought was normal as well. And apparently, that wasn't normal.

He told me that it wasn't necessarily reasonable to cruise

men with one's grandmother. Even when I was young, whenever Virginia and I dined, she would pick out a waiter she found amusing and ask my opinion. And though I was closeted, I still had my type. I liked older jocks. Blond businessmen with tanned skin and big shoulders, who wore powder blue favorably. Usually I found the men Virginia desired to be just a bit too slippery, all hair tonic and stinking of Brut aftershave. But I'd agree they were hot. It was better that way. I was more likely to get some quick cash if I told her, in a diplomatic way, that the Argentinian busboy was fuckable.

CHAPTER FOUR

Place bird on rack, uncovered

It wasn't until I was in love with Mark that I felt brave enough to tell my mother I was gay. My therapist at university had been encouraging me to tell my family, but I wanted to wait until I felt secure in my relationship, so that I had some emotional support and a place to stay during the summer in case my family was too horrified by my queer cock.

And in his own way, Mark was there for me. He wanted to tell my family that we were lovers, and I almost let him, until I realized he just liked scaring families. He had been 'out' to the world since he was twelve. He'd hoped the news would send his folks over the edge, resulting in mass suicide. Young queers are such dreamers. When the family just shrugged, claiming his homosexuality was a 'phase' he'd grow out of, Mark needed a new plan of attack.

So he slept with his stepfather, Ralph, which apparently was not as hot as it sounded. 'Ralph always called out my mom's name when we were in bed together.'

Which I guess would've been distracting. And alarming, for dear old Mom. When Mark told the rest of his family what was going on, they figured he was lying and sent him to a doctor. Then Mark fucked the doctor. So they sent him to a psychiatrist, whom Mark fucked. And then, well, you can guess the pattern. Mark fucked his way into premium government-assisted programs, like dance workshops that included month-long trips to the Big Apple and backstage passes to the New York City Ballet.

When I met Mark, he'd humped his way into university, with a full scholarship for 'emotionally disadvantaged youths'. Whatever. He was like a federal subsidy whore. The welfare system had replaced his real family. And you haven't heard lies until you've heard the shit welfare workers spew. When he'd inquire about his subsidy, his caseworker would act as though money hadn't been invented yet.

'Your what?' she'd say. Mark would put her on the speakerphone in his apartment, and I'd watch his eyes roll so far back his pupils disappeared. 'Did you say, your subsidy money? I'm not sure what you mean. Is this Mr Benini I'm speaking to? Do we have a bad connection?'

'No, Connie, we don't have a bad connection.' Mark's voice would lower in volume, as he pressed his mouth closely against the receiver. 'It's just my voice is weakening, since I haven't eaten in three weeks. My student loan dried up months ago. I barely have the strength to breathe, much less dial the phone. Thank God your supervisor's number is on speed-dial.'

Mark had been dealing with these people for years, so he usually got what he wanted. But I was surprised he never went postal. I think his welfare worker invented the old 'the check is in the mail' line.

I eventually told my mother about Mark because I was trying to get out of going home for Christmas. I figured, if I was lucky, she'd at least need the holidays to recover from my confession.

My plan failed. Actually, my mom was thrilled. She needed a gay friend to explain things to her, like the never ending popularity of ABBA, and why drag wasn't sexist. Leaving San Francisco to live in a rich white suburb had made my mother lazy and guilty. I was her penance.

So she told everybody! My dad, my cousins, Virginia. I suppose Mom sent out chain letters. Or maybe Indian runners, because when I returned to college after the holiday break the entire campus and its environs seemed to welcome me with open legs. Suddenly, my auto mechanic was winking at me and wishing me the best, and my postman was leaving condoms in my box. I was waiting for my sexuality to hit the headlines, or at least be announced on television before the next big lottery draw. I think the Pope was faxed. Everyone was alerted.

And as the months went by Mom kept everyone up to date on just about every aspect of my relationship with Mark. Well, everyone who could stomach it, which was mostly a gaggle of friends in her aerobics class. Those middle-aged, frozen-yogurt-eaters were hungry for news from the front. Everything I told her, from the first kiss to the first poke, was shared over a non-fat vanilla classic swirl with chocolate sprinkles, and the resounding response was 'Yes! We need more details! And more napkins!'

Remember, these were pre-AIDS days, when faggots were still amusing. With my mother's blow-by-blow updates, those geese giggled their way through just about every important moment Mark and I shared. Or at least, the moments I shared with my mother.

Then, around the time of our graduation, my dispatches stopped. Mom was concerned. Her friends were demanding trivia. So I told her the truth. Mark had slept with a black pianist. 'A *black* pianist, for God's sake?' she responded. 'That part I won't share with the gals.' Mark and I had met the guy – named Patryck, with a 'y' – while he played at a piano bar near the beach. I found out they'd fucked, in our bed, while I was in class. Of course Mark didn't tell me that. I read it in his diary. Stupid cunt. I mean me, of course. And when I confronted Mark about the indiscretion, he decided to be honest, unfortunately, and he admitted that yes, he and Patryck had fallen in love. Two weeks later they were living together.

My mother shared the news of our separation with her klatch, but this time, solemnly, like the death of a president. And in the yogurt store, those ladies bowed their headbands, in silence, for sixty beats. My dentist sent me a sympathy card. Everyone knew about the break-up.

Everyone except Anne, my father's mother. After all, Anne hadn't been informed I was gay, so why tell her about Mark? Actually, we'd all learned to tell Anne as little as possible about ourselves and about one another. She was just too delicate. She was the kind of fragile old woman who got shaken if someone rang her doorbell too loud. That's a picture of Anne and my grandfather, Carlo, on the wall, right before they got married. I think they're at Santa Cruz there. Isn't she beautiful? She looks like Ingrid Bergman in *Anastasia*. Anne could've been a princess, too, if only her family had just a little bit of money. But they were poor Italians, real 'greaseballs', and she was the only one among all her sisters who bothered learning English. My grandfather's family were wealthy wops, and they hated Anne. They thought she was total Eurotrash. But she and my grandfather Carlo had to be together.

It's all so romantic. Until you turn the page, and find out Carlo had a mistress, and when he died he left Anne with a huge gambling debt. But she never stopped loving him. She had to be dragged kicking and screaming from his funeral. When I was a kid, I thought it was because she was angry at him for leaving her alone. Now of course I know it had more to do with the fact that too many people had shown up and there wasn't enough food back at her house. Once she was sedated, and pizzas were ordered, she was fine. Well, as fine as a woman who was still in love with her freshly dead husband could've been.

She was very 'old country', uneducated and superstitious. Wind scared her. She wasn't stupid, just severely Catholic. She could roll her own canoli, but if the phone rang she'd jump out of her fuzzy slippers. Sweet, but defenseless, and incredibly uncomplicated.

My mother saw no reason to tell her about my being gay. Anne would've only misunderstood, not known what it meant, blamed the heat. And none of us had the time to explain it all to her.

Except Virginia. She had the time. She was between marriages. And without any men around the house to punish, Ama tended to look elsewhere for entertainment.

My demonic grandmother was a bit disappointed I was gay. She'd hoped I'd marry a girl just like her. Little did Virginia know how much like her my Mark actually was. They were both Aquarius, born in different years of course, but only seconds apart, on Valentine's Day. They both had very neat underwear drawers, with a lot of dirty little lies hidden underneath each pile of panties. And, like most sociopaths, Virginia couldn't spot the similarities between herself and other freaks.

What she could do was formulate a plan. Socios always have a plan. It may be an evil plan, an intricate, damaging plan that might rival those constructed by soap-opera writers, yet a plan nonetheless. When mom told her I was gay, and in love, Ama didn't cut me off financially. That would've been too easy. She waited until the relationship with Mark was over, until I was at my most vulnerable and least able to defend myself against recriminations. Then, and only then, would she try to undermine the small bit of self-esteem I still had left by destroying my comparatively warm relationship with her only true competitor for the Grandmother of the Year award.

Virginia has always felt that if she is suffering, then everyone should be suffering. Why should she be the only grandmother bearing the burden of truth? Of course, because we'd all told Virginia that Anne was not to find out anything about my proclivities, she wouldn't bring it up directly. But if my sexuality sort of slid into conversation between courses, who was to blame? Unfortunately subtlety was not Anne's strong suit. This would have to be handled cleverly.

First things first. The restaurant. Where could they both dine comfortably? What establishment would cater to both Virginia's velvet moods and Anne's salt-of-the-earth sentiments! In other words, Virginia had to think of a place where being seen with Anne wouldn't ruin her practical reputation as a sophisticate. Ama considered Anne to be peasant Italian stock. When I was younger, she told me with a sneer that Anne only started wearing nylons when the doctor told her they'd help prevent her from developing varicose veins. 'Like it matters.' Virginia said, while turning mens' heads on the way to our table. It was my thirteenth birthday, but more importantly, Ama had just had her face lifted. She was cleverly celebrating both events by covering a shockingly small amount of her ivory skin with a skin-tight, midnight-blue velour pantsuit with straps at the shoulders and no jacket. And as always, she wore a bra two sizes too small, so that her boobs were pressed up under her chin. Her nipples danced. She was sixty-seven. She looked forty. Men half her age wanted her. 'The woman has legs that don't taper. They are thick at her thigh, and they remain decidedly so all the way down to her toe. No change in circumference whatsoever. Why bother dressing them up? They're like piano legs.' She sat, crossing her own, while returning a stranger's gaze. 'And who looks at the legs on a piano?'

Later I noticed that Anne never shaved her armpits. And that she had a beard. Not just a couple of hairs that might distract you during conversation. NO. We are talking full, perhaps scraggly, yet well-entrenched and well-documented facial growth. She was one testosterone shot away from sideburns. Of course, when I was a kid, I didn't mind, because Anne was nice to my sister and brother and me. She took us for haircuts and bought us new shoes in her little Italian neighborhood in San Francisco. It was all old ladies then, and Lisa, Rob and I would buy comic books and cigar gum from old Mr Fitzsimmons, who always wore a smile, unless some 'darkies' came into the shop. What a sweet old racist he was. Or perhaps Mr Fitzimmons was the shoe shop owner. Now I can't recall, actually. I've had one too many. Disappointments, that is.

The thing about old people is they smell like urine, and then they die. Well, not in my family, just everywhere else. All those old shop owners bought the farm by the mid-1980s. Suddenly, even earthquakes couldn't keep the yuppies out. Now, the marina is Satan's asshole, full of frozen yogurt shops with neon displays, where caffeine addicts commute between Starbucks and home on roller blades. Horrific.

But it will never dim my memory of strolling up and down Chestnut Street with Anne. Well, actually, we were always 2 feet behind Anne. She was northern Italian, after all. Physical contact in daylight embarrassed her. But with my freshly shaven neck, I was happy. I often wondered why she didn't get her neck shaven too.

Of course, Virginia would always swoop down and buy us shinier shoes and better outfits. She made fun of Anne's taste. Still, I wore Anne's gifts, even though I knew that she hated my father. My dad drank and gambled and whored around just like his dad. And I'm pretty sure she assumed that my dad's sons were – and are – the same. She was never cuddly with anyone, but she seemed to offer a particularly cautious embrace to both me and my brother. As a child, I thought Anne just hated all men, which confused me, since she was the most masculine person I knew. Now I know she just hates people's flaws.

Maybe she should put that on her 5 x 7 card.

Maybe she and Virginia should have exchanged cards at my coming out luncheon. Or, Virginia could've just written 'Tom is queer' on a cocktail napkin and saved them both a lot of time. But again, that would've been too easy.

Instead Ama chose the table, the food and the topic of conversation. The restaurant was probably something windowless. Virginia has never liked having her back to a window, in case of snipers, and she's always avoided the hazards of natural light. I'm sure the booze was as heavy and dark as the subject matter.

Without wasting any time, Virginia lifted her Manhattan to toast the family.

'To a job very well done, Anne.'

Virginia hoped Anne would return the compliment. Instead Anne sipped, checked to make sure her purse was somehow attached to her body, and said, 'We're not talking about the family today, are we Virg?'

I'm sure Virginia thought, 'Well, what else will we talk about? Your polyester flared trousers? Or maybe the fact that you smell like a dead chicken that's been left out for too long?' They weren't the best of friends, and really the family was all they had in common. That, and the fact that Ama had also slept with Anne's deceased husband. Although, to Virginia's credit, she did sleep with him while he was still alive. Oops! Hadn't I mentioned that? It might've been what killed him. He probably contracted cancer through her vagina. I think I read a Stephen King novel where that happened. Or maybe I saw a story about it on CNN. But I digress.

When Virginia told me this story, years later, about the time she 'outed' me to my other grandmother, she garbled that she and Anne just sat in silence for the longest time. Ama wanted to talk about all their accomplishments as grandparents before she dropped the bomb about my cock. Just to soften the blow.

Discretion was of the upmost importance. She must have chosen each word very carefully, the way Mark did when we first met.

Sly a. (*slyer, slyest*) unpleasantly cunning; mischievous and knowing; *slyly* adv.

'Tom is taking guitar lessons.'
'Guitar?' Anne asked. 'He didn't mention that.'
'Yes. He's quite, well, musical, you know.'
'No, Virginia, I had no idea. How are your . . . outfits?'
'Fine. Segregated. Anyway, my neighbor, Helen, has a grandson who is a bit older than Tom. His name is Jason. Jason studies guitar, and he's tall, as well. He also takes ballet classes. That Jason. He's very imaginative.'

Subtle a. (-*er,-est*) slight and difficult to detect or identify; shrewd; ingenious; *subtly* adv.

'You know, Anne, maybe we should send Tom to some dance classes. He loves to dance. And we don't want him to be clumsy as an adult. What with all the problems he might have to face.'
'How is your salad, Virginia?'
'Fine. Tart. Just the way I like it. Maybe I should introduce Jason to Tom. They might have a lot in common. Music, dance, color coordination.'
'Well, it's always good for young people to have lots of friends.'

Smooth a. (-*er,-est*) not harsh in sound or taste; pleasantly polite and perhaps insincere; *smoothly* adv.

'What would you think if Tom was gay?'

'What?'

'What would you think if Tom was a gay person?'

'Do you think he's gay?'

'I asked *if*?'

'Why are you asking that?'

A long, slow sip before Virginia lifted her left painted-on autumn khaki eyebrow and said, 'Oh, Anne, I've just noticed some . . . flaws in his character.'

'What flaws?'

'He seems so resistant to any feminine contact. Lately, whenever I've taken his hand in mine, he's tried to pull away.'

It's true, I did try to resist her Jurassic Park grip. I was eighteen! I mean, it's really not that I was afraid of women. Pussy doesn't drive me wild, but it doesn't disgust me either. Okay, once I threw up on a vagina in high school, but I never told Virginia that. Don't smirk. It's so embarrassing. I tried to pleasure this gal from my acting class who was blonde and skinny and I should've wanted her. All the boys did. And I got her, but that was no surprise. Of course she wanted me. I didn't want anything from her. At least, that's what I kept telling her, until we got drunk one night, and I tried to eat her out. I don't know why. I just thought, well, I've been there once before. And since I have no memory of birth, it couldn't have been that bad. So I dove in, but I didn't get very far. It's not that it smelled bad. Sort of like, well, filet of sole only saltier. It's just that we'd been dancing, and all that motion had made me dizzy. Or maybe it was the Chivas Regal. I'm not sure. But I'd barely unzipped her Dittos, when I barfed all over her muff. I'd eaten some vegetable casserole for dinner. It wound up all intertwined in her bush. To this day, I still can't even be near diced carrots. But I've never hated women.

I just hated Ama's wizened, wrinkled, spotted claw. It would always appear over the front seat of her Impala, poised, waiting for me to offer up my young, virginal soft white hand. What a shame it seemed, to encase my lovely little paw in that leathered trunk. I'd try to pull away, but she'd increase the pressure. And there we'd sit, hand in vice, while Soupy or Myron or whatever husband she was violating drove us to the racetrack or the mall or to Denny's. You'd never know my grandmother had money from all the down and out rat holes she frequented.

Though deadly, her grip was also pacifying, like Dracula's bite. Once insulated, the victim was under Virginia's spell.

And that's when Ama asked questions. But remember she wasn't using truth serum. She never wanted to hear the truth. She only wanted to hear what would make her happy. Well, if not happy, powerful.

'Who's your favorite grandma?' she'd ask, sweetly.

'Huh?' My brother and sister ignored us, and looked out the car windows. Even then I was the only grandchild who could stand being near her.

'Who do you love more? Me or Anne?'

'I love you both.'

'But who buys you more things.'

Well, you couldn't argue with that. Ama always kept all three of us well dressed. In fact she always made my brother and I wear a bow tie to dinner. A bow fucking tie! On a kid. God, we looked like midgets. Sad, little angry midgets, beating each other up in the lobby of some poorly carpeted restaurant. Why we were the only ones who ever dressed up to go to diners always confused me anyway. I mean, most of the clientele looked like they were going to a food fight. Big pants. Big blouses. Fat, toothless, bald bastards. And us. The bitter youth in the corner booth. With my sister crying the whole time because her braids were too tight. And, of course, throwing up at the end of every meal. My sister has always been able to throw up all the time. She's never been bulimic. She just always had the gag reflex of a sparrow feeding her young. So when her tears came, we knew that bile was just around the corner. She'd cry, cough, choke, and barf. Not always in that order. Sometimes, the barf would cause the choking, coughing, and then the crying would come. But those four elements always persisted. Oh sure, it all sounds fun now. But, as a child, barf and bow ties just mortified me.

Still, I was under the Virginia trance, and so, of course, I said, 'Oh, you give us the most Ama. I love you the most.'

Stooge n. subordinate; person who is another's puppet.

I could feel my siblings repel from me in abject horror. They pressed their bodies against their various car doors, gripping the handles ready to jump out at the next stop sign, rather than betray Anne. We all knew we liked Anne more. She left us alone and let us watch TV all night. My sister didn't throw up as much around Anne. Yet I gave in to the Wicked Witch of West Virginia.

And then, years later, as Ama outed me to Anne, my words as a child were being used against me.

'It's odd Tom's afraid of my affection. He always used to hold my hand in the car, and tell me he loved me more than he loved, well, any other person in the whole world. He'd cry if I didn't let him sit right next to me in the front seat.'

No way! She'd never let us near the front seat. We smelled too much like kids, and we would've wrinkled her skirt or smudged her shoes or KILLED HER!

'And, Anne, he always told me how he wanted to marry me, to live with me for ever. He'd wrap his long arms and legs around me and I'd practically carry him.'

'That sounds like a lot of work.'

Either Anne was too dense, or had too strong a sense of irony to ever let Ama get to her.

Unfortunately, the truth probably is that she just didn't care about me.

And that's another reason why I'm in therapy. And talking to you.

CHAPTER FIVE

Insert the thermometer

D on't get me wrong. I wanted to talk to you after we first met, but you were impossible to reach. Every time I called, all I got was your goddamned answering machine.

'Hi. I'll try to return your call. Who knows when that will be.'

Well, shit, I guess playing piano and practicing law is a lot of hard fucking work. I was annoyed, because being busy had always been my excuse. You'd usurped my reason for not calling. Now, if I tried it, it would only seem as though I was copying you, trying to match you in importance by being unattainable.

So instead, I called again. Three times. I left three messages, each more pleading than the last. You didn't return any of them. I knew what you were doing. I'd played those stupid fucking games before. It's just that, in the past, *I* was in the driver's seat. *I* was the one who had to avoid some guy who couldn't get the hint. I was YOU!

I tried to wash you out of my sheets and forget about you. I couldn't. My therapist thought I was angry because you were the first guy in a long time to make me feel anything, and now you were avoiding me. Actually, I was angry that you made me feel anything, period.

Feelings. I don't like 'em. They're just not my cup of tea. And I tried getting rid of them, with all the usual tricks, and some new ones, but nothing seemed to work after I met you. Pot, speed, booze. They all left me alert.

Then I tried GBH. That's this clear liquid that you drink and it makes you feel tingly from the neck down. Sometimes. I guess it has different effects on different people. GBH made River Phoenix fall down and do a fish dance on Santa Monica Boulevard. They say that's because he was a vegetarian. His system was so pure, that he experienced the full effect of the drug. Of course, pure or not pure, he still died after flopping on the cement like a salmon. Maybe that's because he mixed GBH with cocaine and acid. Maybe if he'd had a couple of steaks first, he might still be alive today. The red meat might have buffered his innards. But then he wouldn't have had that ultimate high, which I guess is overdosing on drugs.

Maybe the next time I do GBH, I'll skip that burger for lunch. Kind of purge, so my system is pure and I can achieve the fullest experience. Of course I'd also have to forget about you. Then maybe the drug would work.

Because, I'll tell you, no matter how much GBH I poured down my gut last week, you kept creeping back into my consciousness. After I drank it, I just sat on the sand, staring at the ocean. I wanted to be close to the sea in case I did the fish dance. I thought I'd end my life metaphorically and figuratively at the same time. Like Jesus.

But nothing fucking happened. I mean, I drove home from the beach, that's how fucking awake I was. I really don't think I was asking for much. Just a numbing high. That's all. Is that too fucking much? Why did River Phoenix enjoy such a glamorous death, and all I got was a chill from the sea breeze? I could've done without the fish dancing, and still have been quite happy with the death part. Or vice versa. But I didn't even tremble. No numbness, no vomiting, no denial. Nothing.

So even if you had returned my calls, I would've been upset. But I wouldn't have felt spurned. I guess the irritated/spurned combo is what made me do something I'm still not very proud of. I tried to access your messages on your answering machine. That's awful, isn't it? It's like reading someone's mail without their permission. Which I think is a federal offense. Of course a minor felony is the least of my worries. Still, I kind of feel bad about it.

I just wanted to know what was going on between us. And I thought I could figure out the reason or reasons you were ignoring me by listening to the messages on your answering machine. THIS IS NOT AN EXCUSE! It's merely an explanation. If you had a boyfriend, and he left a message about your upcoming domestic partners ceremony, then I could've understood why you weren't calling me. Or if you'd joined a cult, and they needed your help rounding up followers and such, then I might have seen why you were too busy to pick up the phone.

See, I wasn't maliciously trying to spy. Just like I wasn't trying to spy on my friend Alison the last time I called her machine. But I heard some of her messages nonetheless. A few months ago, I called my friend Alison in Los Angeles, and I got her answering machine. While her outgoing message played, I yawned. It was kind of a high, long yawn. The kind of yawn that requires the closing of eyes and the stretching of limbs. And I guess I yawned a note that matched one of the numbers of the code that Alison punches when accessing her messages from another telephone, because Al's greeting suddenly stopped. And instead of asking me to record a message of my own for Alison, her machine rewound all her incoming messages, and played them back for me. It was scary. I learned way too much about Al, in a really short amount of time. I simply didn't need to know that Alison's strap-on dildo had arrived. I wasn't even aware that Alison shopped for dildos. I've never even seen a dildo. Well, not a real one. I've seen a fake dildo, which, I guess, is an actual penis. And I'm still not sure why anyone would want their dildo to have Velcro attachments. I hung up the phone before Sandra from Deja-Screw could elaborate.

Bewildered and abruptly suspicious of anything to do with rubber veins, I'd all at once discovered in myself a certain talent that, though capably manipulated by anyone with a voice and a hangover, few were aware of possessing. Yet I kept this weapon, this high yawn, in check. Until I met you.

And there I was, one warm day, hovering shamelessly over my telephone receiver, singing high and low. I should've been out, in the park, cruising guys who use their dogs as dude-magnets. Instead, I was dejected, and hitting every note imaginable, trying to play back all your messages. Trying to figure you out.

'Ah! No, that was too low. (Cough) Ah! That was still too low. Shit, I've got to stop smoking. I sound like a really sad drag queen. Maybe I should inhale some helium. Ahhhh! Ouch. That note hurt.'

Fuck, it was hard to find the right fucking note, especially after I'd been drinking vodka all afternoon. Now I know how Liza Minnelli feels.

I never heard any of your messages. I never heard from you. I was convinced you'd gone on a long trip. Or, better yet, that you'd died in an unnecessarily violent car crash.

Then, a couple of weeks later, there you were, on the beach, resting on your stomach, with sheet music in front of you, while you were conducting an imaginary orchestra! Why the fuck did you have time to sunbathe when you couldn't find the time to pick up a phone and call me back? And what were you doing on the 'gay' beach? And why were you reading sheet music? What sort of ploy was that? I mean, if I had ever thought you were lying to me before, then I was sure you were. Musicians, especially pianists, don't carry their sheet music on to the beach. Unless they're starring in some stupid MasterCard commercial, or unless they're trying to look like an artist. It was all a façade! And not even necessarily for my benefit!

But you looked so cute in your underwear.

I really admire people who can comfortably wear their underwear to the beach. It's so freeing to watch someone casually tear off their togs and trip through the surf in their skivvies. I never go to the beach unless I have full beach attire: lounging jacket, open-toed sandals, binoculars. I do have a certain image to uphold. But for an adorable nobody like you, I say go for the panties! I've never looked too good in underpants. My skin tans unevenly, and my clavicles stick out. I'm bony and flabby. It's genetic. My father is ET.

But your big ass in white underwear looked like two tall piles of fresh snow. Each cheek seemed to have its own life. I worried they might melt, being exposed to so much sun. Fortunately they stayed solid, individually shifting, ever so slightly, with each stroke of your arms. I wanted to rest my face in the snow, cool my skin in your soft mounds. I wanted to dive right in to something I so pleasantly remembered. I felt like a kid in a playground.

I checked other favorite parts of you. You, in the sand, in your cute white underwear, memorizing Mahler. I was relieved to see your hair still in a silly pageboy cut. Or, if I was going to be mean, actually sliced into an extended wedge cut made famous by that perky American ice skater, Dorothy Hamel. You're too young to remember her. She won a medal in the Olympics a long time ago. She did this move, balancing her weight on one leg while she flipped the other leg up behind her. Then she spun around. It was called the Hamel Camel, and even though she didn't resemble anything more than a girl on skates trying to win a medal, America went wild. The move was kind of pervy, actually, since you could practically see all her bits on national television. But that's true of most ice-skating. Especially if there are two people skating together. Ice skating duos perform like they're constantly on the verge of fucking each other. Like they're one Hamel Camel away from fornication. I mean, hell, he's got her ass balanced on his fist. She might as well take it up to the elbow. Isn't that why most people watch skating? To see all the bits rubbing against all the other bits?

I guess some people still wear their hair in a wedge, like Dotty. People in Omaha, that is. Does that mean you had to fly thirty years away every time you needed a trim? Why did you bother living in San Francisco when you looked and dressed like a librarian from Nebraska? But then that was part of your allure, wasn't it? Oh, yeah, I'm figuring you out.

And as I walked closer to you, I thought, I hope that those blond streaks are from the sun, although I fear they might be from a box. Fuck. A liar, a lawyer and most probably a bleached blond. Three things I couldn't tolerate in a waiter, and there I was, obsessing about you as a lover.

I panicked, realizing I wasn't stoned enough to handle seeing you. Then I remembered what I always try to do when I'm in love. I merely listen. At that point, you and I had only exchanged a few pleasantries in a bar and then I'd taken you home and licked your ass, but I hadn't really listened to you. And, often times, if I hear what someone has to say, and I mean really hear them, I realize what a psycho they are and how they need to be expelled from my life immediately.

'Hey,' I said, as I blocked your sun. You were resting on your elbows. Your beach towel was one of those New York City Ballet beach towels that were really popular in the '70s, only yours looked new. The black was still very black. How do you keep your retro items so fresh and new? And why do you? I thought that the beauty of retro products is that they looked old! Christ, I wanted to come all over your face.

'Is that what you say to someone when you're attracted to them?' my therapist asked me, in his signature toneless tone. 'That you want to "come all over their face?"'

'No, usually I say I want to make them bleed. But I say that in a loving way. Not in a Wyoming sort of I'm going to tie you to two posts and steal your shiny shoes sort of way, more in a group hug sort of Hollywoody sort of Come on, baby, let Daddy have what he wants kind of way.'

'And that works?'

'Listen, it's tough to find a top in this town.'

'A what?'

'Oh, come on Dr Lewis. You must know what a top is. The pitcher. The agressor. The penetrator.'

'Oh, yes. A top. Go on.'

'Anyway, most guys cannot wait to get nailed. They spend most of their time in bars looking for a real man who can really do the job. Guys like me don't come along too often.'

'Is that right?'

'Oh, don't be so coy, Doctor. You must have other patients that bitch about the lack of masculinity in San Francisco. I'm probably the only true top you treat.'

'Oh, really.'

'Sure. And the few guys I've met who claim to be tops are lying. They're about as top as the *Titanic*. Their feet are behind their heads with the expediency of a gymnast. They're dancing on the ceiling before I can even get a CD going.'

'How predictable.'

'Yeah. But sometimes you find a surprise. Like that guy I took home a while back.'

'Was that Taylor, the pianist/lawyer with the sugar bowl haircut?'

'Your memory both impresses and frightens me, Dr Lewis. All this is confidential, right? You won't blather any of this on the outside, right? You'd wreck my career if you told anyone about me being with guys.'

'Tom, this is all strictly between you and I. And a hidden tape recorder. I'm kidding, Tom. Go on.'

'Well, when I saw him in the bar, I was sure he was straight. And straight guys are always on the bottom. They act all indifferent and reserved, but the whole reason they're in a gay bar is 'cause they wanna get what their girlfriends can't give them. Cock. I mean, let's face it, a strap-on just isn't the same, right? Ask any dyke. She'll tell ya'. Anyway, I was really looking forward to sticking it in him, especially because he was unknowingly featuring his ass in these really tight, stupid, straight-guy jeans. But no way. He fucked me like I was a natural woman. And it was great.'

'Will you see him again?'

'I did. On the beach last week. I almost didn't recognize him at first. He looked so soft and comfortable. But then I saw his sweet ass. He was on his stomach, working with some sheet music.'

'Did you two speak?'

'Sure. I asked him, so, how's the music going?'

'And what did Taylor say?'

'He said, "Cool". That's a pretty bad impression of him. Let me try that again. "Cooolll ..." He always draws out his vowels, really lightly. "Cooooooooollllllll ..." That's better. Anyway, after he said "Cooooooooollllllll ..." I smiled, because ... well, because ...'

'Tom, what's wrong. What just happened there?'

'Well, I realized that he had no idea who I was.'

'Are you okay? Do you want me to sit next to you on the couch?'

'No, I'm fine. Is there any tissue in here? Thanks. I realized he just thought I was some freak with nothing better to do than walk up and down the beach, stalking liars. Right then I was so over him. I was so over all men. But then he started flirting with me. Maybe because he didn't remember me. Maybe he only fucks total strangers. Anyway, he tossed back his hair, squinted his eyes, and said to me, "Cute outfit".'

'And what did you do then?'

'Well, I popped a woody.'

'A what?'

'A woody. I had an erection.'

'Why?'

'Because, Doctor, he made me upset, and then he complimented me.'

'Just like your father does.'

'It totally turns me on.'

'Was that embarrassing for you? "Popping a woody", as you say.'

'No, Taylor couldn't tell. My outfit included a short jacket that ties at the waist. It's called the "Beachcomber". When I told him it was a gift from an ex-lover through the International Male catalogue, all I got was a blank stare. He had no idea what the International Male catalogue was.'

'Neither do I.'

'Christ. I know it's none of my business, Doctor, but aren't you gay?'

'Go on, Tom.'

'Sorry. The International Male catalogue is a bastion of gay fashion, in print. Lots of flowing linen for those trips to Ibiza. Loads of porn stars posing in tight camouflage. As if they'd ever be satisfied by just blending in. I can't believe neither you nor Taylor have ever even taken a glance at that mag. How envious.'

'Continue, Tom.'

'Right. Anyway, when he complimented my outfit, I said,

"Thanks. I think it suits me." That was a pun. He didn't get it then, and you obviously don't get it now. I'm wasting even my minor talents on you both.'

'Stay focused, Tom. What happened next?'

'He adjusted his cock in his Calvins and said, "Well, you look bitchin'." And I thought, "bitchin'"? There's that vernacular again. I looked around to see if he was reading off cue cards. Then I looked down at his work, tilted my head and said, "That is music, isn't it?" I knew the answer, but when I'm shy, I look younger.'

'How interesting. How did he respond?'

'He told me that yes, it was his music, and he was preparing for a recital. Lies! That he was going to a rehearsal that night. Lying! And he had to memorize a big solo. Liar!'

'There's more tissues there.'

'Thanks, Doc.'

'Use as many as you need.'

'Great.'

'So tell me, how did his disclosure about his recital make you feel?'

'It was weird. I went into interrogation mode. I was like, "So, where is this recital?"'

'And what did he answer?'

'He said, "Fort Lauderdale." I thought, fucking hell, for his sake, I hope he is lying. And then he finally asked me about myself. What I was up to.'

'And what did you tell him?'

'I'm like, "Oh, I'm rehearsing too." Suddenly, I couldn't remember if I'd told him I was a comic. "I go up and down the beach, practicing, uhm, monologues, trying new, uh, intentions." And he goes, "Coooooollllll . . ." He still had no idea who I was. He must've thought I was a juggler or a mime. It was so humiliating.'

'How did you end it?'

'He wanted to get back to work on his conducting. So he said, "Listen, give me a call ..." And I reminded him, "Tom." And he goes, "Right, Tom. Give me a call, and let's get together."'

'Well, that was nice.'

'Yeah, whatever. And then, as I walked away, I said, "Good luck tonight, Taylor." And he looked confused and said, "Huh?" Then he looked down at his music, smiled, and said to me, "Oh, right. Thanks. Good luck to you, too. Tom."'

It didn't feel good telling all that to my doctor. His style of empathy is so uninvolved. He wouldn't cry with me, he never really commiserated. He just kept telling me it was good I'd opened up communication with you.

Maybe it *is* good we have dialogue, because now I've got to take a shit, and I haven't shit for days. Should I close the door? Man, this is a three-alarm fire! I'm gonna need a shower after this.

Anyway, after I saw you on the beach, I went home, and ... oh, fuck, I'm out of toilet paper again. Maybe these paper bags will finally be useful.

I hope I don't have a Safeway logo on my ass. Oh, what do I care, no one ever sees my ass anymore, except you. And you love my ass unconditionally, right?

After our beach visit, I couldn't sleep, couldn't eat. My whole body just shut down. I started having memory loss on stage last week, too. I couldn't remember my punches. I kept setting up jokes, then forgetting where I was.

So thank God for this stuff. It really wakes me up, makes me alert. It helps if you're having a hard time. But, like I said before, no matter how good the speed, it didn't make me feel better when I thought about you. Actually, I just got more frightened. I mean, I had no idea who you were. What you were really doing. I suddenly started to doubt that your name was even real. I was going nuts. I needed more help. More information about you.

So last week, I finally called my father's brother, Carl. He is the only man I know who can trace down a person's past, find out how they've wound up where they've wound up.

He's Uncle Carl. The cop.

CHAPTER SIX

Slide it in for 15 minutes

Now, it wasn't my choice to call Uncle Carl. I wanted Trish to do it.

'Tom, I'm not calling your uncle. He used to corner me and talk to me for hours.'

'Trish, he really likes you. He could never figure out why you and I broke up.'

'Did you tell him it was because you're a dicksmoker?'

'That's exactly what I said. "Uncle Carl, I smoke dick." Maybe I was too subtle.'

'No, it's just that Carl has good taste. I mean, how could you have given up these tits.' She was probably grabbing her big boobs with both hands like she always did whenever they were mentioned. 'Most men would kill for these casabas.'

'Yeah, especially now that they're the size of honeydews.'

Trish was pregnant. Her breasts were twice their normal size. And so was the rest of her. She was 30 pounds over her pregnancy weight. She blamed it on the girl scouts.

'Those little bitches show up every day at my door with their boxes of cookies. I think they're stalking pregnant women. I think they break into hospitals and steal our records and hunt us down. In their little spotless brown outfits. Decorated with all their badges. They look like soldiers. Little tiny soldiers with cookies as their ammunition. And I buy. Oh yes, I buy the cookies. Better that, than be pummeled by them.'

'What kind are you eating right now?'

'Mystic mints. They're better than sex. It's my third box. I'm huge.'

'Well, Trish, I have an idea. Call Carl, and he'll come to your house and chase away the girls with their cookies. He's a cop. Those little troops will do what he says.'

'Don't patronize me. I'm not crazy, I'm just pregnant.'

'Carl would love to hear about that.'

'Yeah, exactly. And Tom, you know he'll ask me loads of questions, like, who's the father? And other things I don't know the answers to.'

'Isn't Michael the father?'

'He might be. Ever since that wild solstice party, it's difficult to tell.'

'So things are a bit messy between the two of you?'

'I guess I just don't have time for Michael's fear of intimacy bullshit, and I don't have time for you. Jerry Springer is on soon.'

'Well, I guess I could call him.'

'Don't call Jerry Springer. He's got nothing to say to you.'

'No, I mean I should call Carl.'

'Don't call your uncle, either.' Trish sounded distracted. She was watching *Ricki Lake*, so lots of absent-minded opinions were flying out of her mouth. 'You'll just anger him with your inquiries.'

'What are you talking about?'

'Tom, you know that you interrogate people. That's why my family won't have you over on Christmas Eve anymore. You scare the children.'

'All I did was ask your niece Gabriella if she knew what her grandparents did during the Second World War.'

'For Christ's sake, my mom and dad were both five when

they did that! They had no choice. All their friends were in the Hitler Youth.'

'So, if your parents were such innocent little Nazis, then why doesn't Gabi know about it?'

'Because we were afraid she'd tell other kids at school that her German grandparents had, well, worked for the bad guys. Which she did. Now all her friends torture her by yelling out "Hotsy Totsy, Gabi's a Nazi." Happy?'

'Listen, it ain't my fault your parents were National Socialists.'

'God, I hope fascism isn't genetic.'

'You've been watching Woody Allen films again, haven't you?'

'Well, fuck, Tom, what if Gabi becomes a malevolent little brownshirt.'

'Then she can join the girl scouts.'

'Or,' Trish paused as she swallowed another cookie. 'I could put her on *Ricki Lake* and let her defend herself.'

'Yeah! Put Gabi up there with a rabbi, some shaven-headed neo-Nazis, a couple of black guys with retro-afros, and a psychologist wearing too much make-up. They could go after each other. Sure, some hair might be pulled and some lipstick might be smeared, and yes, Gabi might be emotionally scarred, but think of the ratings!'

'Speaking of ratings, Ricki Lake is crying.' Trish said, as she took another bite of the chocolate and mint wafers. 'Is it sweeps month? That bitch only cries to increase her ratings.'

'Who doesn't.' Then I got excited. 'You think she'd have me on her show? I could hold up a sketch of Taylor' – because I had your faced etched in my memory – 'and ask anyone watching who recognizes him to contact me with any information they might have.'

'Can you cry?'

'Can I cry? Is Celine Dion a talentless cunt?'

'Quit bragging.' I could hear Trish searching through papers for something. 'Oh shit, I've lost my *TV Guide*. If I don't find it soon, my afternoon is ruined. And anyway I've got to call my family and ask them to pay my rent again this month. What did really pregnant women do before telephones and TV?'

'Drank and smoked?'

'Don't remind me. I haven't had a drink in seven months. This little fucker better pop out soon. "Come on out, Gina or Parker. Momma needs a vodka enema!"' She dropped her remote control. 'Ah, fuck! Listen, I've got to go. My entire home entertainment world is slipping away.'

'But Trish, what should I do about Uncle Carl?'

'Just call him. But don't let him know Taylor is your newest obsession, Tom. I mean, Carl is a cop. He might not understand. Just tell him you're hiring somebody new to help you write some jokes, and you want to know about his past work experience, if he's had any trouble with the law, blah, blah, blah. That way, Carl will feel like he's doing you a practical favor, instead of what he'll actually be doing, which is feeding your neurosis.'

CHAPTER SEVEN

Bring down the heat

My father's side of the family have used my uncle's expertise as a cop to get various family members out of drunken-driving charges, which only seems fair, since most of those charges have been accrued while returning from family functions. However this time I offered Carl a new challenge, by which he almost seemed intrigued.

'Sure, Tom, I'll find out what I can. Listen, how is that Trish character?'

'Oh, she's fine, Carl. She's pregnant.'

'Aw, that's great. I always liked her. Who's the lucky guy?'

'Well, he's uh, a guy she . . . married. Yeah, that's it. The lucky guy is her husband.'

'Right. That makes sense.'

'Uh huh.'

'You really gave up something good when you lost her, Tom.'

'Well, we're still friends.'

'Yeah, but those tits. They're the best! How could you give those up?'

'Gee, I really regret that.'

'It's just too bad. Just too bad you dumped her.'

'Lou, she dumped me.'

'Oh, yeah. Why was that?'

'I'm a dicksmoker, Carl.'

Pause. 'Anyhow, Tom, I'll find out what I can.'

Why do I bother telling my relations the truth? Because really, they don't want to know. They probably hope I don't have sex. They're worried about the AIDS thing. Little do they know that the booze will kill me first.

I think they'd rather imagine I was celibate. In fact, when my Dad found out I was gay, he was sort of excited, because we're Italian, and the family needed a priest.

'Dad,' I said, in my best queer droll, 'I'm gay, but I'm not *that* gay. And anyway, drag really isn't my thing.'

And that was the last time Dad and I talked about my sexuality. Which is fine by me. I don't want to hear about his sex life either. So we just avoid the topic all together. It's not that my family hates my being gay. Well, most of them do, but they don't hate it as much as when my sister dated a black guy. She's only recently been added to several holiday guest lists, and that's only after having been married to Mr Unbearably White for seven years. Of course, if I bring home a black boyfriend, I might as well kiss my inheritance goodbye. But who needs an inheritance, when you're a member of an inter-racial gay relationship? Hell, between grants and talk show appearances, me and Mandingo could live quite nicely.

I guess some of my kin feel sorry for me. I'm just a lonely gay clown, with a bit of a drinking problem. So they bend over backward to help.

For instance, Uncle Carl shouldn't have looked up your profile down at City Hall. I think it's illegal, but he wanted to help. And anyway, he's Italian. If it were legal, he might not have bothered. He couldn't come up with anything. Either the name 'Taylor' is fictitious, or you've never really existed. I was sure I'd made you up. I was sure you'd happened because you had to happen, like a character in a novel, but you were still fiction. A fantasy. Nothing more than a figment. A fig, rolling down my back, making me tingle, then rolling off.

CHAPTER EIGHT

Allow 25 minutes per pound

I only communicate with my dad's family on special occasions, like holidays and weddings. Which is probably poor planning on my part, since those are the most stressful moments in any heterosexual year. All their expectations for a perfect communal event go out the window after the second whiskey sour. Then all my uncles start fighting over Anne's star sapphire wedding ring, and everyone runs for cover.

I do like certain members of Dad's family, and if I weren't so lazy and self-obsessed, I'd call them during off-peak dates, so we could hang out and make fun of the family the way we did when we were kids. Except now we wouldn't have our parents around editing us. We could be a lot more explicit and more cruel, aware of what we know of one another.

For instance, I know that my father dumped my mother to marry his second wife, Flora. As a child, I'd been led to believe that Mom and Dad just didn't get along, and so they separated. Then, by chance or perhaps by fate, my father, in need of a stable family life, met Flora at a conference. Before they even knew what was happening, they were swept away by love and were soon married.

A dubious story, since my father sold booze at Dean's Liquors on Polk Street. Perhaps the word 'conference' was used euphemistically, in a poetic sense.

What actually happened was that Dad met Flora in a

bar down the street from Dean's Liquors, where Flora was a cocktail waitress. The bar was Polk Gulch, known as a trucker and biker hangout. It was 1963, I'd just been born a few months earlier, and Dad was on his lunch break. He witnessed Flora defending herself in the unruly atmosphere of her workplace. Apparently, when pinched by a frisky customer, Flora's instinct was to lift a beer bottle by the neck, breaking it against whatever table was nearby. Then, with lightning speed, she raised the damaged bottle high, and, bringing it down hard across the face of the would-be assailant, slashed the flesh of the scoundrel with the edges of the broken glass. After seeing her so courageously, almost athletically, protecting her pride, my father could not stop thinking about her. Troubles at home persisted, until Flora became Dad's only solace. Finally, he chose the comfort of this simple working-class barmaid over the hysteria of a demanding wife and three sniveling brats.

When my sister and I heard this story, direct from the whore's mouth, we nicknamed her Filthy Flora. And every Halloween thereafter, Lisa and I built an effigy in our garage with the same nickname – Filthy Flora – which we lit on fire for all the kiddies to see. In our own adolescent and angry way, we celebrated what must have been a truly electrifying moment: the union of my cheating father with a Greek guttersnipe.

Yet, even this shameless story was only another sub-plot born in the frighteningly fermented imaginations of my family. Over a couple of drinks at my high school graduation party, Dad figured I was old enough to know the truth, and drunk enough to find out what the truth actually was.

My mother met my father when she was seventeen. She wasn't really ready to get married, but she also couldn't bear living with Virginia. That's easy to understand, yet why she married my father, I'll never figure out. Not that he's a bad guy. Well, he's weak and ineffectual, but that's not the point.

They had nothing in common. My mom was a free spirit who wanted to go to foreign films and stay up late listening to jazz and cursing. My father wanted to listen to baseball on the car radio. My mother wanted to travel and dress up and learn French. My dad liked talking about baseball. Mom wanted to put my sister into ballet and let my brother take a watercolor course. My dad enjoyed baseball. And control. He wouldn't let my mother get a checking account, or learn to drive, or buy a stereo. She was pregnant for five years, and by the tender age of twenty-three she had three kids and no high school diploma. My father worked in a shop. Things were a bit grim.

Now, I don't think my mom and dad were communicating very well when he met Flora. However I know my parents weren't separated. I was only one, and Dad was still living with us in our tract house in Pacifica.

Ah, Pacifica. Pacifica was 'built in a day, yet planned for a lifetime'. Our home had the kind of ubiquitous polyester wall-to-wall carpeting you usually only see on a senior citizen's patio. Durable and practical, and stain-resistant too, but completely charmless. Our walls were gun-metal gray. My father's shiny red Ford, parked carefully in the garage, was the prettiest thing in the house. And everyone in our neighborhood had the same house, the same yard, the same palm tree dying on the same front lawn.

While their balding husbands drove off in carpools to account for other people's money all day, female Pacificans walked about in a daze, like they'd been lifted by a UFO and had all their important areas probed and prodded and examined, and in some cases, removed without being returned. No one really smiled, or laughed, or cried. Everyone just tended flowers that never grew and washed cars that never got dirty. Children went to sleep, woke up, abused their toys and planned their own escapes. Pacifica looked like a scene from *The Deer*

Hunter, just without all the glitz and glamour. And that's where Mom was imprisoned, given $20 a week for all food and household needs, while Dad sold whiskey and prayed for a home run.

Flora must have seemed like a wild animal to my dad, a fiery, earthy chick with a ballsy attitude and lots of fire and music. Kind of like Anne Baxter's character Eve Harrington in *All About Eve*, except without the talent and aspirations and appeal. Eve was clever. Flora was crafty. And self-sufficient. Like a Mormon. Or like a dog that eats its own throw-up. Whichever came first.

I think Dad and Flora initially did meet in a bar. Then, later, they met quietly, secretly, and fucked in the back of Flora's '57 Chevy. She'd had all her four kids by different fathers in the back of that Chevy. Like I said, Flora had walked her pussy around the block a few times. She was tough. She could remove bottle caps with body parts that most people kept hidden.

Eventually the condom must've broke. Hell, that's how I was conceived, too. Flora became pregnant, and sued my father for child support. My parents had separated by then, so I guess Dad figured, what the hell, if I have to support the kid I might as well marry the bitch. And so a new family was started. My brother, sister and I knew he'd remarried. We knew our father couldn't care for himself. But, Dad didn't have the courage to explain his new situation. Instead he'd just pick us up in his red Ford at our new, cramped apartment every Sunday afternoon. Mom would stay in bed, wearing her robe, chatting blithely on the phone while straining to ignore us. She didn't want to see him, and she hated seeing us excited about seeing him.

We would be dressed nicely, our assumption being that Dad would finally introduce us to the person who'd been ironing his polo shirt and khakis. Instead, we spent the court-appointed three hours a week at the zoo. Or at a movie. We saw *Angel in My Pocket* with Andy Griffith about seventeen times. Dad just had no idea how to be a father. He'd been so spoiled by his parents that he had no idea how to talk to anyone unless he wanted something from them. And we were children. We had nothing to offer. We just scared him. I think he always felt scrutinized by us, as if we were our mother's own eyes. He just should've never had kids, and by the time he was thirty-two, he was playing father to several.

Finally, when I was maybe six and my father just couldn't stand spending another Sunday at another Disney film, Lisa, Rob and I met my half-brother, Teddy. He just appeared in the back seat. He was so excited to meet us. I guess that's how we all knew Teddy was related to us. Because non-family members were never excited about meeting us. I have a photo of me and my siblings from Christmas at Anne's house. Let me find it. If I can. I usually carry it with me, to show people. Like David Letterman, when I make my first *Late Show* appearance. Here it is. That's about 1969. Don't we look lost, like frightened birds? My sister is of course smiling. She's not only the middle child, she's also a Libra! Always trying to please.

Dad didn't introduce us to one another. We just said 'Hey' and Teddy offered us gum. Then my father rolled up his window, lit a cigarette, and turned on baseball – where do they play baseball in January? Is this a Japanese radio station? – and off we went to Dad's home to meet Flora and the rest of this new family.

We settled in, thinking we were in for a long journey. Five minutes later, Dad pulled into a driveway and turned off the engine. We realized Dad and Flora lived only a mile from our apartment door. We could have walked to his place. And yet for years we had driven around and around in circles. I think my father had waited for something awful to happen, like the Vietnam War. Something that might have distracted us from the frightening carnage we were about to encounter. It didn't.

Upon arrival at Dad's new tract home, almost undetectable except in taste from the home he'd shared with us, we were greeted by three more children. Three girls. All stretch pants and dirty hair, like their mother. Flora's oldest, Kevin, would've been my father's eighth child, but he'd recently deserted from the navy, so he wouldn't be joining us for . . . ever. And so we all sat down to breakfast.

Flora appeared, cigarette in mouth and huge plates of scrambled eggs in hands. Dad did not speak. Ever again. From then on, Flora did all the talking. In fact, after that day, I only remember seeing the back of my father's head as he drove us to and from our apartment. He became more of a chauffeur than a father, and Flora became more of a stepmother than anyone ever needed.

I was never partial to scrambled eggs. Nor did I much appreciate the down-home heartiness of greasy potatoes. However, when in Crete, one must do as the Cretans do. Although I drew the line at smoking at the breakfast table. Sheila, Shawna and Denise, all ageless, like furballs, just puffed away. I don't think they ate much, although Denise, large and daunting, stared at me like she could swallow me whole. My gag factor, though not ever as sensitive as my sister's, threatened to act up at the sight of brown eggs sprinkled with damp cigarette butts. Even the crockery – a sort of mushroom and butterfly pattern – seemed nauseatingly institutional.

The three girls spoke as if English was not their first language, which in fact it was. Lots of *aint*s and *caint*s and I even think a few *I cain't be doin that*s were thrown about. They seemed to have a particular problem with tenses, as if time was a mystery to them.

'I ain't gonna be goin and doin this now like I's did then though.'

Such sentences baffled me. And frightened me, since they ended almost every sentence with a preposition, like those death row convicts I'd seen in documentaries on public television.

Still, with this influx of new information and the horrifying realization that I might be spending lots of my time with these macabre characters, I rose to the occasion and, at such a tender young age, complimented Flora on setting such a lovely table.

My brother was shocked I could even speak in that Machiavellian atmosphere. He looked at me stunned, like I'd just yelled 'Fuck' in a library.

And Flora responded, 'Well, I'm good at serving food. I'm a waitress downtown, ya know.'

'No,' I said. 'We had no idea.'

'We?' Flora asked, incredulously. Not that she'd have known what the word 'incredulously' meant.

'We, meaning my brother, sister and I.' Of course I actually meant the royal 'we', since my family didn't usually associate with waitresses, but on went Flora.

'Right. Well, you should come down to the restaurant with your father. He knows where it is. Bring your friends. Oh, but, make sure you don't bring no niggers. I don't serve niggers, or faggots.'

And I vomited. It was the combo platter of racism, homophobia and greasy diner food that sent me over the edge. And all over Denise. I covered her with puke. She was, after all, the largest target in the room. Eggs, eggs and more eggs just kept projecting out of me, and then out of my sister. If someone else throws up, Lisa must join in. To Lisa, vomiting has always been like a yawn. Unpredictable and contagious.

We didn't share many meals together after that introductory

brunch. Usually Dad would dump us off at his place on his way to play golf, and we'd spend the afternoon watching cartoons and talking to Denise's newest boyfriend. Denise was seventeen. Which meant she was old enough to date, and, apparently, abort. Flora's telephone had Planned Parenthood on speed-dial.

I never really imagined that Denise even had sex with the boys she dated. Like the woman in a Mormon couple, she seemed much more masculine then any of her male partners. I pictured them arm-wrestling in bed, with Denise always winning. I knew that cunt was strong. She'd thrown me down the stairs often enough.

Sheila and Shawna called Denise's boyfriends 'fags'. I agreed with my two evil stepsisters, although I was too young to know what the word 'fag' really meant. I mean, I was in love with my babysitter, the asthmatic Gary, but I would have never associated my pure love with the kind of polluted friction Denise and her concubines created. I merely observed that Denise's beaus were slender and sibilant and smartly dressed. I assumed Denise dated them for dietary and fashion tips.

But Sheila told me that these boys did not start out effete. When Denise first met her victims in parking lots or at the beach, they were normal, beer-slugging, date-raping studs. Denise simply had the knack, the power, as it were, of conversion. Before long, tattoos were covered by button-downs, and hairs were trimmed or removed. With the brute force of a Greek god, Denise transformed red-blooded hetero boys into Andy Gibb.

Then Denise actually fell in love. With a black man. The news caught like wild fire.

Remember that Flora didn't serve faggots or niggers. Under Denise's tight grip, Leon was destined to be both. Flora forbade Leon from coming near the house, or in Denise.

Denise was enraged. And to get back at her mother, she did what any white trash American teenager would do. She became pregnant. And this time, she wasn't aborting. She was keeping this baby.

CHAPTER NINE

Juices should run clear

U nfortunately in those days we didn't have Jerry Springer to help us work out our domestic difficulties. I mean, if this happened today, Jerry would invite Flora and Denise on his show, and let them duke it out. A few fist punches later, tears would stream out of all eyes, and the problem would be settled before the final commercial break. But in 1972 all Flora had was a cheap frying pan, with which she hit Denise in the head.

Denise moved out.

Dad made bets on the World Series.

And Flora started serving homos at work.

'What can I do? Two new department stores opened downtown. The queers are everywhere. At least they tip well. And they keep their hands off of me.'

Then Denise dumped her black boyfriend.

Then Denise had a white baby.

Then Denise was diagnosed with multiple sclerosis.

Apparently she'd been hanging out in the mall near her studio apartment, when she fell down for no reason. She laughed with her friends, thought it was the acid, but then she couldn't stand without support. Nor was she able to get out of bed the next day. Or the day after that.

By the time the doctors diagnosed the MS, Denise was bedridden, helpless and the mother of two. Of course she needed her family's help. She called her mother. Flora said she was happy to help, with one condition. Denise would have to get rid of the black baby. The white one could stay, but the black one had to go. Denise gave in, and then moved in. My dad wasn't thrilled, because her bed was placed in the family room, partially blocking his view of his big screen television. But he succumbed. After all, the doctors said she'd be dead soon anyway. Maybe even before the World Series was over.

Well, that was twenty years ago, and Denise is still *alive*! And her little white baby is now a faggy, flabby, fat man.

And my father still can't see the whole screen. When we talk about movies we've both enjoyed, it's as if he's left the room during crucial scenes. Dad still has no idea what shocked some audiences about *The Crying Game*.

Whenever he and I are on the phone, I can hear Denise in the background.

'Will someone come and light my cigarette?'

Or, 'Can somebody uncurl my toes?'

Or, 'I need my feet scraped.'

'Dad,' I ask him, while artificially coughing to suppress my own laughter, 'aren't you going to help her?'

'Nah. I just ignore her, and she goes away. Sometimes.'

And that's what my father gets for cheating on my mother.

Which is why it's so strange that I don't mind Flora now. Don't get me wrong. I know that she's an evil cunt. But I suppose we have more than just that in common. Let's see. Well, we're both black sheep. We both exist on the fringes of our family units. And Flora is relentless. To spite all the health warnings, she continues to smoke twenty cigarettes a day. And she eats only red meat. She's like a carnivorous chimney.

Well, a chimney with really bad asthma. Flora is on a respirator. And, because she's active, she has one big respirator for home and a portable respirator for work. At the International

House of Pancakes, or IHOP, where Flora waits tables, she straps a small aluminium canister around her waist, concealing it under her white dress and apron. Customers only see the slim tan oxygen tube jutting up from her collar and circling her right ear then creeping daintily across her right cheek, winding up in her right nostril. It scares children, so the hostess usually seats childless people in Flora's section. Loners. Second World War veterans with newspapers or magazines to read, who won't mind the handicap their waitress so bravely bears. And infertile couples. Older couples. Gay couples. Older gay couples. Couples with respirators, who understand her plight and tip her well but wish she'd stay home.

But she won't stay home. Remember, she's relentless. And she loves people.

'I'm a people person!' She proclaims, while short-changing anyone black, blind or mute.

God knows, she doesn't have to work. My father makes a fine living. He worked his way up, from selling liquor in a tiny store to running a nationwide liquor distribution company. Sweet River, Inc. They're the people who find clever ways to convince minors that drinking alcohol is real cool. 'The sweeter the wine, the sweeter the profit,' my dad always says. See, these days, adults are drinking less, and that makes Dad sad. But kids like fun drinks, and they have lots of money to spend, and that makes Dad happy. He convinces wine manufacturers to add loads more sugar to their beverages and screw-on caps to the bottles. That way, Peter Pan Punch – that name is one of Dad's ideas – looks and tastes like a big bottle of cough syrup. And what could be more harmless? It's easy to open, and easy to store in a backpack, between classes. Kids can always find ways to get alcohol – fake IDs, bums who need a couple of bucks – and now they have booze made surreptitiously for them. My father is helping, in his own small, indefatigable way, to create a whole new generation of American drunks and diabetics. So he's doing just fine.

After he pays off his hookers and gambling debts, he still has enough money to keep Flora in facelifts. She's had four. She's had so many facelifts that when she smiles her ears meet at the top of her head. That's another similarity between she and I. She's also terrified of aging. I shouldn't be worried. I'll probably be beaten to death in the back of a comedy club by some angry audience member before I'm fifty. Better that than having work done on my face. Flora's had so much work done to her face that people mistake her for Liz Taylor. Especially when she's at work, and she has the tube running up her nose.

I think that's another reason she keeps her job at IHOP. All the freaks and senior citizens that go there for the house special – a short stack with one long hair snaking its way through the syrup – tell Flora that she looks like Liz. Maybe, if she'd let them finish the sentence, they'd say, 'You look like Liz Taylor . . . around the eyes. And behind the ears!'

But Flora never lets anyone finish a sentence. That's another way that she and I are alike.

'Hiya. Welcome to IHOP. Ignore my nametag. I'm not Marge. Marge died of uteral cancer last month. Too bad. Nice kid. Her tag was the only tag left in the tag drawer. And you gotta have a tag to serve breakfast, so's the customer knows whose name to put on this customer compliment card we need you to fill out. Here's a pen. I want it back. I used to have my own nametag, but I put it in my purse, and suddenly it ain't there. Like my pens. And like a lot of other things that used to be in my purse. Thank God I've got my oxygen strapped on. I see those busboys eyeing my portable. They could probably get big bucks for this little baby on the black market. Do ya' get what I'm sayin'? These goddamn Mexicans I work with would let me suffocate if it meant an extra gold tooth in their fucking mouths. Anyway, I'm Flora. And I'll be happy to refill your everlasting pot of coffee, if you'll just keep your goddamn walkers out of my aisle.'

When off duty, the doctor insists that Flora use the big respirator. It replenishes her lungs faster. It's like an oxygen tank for divers, complete with a black mask and tube that siphons the air from the tank to her hungry, desperate, gray lungs. It travels on wheels and she drags it behind her throughout the house. It's only annoying to her because lugging the tank around increases her heart rate, which of course greatens her own demand for oxygen. The more active she tries to be at home, the greater her dependency on the tank grows. This makes her more anxious, and she smokes to calm her nerves. Which causes further damage to her lungs, and then she requires more oxygen.

Like a circle in a spiral, like a wheel within a fucking wheel. And each year the tank seems to grow in size. Soon she'll be dragging around a tank that's the size of a space capsule.

Or she'll be dead.

Flora is such an enigma to my vain, precise family. Their self-destructiveness takes more private forms. And that's why I love Thanksgiving so much. The family gasps every time she lights a cigarette near her oxygen tank, horrified we'll all burst into a ball of flames. But let's face it, she adds at least a few thrilling moments to an otherwise dull holiday.

I think the most exciting moment is when Flora moves from cigarette to oxygen tank. You're never sure if she'll make it. This puff may be her last. It's so exciting: all of us at the table, finished with that tasteless Thanksgiving slop, then Flora lights up. We duck! Okay, fine, we're all still in one piece. She didn't blow up the house. And then she takes a heavy hit of nicotine. She exhales. She pauses. Will she make it to the tank? The crowd perches, on the edge of our seats, anticipating, almost demanding, the worst. But, YES! She reaches for the oxygen mask, and phew! She sucks down the H_2O!

The crowd goes wild.

I suppose the family now coddles Flora. We've stopped needling her about her loud wheezing, her loud dress sense and the extra skin behind her head. After all, we're older and just a bit wiser. We've forgiven Flora for her misgivings.

It's doubtful she'll live much longer. Between pushing wrecked eggs and swallowing clouds of carbon, Flora will probably be toast in no time at all. Denise might outlive her mother. And then all Denise's bedsore/toenail-cleaning/bedpan-rinsing duties will fall on my father's lap. And that's what he gets for being emotionally absent.

And I think Flora enjoys the family get-togethers much more now than she did when I was young. She's no longer expected to cook. She can just relax and enjoy Mindi's company.

Mindi is my brother's second wife. She dots both *i*s in her first name with a happy face. She doesn't just blowdry her hair. She tortures it into submission. She's got that mall hair one sees on girls featured in those sad films about towns in the Midwest, once rich in resources or industry, that have fallen on hard times. The bangs are doing a backflip, while the back of her head is flat and shiny. She appears to have almost a satellite dish on her forehead. Perhaps she enjoys Reuters. Or Russian air stations. Maybe she's interested in air traffic control. But everytime I see those bangs, I think of miniature golf and incest.

And Mindi is always pregnant. She's populating small towns in Iowa with her own uterus. God tapped her on the shoulder and told her to! Yes, Mindi's a Christian. And Flora's a hedonist, so she enjoys sitting next to Mindi at family functions, because she loves smoking next to pregnant Christians.

'So, Mindi,' Flora asks, while billowing smoke around the

belly of her ballooned daughter-in-law. 'What are you gonna name this one?'

'We think something evangelical.' Mindi says with that patronizing Christian humility.

'Hmph,' Flora remarks, discerningly, after visiting her air tank. 'I'd name it after its father. I named all my kids after their fathers. Have you met my oldest daughter, Hank?'

Flora then lets out a huge roar, which scares my young niece. I of course recognize it as my stepmother's laughter. To the untrained ear, one might think a giant was farting.

The rest of the family giggle self-consciously. They look down at their napkins, and thank God they're not Flora.

And I wonder, why am I the one on medication?

CHAPTER TEN

Baste frequently with drippings

My therapist makes me take three depression pills each day. These little pills are supposed to make me happy. Problem is, they're homeopathic. They're made of herbs and such. That's why they're brown. They don't contain anything chemical. So I asked my doctor, why bother? Taking herbs for my depression is like putting a Band-Aid on a bullet wound.

Look at these silly little pellets. They're called St John's Wort, named after John the Baptist. I'm gulping down bitter malt infused by a Catholic martyr. That's supposed to make me feel *better*? Why couldn't they have been named St John's Jizz? That would've been a lot easier to swallow. And they look like vitamins. I'm even supposed to take them with food, unlike Valium, which I absorb with Vodka. Like so. Yikes. I should have chilled that vodka first. It burns more when it's warm. And cheap. Valium cocktails make me happy, but these shitty puny turds are pathetic.

I wouldn't even bother taking the Wort pills. But I want to stay on my therapist's good side. I could throw them away, and then just lie when I see him and tell him that the pills are working just fine. But part of me would kind of like to see if the Wort works. My problems might stem from a chemical imbalance, and these can fix that. Loads of depressed people have reported great results with these Wort vitamins. But those are probably people with minor depression, like fashion designers who have only recently grasped the banality of their lives, or housewives with liver spots.

Fuck them. I have real depression. My depression is so intense that I need a bit more vodka. My depression is so bad – how bad is it? – my depression is so bad, that I wish everyone felt this badly, so they'd know how I felt, and would stop blaming me for everything that is wrong in the world. When I was younger, I thought everyone felt this hollow. The way I feel right now. I used to think everyone felt like they lived in a black tube, where something was sucking the oxygen out of them. I had to think that everyone else felt like they were suffocating, or else I would've been totally alone. I was really young then. I think I was still a virgin, but I knew I was gay, and that made me feel alone too. I figured that what I suffered was just teen angst.

'Once I'm "out" and in love,' I told myself, 'I'll be happy.'

Now I know I wasn't just sad or lonely. I was clinically fucked up.

And it's gotten worse. I have the kind of depression that haunts people who've committed a violent crime. I feel backed up into a corner. A corner of a cold, dark room where the walls are made of damp blocks of stones. Everything is wet and rough, and I am not even really there. No one hands me food. No one else exists. And I have no options. Even suicide won't help, because I don't feel alive.

I'm asking an awful lot of St John and his Wort, aren't I?

That's why I like to boost my medication with just a line or two of crystal. Clears my head.

Who do I think I am? Blathering on and on about my depression like that. I'm sorry. Sometimes, I act like I am the center of the goddamned universe.

What made me so self-centered? Good breast-feeding

experiences? Bad breast-feeding experiences? Who knows? Who cares?

Who exists? Me. Only me. Maybe I feel responsible for everyone, because I created everything and that's why I feel so alone. When I leave the room, not only do the other occupants disappear, so does everything they've ever created. Without me, they're nothing.

So it's always strange to me when I find out people in my world are thinking about things when I'm not there. Thinking and talking! How is this possible? Perhaps when I don't require their company, they gather somewhere.

I imagine everyone I've created huddling together in a huge ball of flesh, waiting for my next command. Maybe they go to some small, remote island and crowd together, in limbo, waiting for me to beckon them. And in those quiet moments, while they wait for my signal to join my world once again, they find themselves conversing with one another about me. But then, what else would they have to talk about? I have created all they see!

Of course, my mother would disagree with that.

'I was wiping the shit off your penis before it became a habit.'

That's Mom on Christmas morning, after seven egg noggs. I'd left the house to contemplate my future. And cruise for cock. I was wearing a long black overcoat and I had a Flock of Seagulls hairdo. Short on one side, long on the other, and dyed blond. Black liquid liner surrounded my eyes. I weighed about 40 pounds less. I was nineteen, and I wanted to be adored and ignored, simultaneously.

'I've known you your whole life,' she reminded me, while mixing stuffing from a box with fresh apples. 'So don't try that theatrical crap with me. Going off on a walk. Hmph! When I've got a turkey to fist, the last thing I need to worry about is whether or not you've been kidnapped. So knock off the amateur dramatics. That Academy-Award-winning performance of yours doesn't work with me, Mr What's His Name. Oh, shit, who won the Academy Award for Best Actor this year? It doesn't matter. Look, if you want to be the centerpiece, then stick some maple leaves up your ass and stand in the middle of the table. Actually, just go sit somewhere, and stay out of my way. I've got guests in twenty minutes.'

That was before my mother's third marriage to a rich car salesman, but after her second husband, Jay Sky, left her. Jay's real last name wasn't Sky. It was Simmons. Sky became his last name right before he went on his spiritual journey to the Hopi Indian Resort. Jay had been a dog-walker – that's someone without ambition, who walks dogs for a living – and one night he had a dream where he was visited by a flying Indian. A flying Hopi Indian. And the flying Indian picked up Jay Simmons, and carried him across fields, and through a ski cabin – don't ask me – and then the flying Indian dropped Jay off at a bus stop in the desert. Apparently, as Jay later read in a pamphlet that he picked up in the vitamin section of his favorite organic market, Rainbow Foods, all Americans have a soulmate who is actually an Indian ghost who follows us around and protects us. Jay's aboriginal guardian came to him in his sleep, and another dog-walker told Jay that he must now follow this ghost on a special pilgrimage. So Jay packed a bag, sold his car for next to nothing, which is what it was worth, and changed his last name from Simmons to Sky. Sky is a Hopi word meaning, well, sky.

And then he left.

Then my mom had to buy a new car, and that's when she met rich Ray.

Last Mom heard, which was years ago, Jay had grown a really long ponytail and was leading rebirthing seminars in

Arizona. Those are seminars where people go through their own birthing process all over again. To see what they missed the first time, I guess. I wonder if he's still there. Maybe he's moved on to a new spiritual path. Maybe Jay is braiding beads into a lesbian's hair on a gender-free vegetarian commune in Colorado. Maybe he's following a comet. Or maybe he's still in Arizona, spending his afternoons spritzing rich blond women with placenta mist while they writhe about crying and gasping for air.

Clearly, Mom's glad Jay left, because now she's got a husband with enough money to hire someone to baste her bird. And bleach her hair. In fact, Mom's hair procedure is so expensive it's no longer called 'bleaching'. Now, my mother has her hair 'tinted'. Isn't 'tinting' what serial killers do to van windows to hide the violence inside? Well, I guess if Mom's head was a car window, I'd have it tinted too. There's an awful lot of creepy stuff in that cranium. Past, present and future suicide attempts coexisting with B-movie plots and regrets. It's hard to imagine there's any room for reality in there. Maybe there isn't, but it wouldn't matter. Mom never leaves the suburbs.

As Liz Taylor says, 'Money is the best deodorant.' Or maybe Flora said that. Either way, my mom has more cashmere on her back and more time on her hands, than ever before. She lives in a house that is so expensive that mailmen are not allowed near the mailbox. After all, those postal workers are so common. They wear such sensible shoes. Nothing but overpriced, heavily polished Italian shoes are allowed on my mother's gravel driveway. Actually, Mom and Daddy Ray – that's my current stepfather – they don't even own a mailbox. Mom has to stroll down to the post office to pick up her mail every day.

Maybe that's where my minions gather.

Daddy Ray likes that Mom has to complete this retrieving chore.

'It's just like back home in Oklahoma.'

Daddy Ray always spouts about his roots. He doesn't want us to think he's grown 'too big for his goddamned britches', so he often reminds us he's from that regressive, backwater state that's somewhere above Texas and below Satan's asshole. Like having to call him 'Daddy Ray' isn't enough of a reminder.

In fact, Daddy Ray likes everyone to know he's just the same ol' spit that he always was. He's especially concerned the working classes know of his humility. He feels a great affinity for those kind, simple folk. After all, he often says, his own daddy was a workin' man.

My mother regards Daddy Ray from a distance. She knows he butters her white bread, so she lets a lot of what her husband says slide.

Until we're alone.

'If he tells me one more time about his trashy family in Oklahoma, I swear I'll solicit another Timothy McVeigh. I mean, my family is trashy, too, but I don't advertise it.'

It's just embarrassing. Whenever we are out in a restaurant Daddy Ray has to flirt with the waitress and make her feel like she's part of the family.

'You're a pretty young thing. What's your name, girlie?'

'I'm Nancy, sir.'

'Well, Nancy, I'd like a nice, big, plump piece of beef. And I want it pink. Pink and juicy.'

'So, you want it rare?'

'Rare as it can be, Nancy sweetie. Hell, why bother cookin' it? Just rip off its horns and wipe its ass!'

Yee haw.

'It's so fun, watchin' your momma shuffle off to the post office every mornin'. My momma . . .' oh no, I thought, this homespun musing I have to listen to is going to ruin this free meal, '... she had to ride a pony into town to pick up our mail. Course, we only got mail once a month in those days. And gooks didn't sell us our stamps. But other than that, it's just like back home.'

Picking up the mail is only one of my mother's daily chores. She also has gossip to impart. This leaves her ample time to think about me. As one does.

And she's been watching daytime television. As most do.

Mom obsessively inspects chat shows. She's on a first name basis with Ricki, Jerry and Oprah. Lately, I think my mother has actually been attempting an Oprah metamorphosis. She asks questions all the time. About everything. Including the gay thing, which I guess is discussed incessantly on these chat shows.

Fortunately, Mom's not Oprah. One Oprah is enough. And depending on her size, sometimes even one Oprah is too much. However, my mother does have Oprah's hair. Actually, Mom's got the white girl version, which is truly the kind of hair Oprah craves. I mean, let's face it, forget all the power and applause. I think all Oprah really wants to be is a regular cast member on *Friends*. Then all her pretty girl fantasies could come true. She'd be anorexic, untalented and overexposed.

Well, two out of three ain't bad.

Mom's even started drinking decaf. She makes decaffeinated cappuccinos. They're chic, if your hair is bleached. Sorry, tinted. Mom has the gals over for decaf caps and croissants. Croissants are crescent rolls if you're rich. And 'gals' are rich women, who might be identified as 'bitches' if they were poor or if my mother drank alcohol, which is against the rules in her new husband's home.

And the gals have begged Mom to get answers about the gay thing. I call it a 'thing', because I don't know what else to call this process of engaging in homosexual behavior. I suppose I have to come up with a name for that, too. It's tough being Zeus.

Mom is a woman (alien concept #22) and so she is more rational. At least, that's what she tells me. And she wants to know how it all works. The ins, the outs, the ups and downs of being a deviant. Her word, not mine. When did it happen, and why? Questions, questions and more questions! And often times she fires her queries during holiday meals, which leads to public discourse.

'Honey,' she asked at Easter, with a knife so high in one hand that I thought she was either about to stab me, or use it as a mock microphone, 'when did you find out you were gay?'

I always knew this day would come, when my parent would ask about the birds and the . . . birds. My therapist and I had talked about my being more direct. I wanted to tell her, so that she could tell everyone else. All the little people needed to know the truth. Once and for all, I wanted to alert the tabloids, spread the news, and end the controversy.

'Mom, I knew I was gay when I had a dick in my mouth.'
Stop the presses.

CHAPTER ELEVEN

Don't scorch the bottom

S ometimes even vague family members, cousins I've never liked who don't even share my ethnicity, ask me questions about the gay thing. I'm sorry. The 'Gay Experience'. Again, conversation suddenly becomes an interview. What am I, the gay spokesperson? Isn't that Ellen Degeneres' job? I'd rather be the gay spokesmodel. Although I'd have to wrestle Rupert Everett to the ground for that position. What is Rupert's job anyway? With those little girlie shoulders, he can't lift anything, including his sinking career. Maybe Oprah's job is to make both Ellen and Rupert seem normal, and worthy of the public's respect.

Oprah is a pimp. She should be shot at sunrise in the back of her pumpkin-sized head. I hate that cunt. Telling all of America what to read and think and eat. And then she complains that she's had it tough because she's a 'black woman in America'. Fuck off, Oprah. The only reason she is anything is because she's a black woman in America. You think anyone would give a shit what she thought if she were white? We've got loads of white bitches going on and on about abuse and incest and drugs on daytime TV. But she's the only ugly black chick doing it. And America loves a bit of ugliness. Oprah gives us all something to compare ourselves to.

'Well, yeah, my ass is huge, but at least it's not the size of Oprah's ass.'

The stock market rises and falls based on the size of her ass. I swear to God, Uncle Taz told me they've done studies. When she's big, the public feels more confident and better about their own selves, and they buy, buy, buy. When she's skinny, like in the late 80s, the stock sales go way down. That's why we had that crash in 1987. Oprah's shrinking ass was destroying our economy.

I'm glad not to have her responsibilities. However I do wish in various moments I contained some of Oprah's diplomacy in my character breakdown, because when a stepbrother tried to ask what I figured would be a gay-genre question during a family meal, I ignored him. I know it wasn't fair, but I was tired. Defenseless. Although I should've seen it coming. Kevin, Flora's son, had been staring at me for about an hour. And he scared me. He'd only recently reappeared in our lives, after a long absence. I'd written him out of my story before I even met him, when he went AWOL from the navy. Then, last Thanksgiving, he turned up at the holiday table. I asked for stuffing, and a thick, trembling, pale hand with yellow, stained fingertips handed it to me. I thought I was sitting next to Quentin Crisp. However the hand belonged to Kevin, watery-eyed and surrounded by cigarette smoke. Like Flora, like son. His dead stare remained on me all Thanksgiving afternoon.

And now, at Christmas, Kevin's hapless attempt to keep the saliva in his mouth almost endeared him to me. He seemed nervous, afraid, and in need of my approval. I like men who are like that.

'Is he cruising you?' my nephew Christopher asked me. Christopher is eight.

'What?'

'Uncle Tom, I know you're gay. Mom told me.'

Great, I thought. Cindy, my brother's first wife, told Christopher I'm queer. And yes, my brother's first wife has a name that sounds similar to his second wife Mindi. Cindy and Mindi. They might be sisters in a Broadway musical. In Californian suburbs, there are only so many names to go around. Even meager variations are encouraged. For lack of confusion, we'll call my brother's first wife Ignorant Cunt. Ignunt, for short.

I was mad. I wanted to tell Christopher I was gay. Or let him find out when he read my obituary. Whatever. I just wanted it to be my choice.

Hell, I didn't tell Christopher that Ignunt fucked her boss at the Pizza Hut and that's why my brother dumped her. Well, it was mutual. Okay, Ignunt dumped my brother. So what? The point is, I would've never told Christopher that his mother was a slut whore. Well, not unless I had to. Not unless lives were at stake. And if I did tell Christopher that his mother rolled around in flour and diced mushrooms with a pizza jockey, I would've done it in a loving way. But I know that Ignunt was not caring when she blurted out something along the lines of . . . 'Your Uncle Tom is a fag!' Only she wasn't that clever.

Oh, what difference does it make? Virginia would've told Christopher someday. I can just see it all now. 'Christopher, come here and look at pictures of your Great-grandma's last surgery. This is a rectum. Do you know what a rectum is? It's an area that your Uncle Tom knows a lot about. And here is why . . .' But all my anger didn't eliminate the fact that Christopher was wise about my proclivities. So why deny anything?

'I don't think Kevin is cruising me, Christopher.' Secretly, I wished he was. I'd have fucked Kevin in a second. He's dumb, so he's perfect for a one-night stand. See, dumb guys won't remember a number, or a name. They're too dumb! They'll never call or drop by. And during the holidays, trashy sex is the only thing that will pull me out of that mundane, humdrum waste of twenty-four hours called 'Christmas'. 'He fried his brain on acid. When he stares, he's not looking at anything in particular.'

'So you could be a girl for all he knows.'

'Exactly. Who knows. Maybe I am a girl. After all, I've played a girl before.'

'That's what my mom said.'

Thank you, Ignunt.

But before Kevin could ask me anything, before he could barely form a sentence or perhaps a thought all his own, I tastefully moved on by passing the salt and asking my stepsister, Shawna, about her recent separation from her husband, Rick.

Rick used to spend his weekends running his car over his neighbors' children. Well, okay, I shouldn't exaggerate. He's only driven over one child twice. Rick backed his car up over a neighbor's three-year old daughter. Oops.

Rick used to be home a lot. He injured his wrist lifting something heavy at work. I think it was his ass. Anyway, since that injury, in 1988, Rick had been on disability. He'd become a househusband, and he guarded his trailer with enthusiasm and beer nuts. Rick was just not the shiniest hair in the comb, and one day, after drinking twelve beers while watching several episodes of *Bewitched* during a cable-sponsored sitcom marathon, he decided to take a break in the action.

He stumbled to his carport, determined to get to Safeway and buy more Bud before the next episode got underway. Perhaps the excitement of ornamental witchcraft and microwaveable popcorn was too much for him, because Rick blacked out while backing his back tires over something mysterious. If he were awake, he would have felt a sort of speed bump bounce beneath his wheels, which he might have mistaken for a child's toy. As one does, when one is shit-faced. Anyway, he continued to reverse his '74 Ford Escort – or did the Escort continue to reverse him? – only to encounter a second hop, this time under his front wheels. I suppose that was the 'shock' that woke him up. He threw on his brakes, cursing his own children for leaving a Big Wheel in the driveway. However, it wasn't a Big Wheel. It was a big problem, in the shape of a crushed kid named Claudia.

By the time Rick stumbled out of the driver's seat, it was too late. All that was left of his teeny neighbor was a pile of pink pajamas stained with tire marks.

'Now,' Shawna informed me, as she licked gravy off the tips of her hair, 'I ain't only divorcing Rick, that driver/child murderer, but I'm also suing him for what the lawyer downtown calls "emotional mistress".'

'Do you mean, emotional distress?'

'Ain't that what I said? I's been shunned from my community. I cain't no longer get invited to the Tupperware church socials. And my tuna casserole has lost that kick that so electrified my buddies at the pool hall.'

I felt bad for Shawna, but I realized that little Claudia was probably better off. I mean, these people were living in a trailer park. What kind of future did Claudia have to look forward to? Christmas lights up all year long. Greeting cards in the venetian blinds. Home perms and flip-flops in every color of the muted rainbow.

But why stop there? The women in Flora's family, and probably the babies in Shawna's neighborhood, have 'personalized' running suits. Shawna, Sheila and Flora buy running suits at the local mercantile, then, when they get back to Shawna's trailer, the females spray colors from cans on to the running slacks, and glue little sparkly things on the backs of the jackets.

Note to myself: find a word for those sparkly things.

Suddenly, as if it were a miracle from God – that's me – they got themselves an outfit! It really is easy, and fun.

And sometimes it's even emotional. My stepsister Shawna told me that she made herself a sort of mourning outfit for the little speed-bump girl's funeral. She bought a one-piece Nike running suit, black, very tasteful, and she drew a portrait of the dead girl on the back of the jacket with white chalk. Then she wrote the dates of the little deceased's lifespan under her chalky face, on which Shawna then painted a single gold tear dripping from the toddler's right eye. She wore the running suit to the funeral, and many wept. It got her on the 6 p.m. news, too! I think they hung the suit in the local Hard Rock Café. Framed. For all the town to see. And mourn.

During Shawna's sweet story, Kevin, my stepbrother, had time to gather his thoughts and reload. When he caught my eye, he blurted out the question it seemed he'd been waiting weeks to ask.

'Can you pass the mashed potatoes?'

I was in love.

CHAPTER TWELVE

Check the skin flaps, and make sure they're still skewered together

S peaking of 'in love', maybe I should call your boyfriend right now. He'd probably understand all of this. He didn't seem like a bad guy.

Don't worry, I never fucked him. I never even talked to him. I just saw you two together, at the Stud.

I usually don't go to that bar. They play all that '70s music and, honestly, I've paid more than enough attention to the Bee Gees. A bunch of young faggots wearing bell-bottoms and trying to look 'retro' offends me. I'm kind of insulted that my developmental years are now considered 'kitsch'.

I was probably there scoring speed. That place is full of tweaked office boys, and it's pretty easy to scrape together a gram or two if that's what I'm after. But buying drugs in a bar can be so expensive. I must have been desperate. I probably was, now that I think about it, because that was last month, right after I'd seen you at the beach. And after I tried to get some information about you from Carl. Trish told me to try to forget about you, so I went out for some speed, and there you were, with someone who was obviously your lover. I think the guy you were with was your lover. Actually, I hope he was your lover, Taylor, because I gotta tell you that the guy you were with was a real dog. Well, not a dog really, just a very unappealing domestic type. I'm not being jealous. It's a fact. As my grandmother Virginia might've said, that boy has been beaten with an ugly stick. He's taken too many ugly pills. A wide, pale face and lots of thinning hair. Yikes. I mean, you looked great. You were doing the yuppie thing, with a button-down dress shirt and tight, pleated slacks. You looked like you sold real estate. But cute. And he was wearing a greasy surfer T-shirt and dirty jeans with holes near the crotch. How could you let him leave the house dressed like a homeless lesbian? Were you angry with him?

Your boyfriend has those dead eyes. Those kind of eyes you see a lot in gay bars. The kind of eyeballs that have way too much white under the pupils. Sanpaku eyes. Do you know the meaning of the word 'Sanpaku'? It's Sanscrit for 'three whites' and it refers to the danger of having too much white around your eyeballs. See, the Indians, or the Hindus, or the Buddhists, or maybe just the author of a pamphlet I read at Rainbow, believe that if the whites of your eyes below your pupils are pronounced, then you're in motherfucking trouble. You should only have white on both sides of the pupil or else you will die a horrible death. Your system is out of whack. You're cursed. Think about it. Marilyn Monroe, JFK . . . lots of others. It worries me. Some days, my pupils are dead center. Right where they should be. The only whites you see are on either side of the iris. But other days, like today, the whites all around are very prominent.

If I die today, it'll be a really awful death. I'd better not leave the house. Of course, I could fatally injure myself in the privacy of my own home. That's where most accidents occur. I might slip in the shower and bang my head, while my right foot flies up and inadvertently turns the hot water handle with my big toe. As I lie there, unconscious, the scorching shower water would boil my skin. When the paramedics arrive, they would lift me out of the tub, and all the blistered membrane that used to cover my torso would just peel off, strip by grisly strip.

I suppose I shouldn't shower today, either.

But what if my agent calls, and the *Tonight Show* people want to meet with me? It's unlikely they'd be in town today, but you never know. Improbability is what showbiz is all about. And wouldn't you know it, the day I might have a meeting with some big Hollywood types, is also the day I'm completely Sanpaku.

I can't go to any meetings, unless they turn off this city. All the buses and cars would have to stop, and without bathing, I'd be driven to the nearest meeting place in a bulletproof limo. Those producer types would be thinking, 'Who does he think he is, showing up in that big car? Madonna? Or the Pope? And why does he smell so bad? Maybe he thinks he's Sting.'

Actually, I think I'm horny. I want to fuck you right now. Do you mind? I'll try not to soil your hair anymore. Does this feel all right? Am I pressing too hard? Let me know if I give you a headache. Why is it that whenever I see you you look so different from the last sighting? When I met you, at the Detour, you looked boy-next-doorish. Remember? You had that hooded sweatshirt and your hair was all messy, not slicked back like it is now. Ow! Sorry, I think I chipped something. I'll try again. Then, at the beach, you were dancing around in your underwear, like a lost, happy hippie. Motherfuck, my mouth is so dry, I can't work up any spit. I really need to invest in some lubricant. At the Stud, with your boyfriend, you looked almost like a dad on a sitcom. And then at the Pilsner, a couple of nights ago, you were alone and wearing a see-through muscle T-shirt. I thought you were a doorman. Then, tonight, when you arrived at my door, you were covered in leather, like some hooker or something. Every time I see you, I feel like I'm cheating on you. You're enough to make me crazy!

Fuck, yeah!

Oh, man, having sex in the kitchen is so much better. The clean-up is so easy. No smeared sheets to worry about. Watch this: the sperm just wipes away!

All this seems so right. Maybe we should tie the knot. My friends would be thrilled to meet you. Really thrilled. After all, they've desperately wanted me to find someone I could love.

Especially now, because they're almost all married. I make most dinner parties odd-numbered. And they say they worry about me, spending so much time on the road, in a rental car, by myself. Dragging my act all over the US is hard enough, but always travelling alone is potentially dangerous. At least that's what Trish thinks.

'Tom, I don't want you to get carjacked. Out there, all alone, with your skinny little forearms, turning that big rented steering wheel. You're a sitting duck. Or a decoy. Or both! You might park at a rest stop on the freeway, and the next thing you know some Vietnamese gang members from some tumbleweed town off the interstate are beating you up for pocket change. Or worse.'

'Yeah, well, what could be worse than getting beaten and robbed?'

'How about raped?'

'Trish, do you forget who you're talking to?'

'That's right. You can't rape the willing.'

'You're more vulnerable than I am. Travelling on the bus, pregnant and alone, every day. You need a husband more than I do.'

'Oh, yeah, Tom. I need a husband. So he can rape me legally.'

'I thought you wanted to get married?'

'I've changed my mind.'

'But who'll take care of you?'

'Look, I'm on the Internet – I'll be fine!'

'That's right. I forgot. Women don't like sex, do they?'

'No, we like sex. We just don't like getting raped. Well, that's if a guy rapes us. I wouldn't mind being raped by another woman, though. Then I could just relax, and take it like a marine, without having to worry about the small cock confrontation.'

'You know, Trish, I don't think rapists worry if their cocks are too small.'

'Oh, you'd be surprised at the extent of a man's ego. And I'm so unlucky, that I'd probably get some Irish rapist with the Irish curse. Some teensy little dick that I could barely feel in me, then I'm supposed to cry afterward to give the rapist the satisfaction of making another person suffer? What pain was I supposed to feel, with something thinner and shorter than a french fry shoved inside of me? No way. Give me a black rapist, or forget about it. At least then I'd have something to cry about.'

'Your obsession with big dicks is frightening.'

'Look who's talking, Tom.'

'Yeah, but I'm a freak.'

'Yeah.'

'And I'm still single.'

'Right.'

'Well, Trish, I'm just saying that maybe I'm single because no dick will ever be perfect enough. I need to make some concessions, don't I?'

'What do you mean?'

'I look around, and I see happy people in love. The men can't all have big dicks. In fact, some people aren't even interested in dick size.'

'Well, I'm not interested in those people.'

'But you're a woman. Aren't women supposed to be more internal and less competitive?'

'Yeah, that's why every woman I know owns a dildo the size

of Texas. One woman I know even owns a dildo the size *and the
shape* of Texas.'

'Speaking of Texas, I'm in Austin next week.'

'Oh, Tom, be careful. Those redneck audiences will eat you
alive out there.'

'Yeah, but what a way to go.'

I was fine in Texas. At least, I didn't get beaten up. But those
big hotel rooms and desolate airports do become torturously
solitary after a while. I suppose I could adopt a pet. A dog
that could fit in my carry-on would be good. But Christ, I'd
look like Auntie Mame, with some poodle's head sticking out
of my straw shoulder bag.

And anyway, I kind of need human companionship, don't
I? If nothing else, a boyfriend would mean that I wouldn't be
sat at the kiddy table during the holiday meals with my family.
Which would be a relief. After years trying to entertain those
brats, I've finally realized that kids don't like dick jokes. They
don't understand the irony.

Actually, if I had a husband, I probably wouldn't be invited
to holiday functions at all. I'm pretty sure Sheila and Shawna
would say that a gay couple might scar the children. If my
stepsisters only knew what I've already told those little punks.

'Your mothers watch you when you poo.'

That one really scares little kids. I'm not sure why, I just
know it does.

CHAPTER THIRTEEN

When will that creature be ready?

Whenever my solo status emerges as a conversation topic among friends, all pitiful eyes turn downward. My ex, Mark, simply shakes his bald head as he focuses on his casual loafers.

'I don't know why you can't find someone. Alex . . .' his boy toy '. . . and I are both very concerned.'

'Why? I'm okay.'

Mark and Alex glance knowingly at one another. 'We just wish everyone, including you, could enjoy the sort of love we feel for each other.'

A kind sentiment, and one that might moisten a mother's eye, but I wonder if they've really thought about that. I mean, say you and I became boyfriends. Then, I might have as little time for my friends as they now have for me. Mark and I did, of course, live together, and since our collegiate break-up, we've maintained a friendship. It was difficult at first. I was pissed off at both of them, but then Patryck got sick, and Mark needed me again. After Patryck died of kidney failure – he had diabetes. I know, you forget queers die of other things, don't you? – anyway, I helped Mark find a place up here in San Francisco, and I think we're closer than ever. Even closer than Gregg and I. That's probably because Mark doesn't drink anymore, and whenever I see him, we're sober, so we actually talk about matters of substance. Ouch.

Good, but ouch. Maybe that's why I see Mark less than I see Gregg.

And, naturally, since Gregg and I are both single, *we* have time for each other. Mark sees me when he can, but after seven scintillating weeks of symbiotic bliss with Alex, Mark has time for one thing. And I think we both know what that one thing is. I don't mind. I've lost status to a new lover in Mark's life before. Obviously. But if I were also involved with someone, we'd never see each other. And then, who would entertain Mark and his freshest squeeze? Boyfriends come and go, but you always need a good laugh. Now, Alex is sweet and stimulating in many arcane ways. 'Totally harmless,' Mark says, as though that were an asset. But to be honest, Alex has no sense of humor. He's soft and pink and buffered by privilege. He's young in a way that will always make him seem young. He has to have jokes explained to him. Twice. And, he's never seen *Now, Voyager*. And what really annoys me is that he has no idea who Dusty Springfield was!

So when Mark wants a good laugh he calls the comic. We snigger over the Internet. Or I join the lovebirds for dinner. I tell stories, slowly, for Alex's benefit, and the three of us howl for hours. Everyone is comfy, as long as I don't make fun of Alex. That is forbidden. In fact, Alex sort of reminds me of Virginia. He only really laughs when I make fun of myself. Or he'll roar if his boyfriend humbles me, which Mark is allowed to do. I think Alex resents me because I was his new lover's first love. And no love can ever match one's first love. At least, that's what I tell Alex, with every gesture, every twinkle, and every goodnight kiss. Alex misinterprets these gestures, of course. He thinks Mark and I share a nasty private joke. We don't. We just have a past.

Lamentably, at nineteen, Alex's past hasn't yet happened. So I subtly torture him, while winking at Mark, all the while remaining the self-deprecating, sad little clown who desperately cruises gymnasium saunas, stumbling over used condoms, ex-Wham! members and 'lost' German tourists. I'm making Mark happy, I'm making Alex happy. It's actually a lot of work, like a threesome without the fun sex part. How long can I keep this up?

For their sake, as long as they stay together. My being unhitched remains fodder for everyone's act. Because let's face it. Unless I'm single and sad, the laughs are over.

And anyway, if I were in a relationship, my boyfriend would be too jealous to let me alone so I could wander around the Stud, watching people dance with themselves in those tall mirrors, the way you did the night I saw you there. You know those mirrors that surround the dance floor? I also caught you and your boyfriend checking out other boys in those mirrors. And I realized you were scouring the place for a victim. Some sweet lad you'd drag home and perform whatever private rituals you two have created in your long association. I know how weird gay couples who've been together for a long time can be. They create their own language they only use with one another. And they invent about a thousand justifications for fucking other people. Rules and regulations that create the 'understanding' under which they can hump strangers then avoid sexual contact when they're alone and yet remain a 'couple'. It all seems like a lot of work to me.

Thank God I've never had to suffer through all that, since I haven't been a long-term relationship since college. I'm so lucky.

Anyway, you and your boyfriend avoided eye contact with me. I hate it when I see people I know, and I know that person has seen me, and yet they avoid saying 'Hello'. It's so much easier if they just acknowledge my existence and then move on. Even a wave from across the room would've been okay. Instead, you and your boyfriend acted coy, darting in and out of clusters of strangers. If you'd just mouthed a greeting, and continued your scouting I could've forgotten about it, but your ignoring me turned your presence into an issue.

Your boyfriend seemed more nervous to approach me than you did. God only knows what you've told him about me. That I'm stalking you, probably. Lies! We just happen to be in the same place all the time. Liar! It's kismet. Lying! Not stalking.

When I came back from peeing, you two were sitting in my spot. Kissing. And that killed me. I didn't need to see that. That public display shit was really inappropriate. And you held the kiss for a long time, with your mouths only slightly open. It seemed to last for ever, and then you raised your right hand and brushed your lover's left cheek slowly.

I went nuts. Why the fuck were you doing that there? Why were you torturing me? I left without having said one word to you. I got in my car, and drove so hard and fast that I hit a telephone pole. I didn't even know we had telephone poles anymore. I figured all telephone cables had been placed underground. What the fuck was I doing in the rain, with a telephone pole stuck to my car?

I wasn't sure which AA to call. Maybe I should've called my therapist. I looked for my agent's number in Hawaii. I wondered if my hair salon was open. I was sure that if I could've just gotten a decent haircut, my whole life would've fallen into place.

WHY THE FUCK WERE YOU TWO KISSING IN THERE?

CHAPTER FOURTEEN

Prick the skin to see if it's still moist

N ow look what I've done. The rest of the crystal is on the floor. I've got to get out of here, get some more. Maybe I should take you with me. Somewhere. Anywhere. Wouldn't it be great if we could go away? Far, far away. But getting you through customs would be a bitch, and anyway, who would pay for our trip? I'm broke.

You probably didn't know that. Most people don't. For one thing, I almost never let anyone I might see again visit my place. If they saw this apartment, they'd know I was out of money. Or out of my mind. Or both. And then they'd feel sorry for me, think I have a drug problem, wonder if I'll hurt them, or why I don't own an ottoman. After all, I work all the time. I travel all over the world telling dick jokes. I've been in a few successful feature films. I must have money coming in from all sorts of sources. Wrong!

Mine is a frisky, fickle little business. Look at me, turning down club dates so I can wait by the phone for that one call about that one TV show that will change my life. It's almost adolescent. And until that call comes I'm living on canned baked beans.

I'm bad at saving dough, and there is no way I am taking on a day job. I'm incapable of doing something during the day to make money. If I were placed in the secretarial pool, I'd drown.

Which is why I decided to try prostitution. It seemed my only logical choice. The pay was cash-on-demand, and the hours seemed pretty flexible. I'd heard the drugs were great. And, I've had loads of friends who've tried hooking, so I know the ins and outs of the business.

I've even dated a hooker. Well, Vincent wasn't just a hooker, he was also a stripper. But he had hobbies. He dealt drugs. And he did drugs, to get over that relationship he'd just ended with his girlfriend. Yeah, he thought he was bisexual. Well, so do most queers from Texas. A stripping, hustling, bisexual crystal meth-head. Thank you Jesus!

I met Vincent in a comedy club. He approached me after a show. Usually, I don't talk to the freaks in the clubs, but he was young and had pretty teeth and cherry-red lips. He told me he'd been a fan of mine for a while, from having heard me on morning radio. I promote my gigs on a local rock station, and I've become sort of a regular. The host is this Howard Stern type, and the show is mostly porn stars and stale doughnuts. I'm on there to add observational humor, and sometimes a bitter twist. But between blond girls named Barbie fisting themselves and insane callers claiming that not *all* gay men shave their balls, I rarely get a word in edgewise. And it's so early in the morning that half the time I don't even remember what I've said.

What Vincent was doing up at that hour, I have no idea. I don't even want to think about it. He partied a lot. When I met him, he'd been up for twenty-four hours at a rave. He was hung over, all bleary-eyed and unkempt, but even sloppy he could string a sentence together. I guess when you're young, well, as young as he was, you can pull it all together a lot easier after a long night out. And yeah, he was young.

I wonder why youths intrigue me. I'm amused by their wastefulness and turned on by their callousness. And then there's the fact that I can swallow their candy-tasting come without worrying about catching anything.

I've dated young guys, ever since I became a comic. Young men are easier to deal with. They don't ask questions, or make demands, like, 'When are you going to come out?'

But there are some down sides. Sometimes, when I'm out with a young un', I feel like I'm auditioning to play a role that's much younger than me. I can really relate to what Jane Fonda must've dealt with throughout her career. I feel like I have to make sure I act 'up'. I walk with a bounce, I end all my sentences with an expletive – 'You bought some new workout clothes? That's hot!' – and I make sure I hum a tune that's currently on Billboard's Top Ten pop tunes list.

Like Jane says, it's a lot of work, but it's worth it. Nothing feels closer to the surface than a twenty-five-year-old's shoulder muscles. 'Did you work your shoulders today Timmy? That's gnarly!' Maybe I shouldn't bother. My friend Jacques once told me, 'Maybe what those twenty-three-year-olds are after *is* someone almost twice their age.'

'Yeah, Jacques, maybe they like gray hairs and back flab.'

Jacques is one of those scientists who send rockets to the moon, or something like that, so I guess he's a genius. And, like me, he has eccentric tastes, which is a nice way of saying he's a chickenhawk, too. He works for the government, but his parents were hippies, so he has a FBI file, which means he has to be even more careful in schoolyards than I do. And he's a communist, which I think means he's never had to pay his own rent.

'They think they're ugly when they're that age,' he says over martinis at our favorite piano bar, Martuni's. Sometimes we go there, and he sings songs from *Les Miserables*. He has no discretion. He's a physicist. He can barely tie his own shoes. 'This guy I'm seeing, he's twenty-two. His name is Eric but he spells it A-I-R-E-C-K. I love that he does that. I love that he gets so bored, that he changes the spelling of his name until it's almost incomprehensible. That's how much he hates himself.'

'Hot,' I reply. And we nod our heads in agreement.

'Aireck tells me how skinny he is, and how pale, like those are bad things. I let him go on and on. Of course, the more he whines, the more I want to eat him up. But he doesn't get that. He's just thankful that someone "mature" like me would want to spend any time with him at all. It's great!'

Maybe so, if you want to actually get to know your sex partner. My expectations with young guys are different. I just want their sweet, soft asses, and when they find that out they become needy in an exacting sort of way. Like I owe them something. They act like they're doing me a favor, and in return, I'm expected to pay for dinner, make all the plans, and feel all the sorrow and self-pity a sugar daddy is supposed to feel. But I don't want to feel anything, except my cock in their various holes.

I told Jacques, 'It makes more sense for me to just hire a hooker.'

'Yeah,' he said, sucking on an olive, 'but that gets expensive, trust me.'

Luckily, one came along that I could use for free.

Better yet, one that was even younger than the rest of the men I'd dated. Fucked. Dated. Oh, what's the difference? The point is, Vincent was *really* young. He wasn't pre-pubescent or anything. He was on solids, for God's sake. I mean, after we had sex, I didn't have to change his diaper or kill him or anything. I've never had sex with anyone who wasn't legal, mainly because I don't have any crawl space. What would I do with their bodies?

But he was very, very young.

He was twenty. I know. When he told me that, I was so shocked, I almost dropped his fork. I tried to remain calm, until he admitted that he didn't know who Karen Carpenter was. That's how young he was. He'd heard of The Carpenters, but he knew nothing of the two members. That had always been one of my unspoken dating rules. Never date anyone who doesn't know Karen Carpenter. And never date anyone who tells me how skinny I look, or how straight-acting they are. Those were always my three private regulations. The ones I didn't want to have to mention. They shouldn't be included on the 5x7 card. They are so basic, they should be instinctively obeyed. If not, the date is over. That's it. Of course, all rules are ignored if the guy is very cute.

Well Vincent was, so they were.

I know Karen is spinning in her own vomit. Barfing, then spinning, then barfing some more.

But hey, at least she's finally eating!

But in most ways Vincent was really intelligent and very dry-witted. I guess that's why I hung out with him so much. He was not what one might expect from a potential felon.

And when we met I thought Vincent's jobs sounded fascinating. Especially the stripping part. We talked all about his work on what turned out to be our first date. Actually, we began the evening at a video arcade, where we played games for hours. We ate salty, deeply fried food and walked along a pier. He kept grabbing me from behind and sticking his hand in my pockets while I played pinball. I'm sure the tourists from Arkansas thought we were the gay antichrist, but I felt like a sixteen-year-old girl dating the high school quarterback.

And that was when he let me ask questions about his

stripping job. See, I'm a comic – I've always had a morbid fascination for detail. I wanted to know about the club where he disrobed, and about the kind of customers that paid $15 to see a man strip. I asked about his coworkers, and how they all related backstage.

His answers were, unfortunately, as colorless as my questions. Yeah, most of the customers were pigs. And yeah, the strippers were often drug-addicted survivors of incest who shot their cocks full of steroids before they went on stage.

And as we talked I realized that, strangely enough, Vincent and I seemed to have so much in common. He told me he'd always had this fantasy about stripping; about being the focus in a room full of strangers; about being in control of what other people thought about him. Hello! I mean, the great thing about being a comic is that the audience only gets as much as I give. They have no intuitive sense. They are a mass, and so they only react collectively to whatever is thrown their way, like cattle. They expect nothing more, and nothing less, than jokes. I get to express myself, without the messy personal crap movie actors have to dump on their adoring fans.

Vincent loved that his public had no idea how he labeled himself sexually. He craved ambiguity, and strippers have an androgynous patina. They're sexual beings. They'll take it off for anybody. It's part of their appeal. Just like comics are sexually ambiguous. Oh, come on, most male comics are so femmy. All those comics with sitcoms, they have girlfriends, but they all act like big girls themselves. Seinfeld, he's the most successful, and he's the femmiest of them all! That's why audiences never guess that I'm gay. Look what they have to compare me to in masculine terms. And anyway, they don't want to know. As long as the funny man just stays funny and doesn't try to share too much about himself, nobody gets hurt. Like with a stripper.

And there were other more obvious similarities in our work. We were both solo acts, and we both resented hecklers. We both tried to end our acts with a bang. Neither of us could resist the grand finale. We laughed when we realized that some of his clients were probably some of my audience members.

And that's when he kissed me. Right there, under the Golden Gate. He took my face in both his hands, real slow, and kissed my cheek, and then my mouth, for a long time, and sweetly, with breath that tasted of caramel corn.

I grabbed him and pulled him closer to me.

'Relax,' he whispered. 'Take it easy.'

And I let him take over.

Vincent was so – don't wince – straight-appearing. His face was angular, and his gaze was brooding and intimidating. He had those piercing blue eyes that looked like he wore the kind of contacts makeup artists apply to the pupils of an actor who is about to metamorphose into a vampire on some scary TV show. In a word, he was butch.

Even in bed. I had to wrestle him on to his stomach just about every time we got horizontal. Bisexual, or not, while I was fucking him he looked pretty gay to me. Actually, first time I nailed him, he started to bleed. When I told him he was bleeding, he begged me to keep going. Then he started crying, and made me pull out and just hold him while he shook for a long time. Then I demanded that we continue, and eventually he conceded. I mean, can you imagine anything more hot than some straight-acting twenty-year-old Texan yielding again and again?

He resisted me every time I tried to fuck him. I think that's what kept the passion alive. I loved pursuing him, and he loved controlling me with his mangina.

I guess that's the way it works with bisexual men. After all, they're half straight, right? So, they have to work twice as hard to prove they're real men. Whereas straight guys have nothing to prove so they can just give in right away, bi guys have to pretend they don't want the hot beef injection, when, in fact, that's all they want.

I'd never met a real bisexual before. Well, not a guy I believed was bisexual. Actually, most straight women I've known were one poetry reading away from gladly licking pussy, but bisexual men always seemed so unhappy. They were always bitching about 'how great the blowjobs from other guys are, but I can only emotionally connect with women, boo hoo hoo, blah, blah, blah . . .' I figured they were just closeted fags without the courage of conviction.

But Vincent's bisexuality was a joy to watch. He had it documented on camera. He'd filmed himself having sex with his girlfriend in Texas, and he showed me one of the films. I think he wanted to see if the footage turned me on, so that maybe he could invite a female into our bed. I must have disappointed him when my interest in his movie became merely academic.

I couldn't believe all that had to be done. I'd read about heterosexual sex in school and, like I said, when I was much younger I'd drunkenly and unsuccessfully attempted to sample the evening's fish entrée, but seeing it sober was a different story. It was a huge commitment. He was all over the place, up and down, side to side, and it seemed to take for ever! Like building a national monument or something. I admired his persistence, but I couldn't help worrying that lives might be lost. I felt like I was watching a film about the construction of the Hoover Dam.

And, as in that documentary, the pay-off was unbelievable. He came all over everything. Then she came. I think. Then he came again. Fluids just flowed everywhere. Masses and masses of come filled the screen. Several seas parted. I felt like Noah. Or was it Moses? Either way, I'd never been so seasick.

When he lived near Dallas, Vincent was like one of those beer-slamming, sweaty construction boys with a Caesar cut. Vacationing in Miami. Yikes! When he met me, he made such progress! I was so proud of him. Instead of yelling 'faggot' out his truck window, he just whispered it into my ear. I wasn't sure which turned me on more.

Maybe I fell in love with him because he was adventurous and, in a foreign way, stimulating. And because we both hated the same people. Before I knew it, Vincent and I were spending all our time together.

And he kept inviting me to see his show at the strip joint where he worked. As a comic who often finds himself consulting people on the complexities of sex, I felt obliged. But I wanted to attend, unannounced. That way I could see the show in its gory entirety, instead of some song and dance he'd edited for my fragile benefit. Also, if I attended anonymously and his show was bad I wouldn't have to criticize. I wouldn't say anything.

Maybe that's why I wanted to surprise Vincent. Part of me knew that no matter how fiery he was on stage, his show wouldn't turn me on. I knew what he thought of his fan base.

'They're horrible,' he told me, during one of my interrogations. 'We had some priest die in the front row last night. Massive stroke. He must have been eighty. Luckily, two other priests were on hand to perform the last rites. They should be ashamed of themselves.'

And, as an audience member, I cannot enjoy myself if I know the performer is bored or disgusted. That's why I don't even rent porn anymore. I just cannot suspend my disbelief long enough to imagine that those boys humping each other for the camera are really enjoying the experience.

And they are such bad actors, those porn stars. They all

lack originality. I mean, someone must have told those fucks that the lines 'Yeah, suck it for Daddy' and 'My girlfriend won't suck my dick, she says it's too big' were written by Shakespeare, thus worthy of repeating. Because somehow they find their way into the improvised dialogue of just about every porn film I've ever seen.

But at least those actors make a bit of money. That's why Vincent was interested in the porn film field. At the theatre where he performed he had to hump ten or twelve guys every day just so he could bring home maybe $150. But in a film, he was likely to make ten times that amount just by sucking off a couple of studs.

So he would practice his porn faces all the time. Apparently, actors need different expressions for different positions. If, for example, a porn star is getting fucked on film, then his face needs to form into a bit of a grimace, as though pain were the motivating factor. On the other hand, if the same porn star is getting his dick sucked, then his expression might be one of elation or joy. And that's about all a person needs to do to be a megastar in the sex film industry. And, I remember thinking, if such stars are at the top of their field, then imagine what shitty performers these second-rate strippers in a glorified brothel like the Campus Theatre could turn out to be, Vincent included.

I was worried about offending him. I was worried of losing him. I was just worried. He walked around town like he owned the place. I trailed behind, reminding him to wear a sweater. That was me, doing all the feeling. I guess if I loved him I could've gone backstage after his 'show' and feigned enthusiasm. But Taylor, when it comes to compliments, I'm a terrible liar. If I think a performance is bad, the best I can come up with is 'fun'. And Vincent had seen me pull that lame comment on my friend Alice after her scenery-chewing job in

Summerfolk. I patted her forearm, said 'Fun', and never stopped smiling until we got in the car.

'Do you think she knew I was lying?'

'How could she not?' Vincent giggled. 'Your performance was almost as bad as hers.'

CHAPTER FIFTEEN

Jiggle a leg, and see if the hip joint feels loose

After going there, I realized that not all of Vincent's 'clients' at the Campus were freaks. Some of them were just regular guys. Businessmen attending conventions without their wives, or closeted CEOs. It was easier for Vincent to wiggle in front of them if he didn't see that some of those guys were in many ways just like him. Frightened. Angry. Lonely. Better they fuck at the Campus, where safe sex info and sober attendants were available, then pump some street hooker, sans condom, in some alleyway somewhere.

So, conceptually, I liked the existence of the Campus Theatre. However, realistically, I was annoyed as I drove up to the entrance, downtown, where a marquee promised the 'all-male Campus squad practices man-to-man contact'. The sex business in general functions with an alarming lack of irony. Maybe it's because the customers, even the men with perhaps an amazing sense of bitter urbane sophistication, become one-dimensional, tongue-wagging idiots when a nude photo of some porn star gripping his dick is downloaded on their computer. The captions to these photos always read something ridiculous like: 'Brad gets off just "hanging out" in the sun . . .'

'Yeah,' my friend Jacques says when he sees this on his screen, 'I love tan lines on dudes.'

Grow up, Jacques. Get a haircut, get a fucking checking

account, and grow fucking up! After all, it's just cock. There is plenty more where that came from. Well, in some cultures, anyway.

Maybe, if Jacques knew what I knew, he wouldn't be so titillated. Like I said, the strippers thought most of their clients were total losers. Of course, most employees find reasons to hate their employers. Like Mr Stubby, an amputee. He paid Vincent $100 so he could rub his old appendages, which ended at his elbows, between Vincent's legs. Yummy. Or how about the married ranch owner from Kentucky who used to hug Vincent really hard, then throw his cowboy hat in the air like Mary Tyler Moore at the beginning of her TV show and yell, 'Yippeee! Let me take a look at that ass!'

I think Vincent told me these stories to shock me, but as a stand-up comic I had heard it all. The dim lights of a comedy club make audience members feel anonymous, and the booze relaxes them. People trust me, I have a nice face, they assume I'm harmless, so they answer all my questions. They seem to forget that what we talk about is not just between me and them. There are a couple of hundred other people in the room. I've had people tell me about problems in their relationships while sitting next to their lovers.

'Tom, my wife won't have sex with me.'

'He's lying, Tom!' exclaims the wife, who happens to be occupying the other seat at their table. 'I tell him I'll perform orally, but he says he's too tired. Too tired! I just tell him to lay back, I'll do all the work. But he'd rather watch cable.'

I've had closeted kids come out in front of their parents. I've had married couples proposition me. I thought I could handle almost anything.

But one thing I couldn't have handled was being recognized at the Campus by a fan. To disguise myself, I wore dark glasses and a red curly wig I'd bought a few years earlier when auditioning to play Lucille Ball's long-lost brother in a rather camp, low-budget film called *I Love Brucey*. I looked a bit like a child molester in a made-for-TV movie, which is why I was alarmed when the ticket seller still recognized me. Actually it was my voice he found familiar. He was a fan of mine from the radio. I guess sex workers listen to a lot of radio, since they get overloaded with visual stimulation. That was when I made a mental note to not talk to anyone at the Campus.

And I prayed I didn't run into my therapist in there. It would've been difficult to explain to him and to a judge why I was dressed like a pervert, wandering through a maze of moaning men. I suppose I could've just said I was picking up a friend. But then, wasn't everybody?

I remember I had a hard time when I saw one of my ex-therapists at The Stud. He had a drink in one hand, his crotch in the other, and his powder blue shirt unbuttoned to his navel. All this red chest hair was hanging out, and a big, bronze medallion was dangling from around his neck! I freaked. It was like seeing my father in jail. Somehow he lost his credibility.

Anyway, the club was in a bad neighborhood. The bad part of the Tenderloin. And because Vincent was so pernickety about his Honda, he paid some homeless guy $5 to keep an eye on it. When I parked my car in front of the theatre, I paid the same guy eight bucks, because I consider myself a liberal.

As I walked into the club, I thought, 'Please God, don't let me get murdered in there.' That is just not the way I want to be remembered. Lying in a pool of my own blood and semen, in some dark, dank underworld kind of place, with my cock resting in one hand and my brains leaking out of my head. Oh, but what a fabulous chalk outline that would make!

Once inside, I calmed down. I found the place to be much kinder than I'd imagined. Almost friendly. There was free coffee and condoms in the lobby, and a pool table! I bought a Mars bar, sipped some Java, smiled at a couple of regular-looking middle-aged guys. Okay, they were both wearing tit clamps and PVC short shorts, but who am I to judge? The entire experience started to feel like a twelve-step meeting, so homey I almost forgot why I was there.

'Gentlemen, the next show begins in two minutes, with our hottest dancer, Vincent!'

I gulped my coffee and headed for the 'theatre', a term used loosely in this case. There were no ushers, and no programs. No pre-show music warmed the audience into an intellectual lull. There were, however, exposed light bulbs that dimly illuminated a few spectators scattered on bench seating in the round. That way guys could face each other while they juggled their privates and shot their wads. I was horrified. It was like seeing the opposing victims right before a head-on collision. I took a seat so far up and in the back that I had to crouch to avoid banging my head against the ceiling. And so the show began.

Now, to me, the very word 'show' implies theatrics. I guess that's because the only stripping I had ever been exposed to was in the movie musical *Gypsy* with Rosalind Russell and Natalie Wood. I imagined Vincent's 'show' might contain lots of dancers, some more tired than others, doing clever choreography, in perhaps red sequins, while sporting feathery boas, or at the very least, tossing props. But his performance had a more organic flavor.

Vincent walked into the theatre from the lobby, went over to the 'sound system', again a term used loosely to identify a boom box spattered with paint, and popped in his tape, or 'soundtrack', as it were. He then walked to the center of the stage, where he adjusted his reflective sunglasses. Nice touch, I thought. When the music started, he pulled his army fatigues down to his knees, and in a rather economic two-birds-with-one-bend sort of movement, picked up a bottle of baby lotion that lay conveniently near his right boot. He squeezed a generous

amount onto his palm – if Johnson and Johnson only knew –
and began to stroke his already mostly erect penis.

I felt embarrassed, even though I'd seen his penis erect
many times. I just didn't know where to look, so I focused on
his face, which suddenly looked so different. He had a sort of
tight, pained expression. His eyes squinted, were almost shut.
For the first time, the pockmarks on his neck looked very
pronounced. The bright lights made his blond hair look thin,
almost disappear around his forehead, like he was receding. He
looked corrupted.

But then, with a few groans from the audience, he was off
on his lap-dancing offensive. The more cash in the army boot,
the more naked flesh this soldier offered to the enemy. And, for
the right fee, everything but the penis could be manhandled.
Vincent jumped from one middle-aged lap to the next, while all
I could think was, 'Are soldiers allowed to wear sunglasses, even
in battle? Aren't sunglasses more a police officer accessory?'

It was at that moment that Vincent jumped on my lap.

'The doorman told me you'd bought a ticket, Tomboy. Why
didn't you tell me you were coming?' He licked my neck. 'And
what are you doing all the way up here? I could hardly get
to you.'

And he took me by the hand, and led me to the center of
the stage.

'Leave the wig on,' he said. 'And the glasses.'

I remembered how much Vincent liked being watched. We
had sex on the beach a lot. And in the middle of the day! He
loved it.

Then I got paranoid. Was this being filmed? I was sure they
had cameras in these places. I looked around frantically. I mean,
look what happened to Pee-wee Herman.

'If this shit hits the papers,' I said to myself, 'I'll never get
to produce my own TV chat show.'

I regretted being sober, then reached for some Rolaids or Advil – anything to give me a buzz – only to realize my coat was actually missing. And so were my pants! And Vincent had disappeared too! Wait, no he hadn't. There he was, on his knees, sucking my dick! I heard people whimpering, and one old guy was actually moving toward us, really slow, with his arms outstretched. He was probably feeling his way toward the exit in the dark, but he looked like one of those walking corpses in *The Night of the Living Dead*. I whispered, 'Chalk outline. Chalk outline.'

Vincent said, 'What?' Of course, he had my dick in his mouth, so it sounded like 'Whaaa . . .'.

I thought, oh my God, he sounds like a corpse, too. It was like the final scene in *Invasion of the Body Snatchers* – the '80s version – where Nancy Allen realizes they are *all* corpses! Or pea pod people! Whatever! Oh God! My dick was so hard.

Then I remembered how attractive I always thought Kevin McCarthy was in the original *Body Snatchers* movie. Oh, Jesus! And didn't he have an affair with Montgomery Clift?

And then I came. My head flipped back and my wig flew off as I shot across the stage in front of an audience made up of pea pod corpses.

'Okay, gentlemen,' Vincent said, wiping his mouth. 'That's it. The show is over.'

Lights up, music off, and the peas waddled back to their pods. And I remained standing, with my pants around my ankles and my dick in my hand, feeling like a kid with his parents' car keys. Feeling dangerous and helpless at the same time. Like in a dream.

Later, while he got dressed, Vincent suggested we work up an act together for the fetish room. That's when I realized that maybe I liked him more than he liked me.

CHAPTER SIXTEEN

Make sure that bird is not overdone

Vincent considered himself to be monogamous. With me, I mean. His work was just that – work. When he walked out of that club, he left behind all memory of the sex he'd just had. Of course, after my experience on stage with him, I was a bit suspicious of that. Vincent loved the crowd, and the crowd loved Vincent. In fact, he had a day job in computer programming, but kept on stripping. He liked the approval.

I couldn't help but wonder whether or not he'd try to whip up the crowd by blowing some other cute guy. Someone closer to his own age. He told me he'd never do that, but how could I believe him? He was a hooker for Christ's sake! Don't hookers lie all the time? Isn't that a hooker's job?

Oh yeah, I forgot to tell you: he hooked at the same place he stripped. Quite handy, don't you think? Jesus Christ, I must have been absolutely nuts.

After his show, interested observers lined up to join Vincent, one by one, in the 'shower room'. It was a small room with a showerhead on one wall and a sling that hung from the ceiling. Very Habitat.

Anyway, once alone with Vincent, men paid him $15 to watch as he massaged himself. And if the customer wanted to see more, or touch more, then he had to pay more. And so on. The reason all this was legal and not considered prostitution was because Vincent kept his black army boots on the entire time.

Apparently keeping on his shoes transformed Vincent from a mere whore to a veritable party host! Very Imelda Marcos.

Outside of work he was all mine. Well, most of him. He had to save his ejaculatory fluids for his show. And for the shower room. I saw him come maybe twice, and that was because he had cancelled a couple of shows because of a sprained wrist.

As those spermless months evaporated, the reality of my life with a hooker started to sink in. We spent a lot of our bedtime holding one another. And while I tried to convince myself that affection was enough, and that occasional sex with someone I cared about was better than no sex at all, I also wanted to pull a bullet on a string through my skull. After I'd used the strength of my two hands to push a nail through Vincent's skull, of course.

What had started out a fun affair between two performers with so much in common had become disastrously apocalyptic. I had somehow fallen in love with a kid who didn't really want to be in a relationship. At least, not with a man. After all, Vincent thought that sex between men was dirty. Which is why his work made perfect sense to him. He was turning an intrinsically nasty experience into something financially lucrative. Kudos for him.

And kudos for me, as well. 'You're the one I go home to,' he told me over the phone between his matinee and evening performances. 'All these dudes here want me, but you're the guy I spend just about every night with.'

'Why not every night?' I tried to make my voice sound as if I'd just thought of this idea, although I'd been ruminating for days about the possibilities of our future together. 'Have you ever thought about us living together?'

'Yeah, and I've also thought about falling on a pair of sharp scissors, but that doesn't mean I'm gonna do it.'

He couldn't understand why I wasn't impressed. He was

breaking an important, if not esoteric, 'self-preservation' rule just by going out with me. As far as he was concerned, I should've been applauding my good fortune, instead of complaining about my half-empty glass.

If only I'd had been less intelligent, had more self-worth or even just a vagina, he would've loved me. Eventually I turned to other forms of affection. Booze and drugs didn't mind about my vaginal and emotional handicaps. The whiskey and the coke loved me unconditionally. And when I ran out of those diversions, casual sex took over. Sure, sex took longer, but it was still faster than prayer.

I think I hoped he would find out I'd fucked other guys, so that he might have been jealous and then he would've maybe felt something akin to the ignominy with which I'd become so fucking familiar.

Then I discovered that Vincent didn't mind if I slept with other people. He figured that, because of his work, he couldn't really ask me to be monogamous.

'So,' I asked him, in the car one rainy day, 'I don't have to be faithful, but you will be?'

'Well, yeah. You're the only person I want to have sex with.'

I should've been thrilled. Isn't that every Christian guy's dream? I had the whole virgin/whore thing wrapped up in one delicious little package.

Then why did I feel odd about it? Maybe because when he came to my place after his show I could smell other men's cologne on his neck. Or maybe because if he had a handful of hundreds I knew he'd had to handle a lot of guys to make that sort of cash. Or maybe because I knew that when he clipped his toe nails the foot fetish guy would be visiting him at the club. Which meant it was Thursday. Suddenly, I was marking my time by his whoring schedule.

'Well, if he has a five-man show tonight, then it must be Friday!'

How romantic.

I wanted him to quit stripping. And whoring. He didn't need the money, and why did he need the approval? Wasn't my love enough? If it was the lifestyle he wanted, I told him, why not just join a band?

'Trust me, Vincent. You'll get better groupies, and it's a lot less work!'

But he had built that sort of trust among his coworkers – outcasts, one and all – that a soldier builds among his comrades in arms. He felt he needed to stay at the Campus and protect his fellow strippers. And this I begrudgingly understood. Whenever I've had a really difficult public service job, the employees have often banded together against the common enemy. Which, in the case of most public service jobs, is the consumer. I remember, when I was a waiter in West Hollywood, I was fiercely loyal to the other waiters at The Creamery. I defended them at meetings, I brought them booze and speed during work, and we all commiserated together about living in LA without acting work or a loving relationship.

Of course, the moment any of us got work and could afford to leave that dump, we took off fast and never looked back. We hated the job so much, yet we were the only 'family' some of us had ever been able to rely on. Totally dysfunctional, yes, but we were willing to fight for each other. Until something better came along, like a recurring role on a series. Or a heroin addiction.

So, I stopped badgering Vincent. For the time being. I knew that if a pretty girl asked him to quit and marry her, he might consider it. I was just something that filled his time between customers. At least, that's the way I felt. Like fodder. And that made me real mean.

Of course, Vincent thought the relationship was becoming

difficult not because he was a stripper but because I had a trust issue.

I realized I had to get away from him, but I was too addicted to his lips and his eyes and his smell. I needed an evil plan. Some sort of mischievous plot that would get him so incensed, he'd have to dump me. But where could I come up with a scenario so dastardly?

CHAPTER SEVENTEEN

If the meat is red,
try not to panic!

Now, let me tell you something. If you're ever in need of a good plan to fuck up your life even more, your best source is *Melrose Place*. Those characters act so disparagingly to one another. And they're alarmingly incestuous. If they aren't sleeping with one another then they're stabbing each other in the back. I'm sure that show is written by a queer. At least, I know it's been *lived* by a queer, because, after watching one particularly illuminating episode, I decided to sleep with Vincent's best friend.

Jerry was a slender, charming, slightly ingenious Southerner. He and Vincent had become good friends when Jerry's demand for illegal substances increased. And at first I didn't really see any other reason why my sweet baby found this unemployed sly redneck's company at all interesting. Then we spoke. Jerry's family were at one time wealthy Louisiana oil magnates. And though they'd squandered most of their cash, they still held on to their social status. Vincent's family lived in a trailer park near Dallas. Always had, and always would. Vincent was clearly ashamed of his kin, and that's why he craved not so much Jerry as Jerry's upper-class identification.

Apparently Virginia has been correct all these years: social standing still matters, at least to people in the South. Jerry offered Vincent the chance to thumb his nose at Southern upper crust, and Vincent offered Jerry the chance to pack his nose with south-of-the-border crystal. The two thrived off one another.

And I figured they slept together. Sure, Vincent told me that, outside of work, he wasn't fucking anybody else, but come on. My little stripper's sexual boundaries were, at best, puzzling. What was really unnerving was that the two of them acted like boyfriends. Vincent constantly complimented Jerry, and told him how good-looking he was.

Vincent never complimented me.

Anyway, one afternoon, while Vincent was doing a matinee (which meant it was Sunday), Jerry and I went to the beach and smoked some pot. Jerry told me that Vincent and I looked more like brothers than lovers.

Then he rubbed oil on my back, and asked me if I was a swimmer. Then he asked if I'd ever thought about stripping. That was the first flattering remark I'd received in a long time.

A few minutes later we were fucking in a cave. With three guys watching. A small, cramped cave. I guess I'd become a bit of a sex performer myself.

I thought, 'If Vincent ever found out, he'd be upset. He might throw things, hit me, or even try to run me down with his car. He might feel something other than complacency.'

Wouldn't that have been great?

But before I could tell him, in a really creative, clever, stinging, Albee-esque sort of way, something even more awful happened. In fact, the incident was so dangerous, that it reminded me of a haiku.

> Fly bird like a kite
> and take my worries with you
> in the winter's wind.

That's a haiku my brother wrote in high school. My brother! That big dumb jock wrote a haiku! My mother made copies of Rob's poemette, and framed them and gave them as Christmas gifts. All my relatives received one, and they were encouraged to hang it somewhere, or else my mother would have made their lives miserable.

Unfortunately, my father's brothers, being Italians, had already covered their walls with gold-framed mirrors, and – I'm not kidding, I don't have to – velvet landscapes of the surrounding areas, made to look suspiciously like Italy. Even the Golden Gate Bridge, complete with amber lights, had ivy growing up its girders.

The only open wall space in their homes was in their bathrooms. However, the haiku had to be hung right above the toilet, because the rest of the bathroom, including the wall facing the toilet, was surfaced with mirrored glass. This was originally my father's idea, but his brother, my Uncle Carl, followed suit. These were busy men. They liked getting more than one thing done at a time. Dad had a phone right next to his toilet. 'Just like in a five-star hotel!' he liked to say. I think he meant a five-star hotel on a ten-star scale. Anyway, while doing business from that throne, he'd glance at that haiku's reflection. He said it calmed him down, and helped him make that big business push. It was his mantra.

And it became mine. When I was younger I used to escape into bathrooms during the holidays, no matter what relative we were visiting, just to get away from my family. I was so anxious and closeted and bored. I had to be naughty. I'd get stoned, or masturbate about one of my cousins, or both. Sometimes I'd even poo, but all there was to read was that haiku.

When I was older, but still youthful and scared, and getting sucked off by unsuspecting strangers in public urinals, I'd look up and see the ghost of the poem, scribbled across tiles, omnipresent. When I was a big drunk in a bar, years later, I'd lip-sync the poem to whatever stupid disco tune was blaring on the jukebox.

Sometimes, while on stage, feeling provoked by the audience, I've placed myself back in that bathroom, at my dad's, twenty years prior. Sure, I'd actually be telling jokes to an unreceptive crowd, but in my mind I was just taking a shit. Nothing more, nothing less. Those 'flying birds' seemed to protect me, almost relax me with that inherent safety that comes from knowing what you are and where you belong.

And then Vincent and I had this really unsafe experience. And I don't mean just swallowing his come. I mean something bad. It was right before we broke up. We were at his place, and he was telling me about his dad, who he rarely mentioned. His dad's name was Vincent also. So actually my Vincent was Vincent, Jr. His dad hated the name Vincent. And so, when his son was born, he named his offspring after himself. I guess because he hated himself so much. Anything he created had to be bad. Every time Vincent's dad called him by his name, Vincent told me it sounded like he was spitting. Every time.

When he told me this, he was grinning, sadly, like at a joke made at his expense. I kissed his shoulder and told him I loved him. I knew he hated it when I said that. I said it too often, apparently. He said it back the first time, but he hadn't said it since.

Then he rolled over onto his stomach. His big, white, bisexual ass was just staring at me. And I couldn't find any condoms. And I knew we were both negative. Well, he told me he was, which made sense because he was so young, and I was the last time I was tested. Whenever that was. Anyway, I wanted it so bad, and I felt so close to him, and I thought well, it wouldn't be bad if I just barebacked him for a bit. That's a term I recently read in the *New York Times*. 'Barebacking' means fucking without condoms. It's the new craze, apparently. Everyone's doing it in the West Village. Leave it to New Yorkers to break all the rules. Gay men are even throwing barebacking parties. It's like the Trival Pursuit of the '90s. I like the masculinity of the term. Barebacking. Sounds almost like we're wild, restless cowboys, doesn't it? And at that moment, I sort of felt like I was taming a bronco, like I was his master. So I just stuck it in. It felt so luxurious. Smooth and rippled, like an expensive fabric. And the temperature. That was odd! So hot. Humid. Finally, he was actually mine. He belonged to me. I felt like I'd won! He held on so I had to come inside of him.

I know. 'I had to come inside of him'? My therapist didn't buy that one either.

Jesus, I felt awful afterwards. And I don't mean the good kind of awful. Like the awful I felt after I fucked Jerry. Nope. This was a bad awful. And it wasn't because I fucked him without protection. I've fucked guys that way before. I'm easily swayed in that department. It was because I felt that by not being safe we were diluting our relationship. We had made it all seem so trashy, which would've turned me on if Vincent were a stranger, but I loved him.

I felt so empty and guilty, so of course I did it two more times that night.

Vincent didn't seem bothered. I was practically crying by the third time, but he told me not to worry. When did I get so smug? How often does a person get the chance to fall in love?

I went into Vincent's bathroom and sat on the toilet. I repeated my mantra, over and over.

Fly bird like a kite
and take my worries with you
in the winter's wind.

It didn't work. I still felt like everything was slipping away. I reached for the phone to call my therapist, but there was no phone near the toilet. Then I remembered I wasn't at my dad's house. I wanted out. I wanted to crawl out of the bathroom window, or out of my skin. Like this radio show I heard when I was a kid, where these people turned their own bodies inside out, and pop! They were just a ball of organs. I washed off my dick. I didn't want to be recognized, or responsible, for anything I had done. I wanted to sleep, there, on the carpeted bathroom floor, then wake up, and find Vincent in his bed, different. Innocent. Apologetic. I just wanted everything about the cheapness of us to go away. I felt like everything I was doing I'd regret really soon.

I wasn't really worried about my health. You don't get AIDS from being a barebacking top. But even if I did, my family would've supported me, in their own special way. Like I said, they live around here. In fact, we're surrounded. And the minute I started barfing up blood, they'd have been all over me, 'helping'. They'd have swarmed around my hospital room, hitting on my nurses and haggling treatment prices with my doctors. Everyone except Virginia. She would have stayed home. Illness confuses her. Especially deadly diseases. After all, what does one wear to an AIDS ward?

A while later, Vincent told me about his IV drug-using days in Dallas, and how he watched his best friend die of a cocaine overdose. Then we were both so turned on we barebacked again. That's when I dumped him. At that point I was falling more and more in love with him. The thought of him watching me die turned me on so much that it made death seem appealing. Him, cradling me in his arms, telling me for the second, and last, time how much he loved me. Suicide is another thing into which I'm easily swayed. And at the time that worried me, because I was still at a point in my career where I thought I might amount to something. That was before I became a prostitute myself, before I had speed delivered to my home daily, before I met you. I still had goals. I still had a workout program. I still had a plan for my hair. I just had too much to sacrifice, so I sacrificed him instead.

I wonder what Tiffany on *Melrose Place* would have done?

She probably would've kicked her nasty hooker boyfriend out of her condo, and gotten tested. Then at the end of the episode, she would've appeared as herself, in 'real life', perhaps posing casually in a director's chair, with non-operating cameras and lights all around her. She'd have just been Tiff, the person, not the actress; after work, on the set, making a public service announcement to the kids. 'Use condoms, kids. Every time. They're awesome!'

Tiff wouldn't have been very proud of my behavior. With Vincent, or with you. I even fucked you today, without a condom. But, come on, I've been avoiding caffeine and red meat, so I think I'm probably okay. Ah shit, even if I did test positive, I know I wouldn't change my sexual habits. So why bother?

CHAPTER EIGHTEEN

If there is fruit, baste it

Vincent lives with some bitch now. I think her name is Cyntra, or Jocelyn. Some vacuous name. I can't remember. I always thought it would kill me if he started seeing a woman, but when I saw him with her, holding hands, I wasn't so bothered. She looked like a young guy. Actually, I thought maybe she was a dyke, but I still talked to her. She seemed okay.

Then, when I ran into Jerry a couple of weeks ago, he told me that Vincent and this bitch live together, but she's frustrated because he won't really commit. He's still stripping, three or four years later. That's pathetic, isn't it? Maybe I should send her the haiku.

In fact, I was thinking about her when I wrote the ad for the escort section of our local gay newspaper. Fucking cunt. She probably has her own ad in there somewhere. She probably offers her services to unsuspecting gay and bi men who need some kind of comfort, and then she pounces, convincing them being hetero is more natural. Maybe she's a special agent for the Mormons or the Baptists, out to convert healthy faggots into fucked up straight guys. Like we need more of those. I fucking hate that bitch, and if I see her on the street again I'll run her down with my car. Or maybe I could buy Shawna's husband Rick a case of beer, so he'll back up over her. We'll see how sexy Vincent's whore is when she's got tire marks all over *her* pajamas.

Those escort ads are wild. Let me see if I can find one or two really raunchy ones in all this newspaper. But first, I need another drink. Actually, why stop with the booze? I'm going for a speedball. I mean, fuck it! I'm not driving. Like that would matter. Getting fucked up is something I usually do alone. I feel like there's a documentary being made about me. You're sort of like the eyes of the world, watching my every move.

I bet you've put an ad in a paper before. You're just the type. How would you describe yourself these days, I wonder? Headstrong? Dreamy-eyed? Easy to store? Well, you'd have to do a lot better than that to compete with these escorts.

See, customers require beefcake. 'Prime Choice Beef!' is the headline of one ad. Many of these hookers describe themselves as jocks and bisexual. Like that would make a difference if all the client really needed was someone to accompany him to the opera. Since when do you need a date with an '8-inch uncut piece of man meat' to watch Wagner? Not that it wouldn't help. At least, then, you'd have something fun to play with during the Valkyries.

How about this one: 'Hot Married Guy looking to satisfy your Juicy Boy Butt. Just $80 will get this hot meat up your ass.' Anyone who reads these ads must see that they are clearly about sex. How could law enforcement overlook this stuff? I don't see anything in print about these guys keeping their shoes on. Perhaps it's assumed.

Here's another: 'I'm Jocko. Football fanatic and very discreet. Fuck me, suck me, rim me. Penalize me for my dirty mind.'

That leaves little to the imagination. But why should gay hookers bother being creative? They're selling the same old plot line: the more straight-acting and butch a male prostitute appears to be, the more exciting it is for the customer to get the stud into bed. No ugly old queen wants to think he's wasting his hard-earned cash on some desperate nelly faggot he might pick up at any bar in the Castro with the promise of just a few drinks and breakfast. These 'escorts' have to be special. Coerced. Lured. Yet not at all desperate.

But when I had to advertise myself, I was lost. I wasn't about to use a photo of myself, like some of these guys do. The only quality photos I have of myself are my comedy promo shots, and trust me, those 8x10s are not attractive. Here's one. Look at me here. I'm wearing a fedora, for God's sake. Christ, the '80s were ugly. What kind of guy would pay for sex with me if I looked like this? Maybe a Humphrey Bogart fan. Maybe Lauren Bacall. Assuming that she sleeps with men. Either way, I wasn't gonna use a photo.

And anyway I didn't want to make a big investment into an ad unless I was convinced this line of part-time work was for me. I wasn't even sure I'd make a dime. So I just wanted a few choice words, short and sweet, that would describe me in the best possible way.

But the only words I could think of that were ever used to describe me were 'skinny' and then later, 'skinny and flabby'. And believe me, skinny plus flabby equals loser. It's so sad when everything sinks. I've never had pecs, and now, at the age of thirty-nine, my waist is wider than my chest. Sometimes, when I wake up, I look in the mirror, and I think, Does my butt look good in these slippers? Now, you might say I look fine, and you'd be sweet to say so. And it's true, the extra weight I've added on has sort of made me look more swarthy, and I've sort of 'filled out'. But, comparatively, I'm still just a weakling, a nerd, and that's all I'll ever be. Let's face it: once a geek, always a geek.

Actually, a lot of people tell me I look like other actors. They never recognize me as me. I'm a nobody, remember? Some perfect little Asian kid in a queer bar told me I looked like Kevin Bacon. That is not a compliment to me. I know some people think he's cute, but to me Kevin Bacon looks like he's had his nose pulled off his face from behind. Like he ran face first into a brick wall and all his features got pushed up into his forehead. Scary. But this little perfect, skinny, pale Asian kid, who looked twelve, was telling me at the Stud once that I looked like him. Isn't Kevin Bacon like fifty by now? I think that, to Asians, all white people must just look like shriveled-up prunes. Asians never age. They sprout a wrinkle at fifteen, then they top out until they're eighty-five.

Anyway, this Asian kid was wearing all black. He looked like a model and some other boy I was after was all over him. Then he says, 'You look like someone.'

'Yeah,' I said, letting my self-deprecating guard down. 'I'm an actor.'

'Are you Kevin Bacon?'

He actually thought for a moment I was. Everyone laughed. I told him no, I wasn't Kevin Bacon.

He said, 'Well, you two have the same nose. You look just like him.'

And I took my last gulp of my umpteenth drink and said, 'Well, you look like one-fifth of the world's population.'

I went home alone that night.

And that was all I could think about when I was writing my escort ad. That I looked like some tired actor who couldn't carry a feature film on his own name. Was that ever a selling point for anything? Is looking like Kevin Bacon a cock block, or a money magnet? I wasn't sure, so I had to get some help from Gregg.

He's the only person who knows 'Cameron's' true identity. 'Cameron' is my hooker name. Gregg chose it. He thought 'Cameron' sounded hot. I wanted to call myself 'Evan' because I've never met someone named Evan who wasn't cute. But like Gregg says, 'Cute doesn't sell. Hot sells, and Cameron sounds hot.'

I haven't told anyone else that I'm hooking. Jacques would probably ask for a discount, and Mark would just shrug and shake his head, all disappointed, like a nun. But the one I worry most about is Trish. She'd freak. She works in social welfare, and she spends her day getting disenfranchised women out of trouble. The last person she wants to share a Caesar salad with is another sad hooker. Of course I couldn't tell my family. My mother has always had such high hopes for me. As far as she's concerned, being a comic is bad enough.

She hoped I'd be teaching English to college students. As a kid, I considered being a teacher, and my mother has never let that little dream die. Maybe because neither have I. I still have an application to the UC Berkeley master's program in English stuffed under my mattress. Every time I have a bad comedy set, I alter the dates and think about mailing it. Mom's right. I should be teaching at some brick and cobblestone college, surrounded by ivy and youth, wearing tweed blazers, seducing nineteen-year-olds. Oh well. One out of four ain't too bad.

'The ad shouldn't say too much, or too little. You gotta leave them wanting more, unlike your act.' Gregg spoke with the knowledge of a sage. He used to date a hooker, too. He had to stop. 'Got too weird,' he explained once. 'Every time he blew me, all I could think about was all the money I was saving.'

'Gregg,' I told him, while we were at my computer, 'I'm too old for this prostitution stuff. No one wants to fuck a thirty-nine-year-old.'

'Well, we'll lie about your age. Everyone does. Some of those guys are twenty years older than their ad states.'

'That's crazy.'

'Believe me Tom, nobody will care. Dez' – that's Gregg's ex – 'told me that his clients would shoot their wad about three minutes after he passed through their front door. These guys just want to get off. They barely know you're there.'

'That's reassuring.'

'Trust me, it's the easiest hundred you'll ever make.'

I suggested that maybe we tell people I look like a mildly famous actor.

'Like who?' Gregg asked, suspiciously.

'Well, some people say I look like Kevin Bacon.'

'That tired troll? Are you serious? We don't want to scare customers away.'

'Gregg, some people like his looks.'

'Yeah, his "wife", maybe. She's one ugly nobody too.'

'Jeez, I think they're both kind of cute.'

'No you don't, or you wouldn't have said "jeez". I know when you're lying. You start talking like a child. Just forget about the Bacon bit. As far as we're concerned, you're unique. After all, youth isn't on your side, so we have to cater to a more discriminating crowd.'

We decided to claim that I was a jock. Thirty-three-year-old jocks are sort of sexy in a cerebral way. And I do go to the gym. I don't work out. Working out is so last decade. Mostly I just hang out with the pregnant women and ex-dancers, we make fun of people, then I do my half-hour of voluntary work in the showers.

Actually, somewhere in there I do lift a few weights every couple of weeks, usually to impress people who look right through me. So I have muscles I'll never use, unless I'm lying on my back and I have to push something really heavy off of me.

'And you know what,' Gregg said sipping vodka, 'that might happen.'

Gregg told me a story about Dez getting trapped one night under a very fat man. He was beneath his client, being kissed by him, and the old guy had a heart attack and died. Quietly. Dez didn't even know the guy was dead for a moment. He thought he was just resting. But after a few minutes, he realized something was wrong. And when he tried to unpry his mouth from the sexagenarian's, he realized that the old man had somehow locked his lips and teeth around Dez's lips. Dez panicked and, with the kind of blind strength mothers invoke when lifting cars off their babies, he pushed all 240 pounds off his skinny frame. Unfortunately, the corpse took both pairs of lips with it. When the paramedics showed up, they found a hysterical lipless hooker banging on the chest of a cadaver with a mouthful of mouth. The lips couldn't be salvaged. The next softest skin? You guessed it. Testicular flesh had to be grafted on to Dez's orifice.

'He has to shave his lips as often as he shaves his face,' Gregg paused. 'Serves the motherfucker right for dumping me.'

'Are you trying to make me feel better or worse about this ad?'

'I'm just telling you, try to stay in shape. Well, as "in shape" as you can be. You never know when you might have to escape a sticky situation.'

The ad read something like this:

CAMERON THE HOT STUD
6'2", 195 pounds, athletic, handsome.
33. Into light S and M.
Out calls only: (415) 665–8821.

'Gregg, what the hell is "light S and M"? It sounds like a diet salad dressing.'

'Oh. Well, "S and M" is short for "Sadism and Masochism". "Light S and M" means you like to get slightly punished. Maybe spanked. And pinched a little.'

'But I don't like to get spanked.'

'Tom, if you're not willing to make some compromises, these relationships are never going to work!'

I didn't want to lie about my measurements, in spite of Gregg's advice. He suggested that, for the purposes of the ad, I shrank an inch and gained 10 pounds.

'You'll probably be in the dark. Who's to know?'

I just didn't want the client to be disappointed when he opened the door. I'd seen that look on too many people's faces lately.

CHAPTER NINETEEN

Now look at what you've done!

The ad ran for one week. It came out on a Thursday, and at 8.30 a.m. on the morning of Thursday, 12 January, I got my first call.

'Hello?'

'Hey, Cameron, you sound sleepy. Did I wake you?'

'You've got the wrong number, asshole.'

Two hours later, while brushing my teeth, I wondered if that wake-up call was real or a dream.

Luckily I answered the phone on the last ring, so my answering machine picked up the same time I did and recorded the exchange.

When the next call came through, I was awake and ready.

'Hello?'

'Honey, why is your voice so deep? Are you ill?'

'No, Mom, I'm just waking up.' I'd adopted a rather butch voice to impress my prospective clients. As I've said, femmy, slightly middle-aged queens are not cash cows in the hooker department. Not that I'm femmy. My voice is just a bit, I don't know, theatrical. But that day, I deepened my register. I sounded like a drag queen playing Tallulah Bankhead, which is in fact redundant. Lots of scooped vowels and diphthongs. It was the best I could do.

'I just called to tell you that I saw *Your Right Hand* last night.'

Like I said, my mother is the type of person who can never get the name of anything correct. And I don't just mean that every so often the title of a song slips her memory. I mean every title of every artistic project, of every film, book and musical arrangement, has been revised by a faulty synapse in her brain. Artists' names have somehow slipped through the cracks as well.

Mark, my ex, finds it charming. But he didn't have to grow up with it.

Here is a typical telephone conversation with my mother.

'Honey, it's Mom. Listen, Mark's in Hawaii, so I had to call you. What's that movie?'

'What movie, Mother?'

'You know. That movie with that woman.'

'What woman, Mom?'

'That woman. Oh, you love her. Your people really love her. She sings. She's a singer. She sings lots of songs.' As always, Mom is swimming through details, like an aquarium fish, in her own little world of lights and bubbles. 'Well, she sang songs. I think she's dead. She sang that song, what was it?' My mother starts to sing with what is actually an impressive meso-soprano range, '*Somewhere, over the people, they need rainbows too, la, la, la ...*'

'Mom, do you mean Judy Garland?'

'Yes! Gosh, that took you a while. You're getting rusty. Anyway, what's the film Julie Garland was in? You remember. We watched it together.'

'*Meet Me in St Louis*?'

'No.'

'*The Harvey Girls*?'

'Nope.'

'*A Star Is Born*?'

'Try again.'

'Mother, you have to give me more information.'

'Oh, all right. Let's see. In the movie she plays a waitress, who saves a choking boy by giving him CPR. It's called *A Child Is Choking*, or *There's A Child Choking and Waiting*, or *There's A Child Choking in the Waiting Room*, or *Someone Help That Choking Child Before He—*'

'Mom, it's called *A Child Is Waiting*. And, yes, it's with Judy Garland, but she's not a waitress. She plays a child psychologist who helps emotionally handicapped children. Christ!'

'Oh, I'm sorry if I frustrate you.' Oh, here it comes. 'I'm just your mother after all.' Oops. I know I've blown it when she reminds me which of us is the parent. 'Maybe I just shouldn't call you. I'll save all my queries for Mark. Why should you want to talk to me?' Oh no, I can almost hear her dusting off the college guilt. 'I know I didn't go to college. Heck . . .' Tears. Hers of course. 'I didn't even get through high school. So, I can see why I embarrass you. I'll let you go. Fly off. Fly away with your famous friends. Go to your east/west coast parties with all your boys in your limos and fancy dress. Fly away from your home, from the people who care for you. Who am I after all? I just created you. You're part and parcel of my soul. WITHOUT MY WOMB, YOU'RE NOTHING! But just remember this one thing, mister. There's no pain like the pain in a mother's heart. And I hope you die in a fiery car crash!'

Click.

Why do I do it? Why can't I just be sweet and kind and help the old woman across the proverbial street every time she calls for yet another title of another movie of which she barely remembers the plot? I think it's because I find her lack of memory alarming. When I was young I trusted my mom. I believed everything she ever told me. She seemed smart. She read a lot. What she retained from all those books is now questionable. Yet, as a child, I was sure she was the most knowledgeable person in the room. I didn't mind she never graduated from high school. I found it admirable, in fact. Without that diploma, she still managed to raise kids on her own.

But now I worry about all the stories she told me as I grew up. I want to believe those family anecdotes. They are part of my past, too. But who knows what was true, and what was a dream she'd had after too much meatloaf. I don't think she ever maliciously lied to me. Maybe, when I was a kid, she just didn't want to bore me. Maybe she's right: my talent for storytelling does come from her side of the family. Drunks can sure whip up a good yarn, and though Mom never drank as much as the rest of them, she might have still picked up the knack of wowing an audience with a fable or two. Or three.

Maybe Mom didn't try to commit suicide when she was eight. Maybe a little girl next door to my mom did, but my mother got confused. Maybe she dreamed the story where my dad's condom broke. Maybe I was actually born because she wanted a third child. What if all those family photos were just inserts that came with the frames? Maybe I'm not the result of several broken homes and an incalculable number of alcoholics? Maybe I'm a prince! Maybe I am Prince. Maybe I'm an artiste formerly known as Prince Philip.

At that moment, however, I was just a hooker. A frustrated hooker, who was trying to remember the lead actor's name from *My Left Foot*.

'Honey, you know that guy. Didn't he win the Academy Award?'

'Mom, I don't know his name.'

'He has three names. Like Eva Marie Saint. Only he's a guy.'

And worse than a frustrated hooker, I was a lazy, frustrated hooker. For days after my initial forced enthusiasm, desperate gay rag readers left messages on 'Cameron's' machine but I couldn't be bothered to return the calls. Between therapy, auditions for pathetic acting jobs I'd never get, and searching for the cocktail that would've made my whole life seem like a *Fantasy Island* episode, there was just no time to blow out-of-town adulterers.

Then, one day, while at home watching the dirt on my floors accumulate, someone called and asked for Cameron.

'Yeah, this is Cameron.'

'Hey Cameron, this is Tam. How are you?'

God, if he only knew.

'I'm cool, dude. Kind of horny, actually. And you?'

'Oh, I real good. Real real horny also.'

I detected an accent.

'Where you from, dude?'

'Oh, I from Hong Kong. And I read your very hot ad in paper. I want hot man to dominate me . . . everywhere. I need it. Now.'

We planned to meet in his apartment, which was about thirty minutes from me.

'I'll see you in about a half hour, Tam.'

'Okay Cameron, you hot, butch, stud man.'

Curtain up, light the lights.

I actually got to Tam's apartment in fifteen minutes. I drove fast, eager to get this experience behind me. When I rang on his building's door, he seemed a bit panicky.

'Oh, howdy,' he bellowed out of his intercom, 'you here so quickly.'

'Yeah,' I said, bending over to speak into the little square screen, 'there was no traffic.'

'Well, okay. Listen, you come in when I buzz door. Go to elevator,' he was panting, like he'd been running a race, 'and press "1". I pick you up on first floor.'

'Cool.'

I waited in the lobby of the first floor for about five minutes, but for once I wasn't impatient with someone's tardiness. After all, the time clock started the minute I entered the building.

When he appeared, Tam's ensemble comforted me. To me, hospital pants and rubber sandals just scream subordination. I thought, I'll have this guy on his knees and out of my life in about two minutes. He looked older than he sounded – about fifty – but he wasn't in bad shape. Big arms, and white teeth.

'Well, so here you are. Come. I live down hall.'

He walked backwards as I followed. I felt lured. The building was prefab, from the '70s. I was relieved. Even I looked good against these ugly orange walls and that thin brown carpeting.

I had dressed up for this meeting. Grey trousers and a new black sweater. It was an outfit I'd stolen from a commercial shoot. Silly, though, since he was paying to see me naked, not clothed. It all still seemed a bit unreal. As I walked into his living room, passing what seemed like walls and walls of mirrors, I couldn't imagine that in hardly any time he'd be handing me a hundred dollars.

'I never do this before. I'm a bit nervous,' Tam smiled, and offered me a coke.

'No, I'm cool. Look, just come over here, Tam, and relax. Let me do all the work.'

I took off my top. My loose trousers slid off without effort, and suddenly I stood in front of him, all skin.

'Oh, you big American. You so big. You so tall.' He walked up and examined me closely. 'You look more or less what you say on phone.'

'Well, I hope you're not disappointed.'

'Oh, no, you not bad to look at.'

I wrapped my arm around his head and pulled him near me. I shoved my tongue down his throat, and bit his lip. He moaned.

'You like that, don't you?' I growled. 'Yeah, you'll take what I got, won't you.'

Not bad dialogue, I thought. Thank God I'd been to Vincent's show and rehearsed different porn scenes with him. The situation called for some sort of motivational speaking. I was, after all, the supposed sex expert. I felt the need to take control.

'Suck my nipple, bitch. And bite it.' I slapped his head. 'Bite it hard!'

Tam moaned his appreciation.

'Come on Tam, you can suck that cock better than that. Lick my hole. LICK IT!'

Everywhere I looked, I saw myself. He'd covered his walls with floor-to-ceiling mirrors. It was like being in my dad's bathroom, only this time I was actually fucking. This wasn't a fantasy about me and my cousin. Me and Tam were actually doing this. No pretense. No mantra was required. I didn't care if the 'birds flew like kites' or whatever my brother's meaningless piece of shit haiku whined about. I had no worries. I was the winter's wind, pushing my expensive cock into the mouth of this hungry, gaping shadow. Perhaps that's why I took on that Stanley Kowalski-turned-escort character. I had an audience. Tam. And me. I was watching my performance. My reflection made me work harder. I wanted to impress somebody.

And I guess I did, because the reviews were good.

'Oh, you so hot, Cameron. You make a me so horny.'

I sat in a chair, with a towel under me and my feet pushed up around my head, as Tam ate away at my ass. As I watched us over the back of Tam's head, I wondered when my father had walked into the room. And sat in this chair I'd been sitting in. And when did Tam start licking my father's ass? I thought, I can't be staring at me. Look at those hard wrinkles around the eyes. And that gray hair above the ears. And that expanding waist line.

Someone slapped Tam's back. 'Suck harder, bitch.'

This guy was incredible! He looked a bit like me, but he was much more demanding than I'd ever been. Maybe it was my uncle, Carl. Cops like getting physical, and they love watching themselves. Well, whoever it was, his potency made me fucking hard.

I really liked this.

'You yummy,' Tam whispered, as he came up for air. 'I want more.'

So I pushed him back down on my dick. And as I pulled on his ears, punching my cock farther down his throat, I felt something that I thought was a hearing aid behind Tam's right ear. When I looked down, I saw red stitches, sort of Frankenstein-like, running from his lobe, up the back of the ear, to the top of his right sideburn. I then saw the same alarming criss-cross stitches behind the left ear.

'Fucking hell,' I thought, 'He must have had his ears pinned back.'

Then, as Tam gagged, paused, took a deep breath, and then continued, I saw a thin red line running from one ear, around the back of his head, and connecting at the other. From where I sat, with my bird's eye view of his cranium, it looked as though someone had sown something on to Tam's head. I let go of the ears immediately. What if I pulled too hard, and they came off? I'd have had to give him a discount. Or what if one slid off, unnoticed? That wasn't the kind of gratuity I was looking for. The last thing I wanted to find in my underwear later was Tam's organ.

Suddenly the whole scenario took on a gruesome quality. Who was this guy? Maybe he was an enemy, in disguise. Maybe he had a mask sown on to his face. A 'Tam' mask. What if he was my high school gym teacher, Mr Castanova? Eighteen years ago, Castanova swore he'd get even with me for telling another student, Jim Hope, that 'only faggots join the swim team'. A week later Jim jumped from the Golden Gate Bridge. When he hit the water, after plunging for seven seconds, he was still breathing, because they found water in his lungs when they found his body, three days later.

In his suicide note, stuck to his parents' refrigerator with a magnet the shape of a dolphin, Jim outed himself, and then quoted me. 'The whole world knows,' he scribbled. 'Even Tom Basiglieri, who told me that only faggots blah blah blah . . .'

The school grieved, and I think I tried to act miserable, but I was actually annoyed by the word 'Even'. 'Even Tom Basiglieri . . .'

Was I that far out of the loop? I was irritated that this psycho took time out of his busy schedule of self-sacrifice to point out that not only was I uncool but I was the MOST uncool! I was the Pat Boone of Drake High.

Anyway Castanova felt that losing Jim, the best water polo player that Drake ever produced, was the reason his team lost the water polo championships the following month.

'You'll pay, Basiglieri!' the coach yelled out at me from his Camaro. 'I'll come down hard on you one day.'

Perhaps this was the day.

What if Tam lifted up his head, reached behind his scalp, and pulled his Asian face off?

'You thought I was a Chinese queer, but I'm actually your old gym coach, here to . . .'

Hold on. Why would my gym coach suck my dick? He'd never take the charade that far. And, I reminded myself, if Mr Castanova did suck my dick, I'd totally dig it.

No. The truth unfortunately was that Tam was just a desperate Hong Kong queen enjoying the cock of a blue-eyed devil.

You know, if I'm watching a good movie, an hour can just fly by. But when I'm having sex with someone unappealing, sixty minutes can seem like a lifetime. The slurping and sucking went on and on, until finally, after what seemed like enough time to balance my checkbook *and* rotate my tires, Tam shot his wad all over a mustard-colored towel we'd been lying on.

He laid back and lit up a cigarette, while I excused myself to the bathroom. On the counter, near the sink, I saw a pile of thin, white latex gloves, and boxes of stainless steel implements. It looked like the prop table for an episode of *ER*. I wondered, Are they surgical tools? Oh my God, I realized, this guy has been giving himself a facelift. He'd been doing plastic surgery on his face in the privacy of his own home. No wonder he was rushing around when I rang his bell. He was probably tying off the last knot behind his ears. The TV was pulled in a strangely intimate position near the sofa. Perhaps he was following instructions on some scary video from Beverly Hills, bootlegged from some sleazy plastic surgeon out to make a quick buck off pathetic, unsuspecting homos. You read about that kind of stuff all the time!

I rinsed my mouth and washed my hands. I had to get out of there.

When I stumbled back into his living room, Tam was looking at a picture on the mantle of his fake white fireplace.

'This my son.' I looked as I pulled on my shoes. 'He younger than you.'

'He's cute. Is that Hong Kong?'

'Oh, no, we on vacation there. In Singapore.'

'Does he visit you here in San Francisco?'

'Oh no, this country too crazy. No kids his age with any morals or values.' He reached in his pocket. 'Here your money. Count it.'

'I'm sure it's all there.'

'Count. I no want no trouble.'

I counted five twenty-dollar bills.

'Well, Tam, thanks. It was fun.'

'Yeah, fun as the day is long! Bye Bye.'

When I got home, I changed the message on my machine:

'Hi, leave a message, and Tom will return your call. By the way, Cameron can no longer be reached at this number. So long.'

Gregg was disappointed. 'After all our work,' he sighed, 'then you panic and drop the ball.'

'Gregg, I just can't do it. It was too sad and scary.'

'Scary? You know your trouble. Not only are you a hooker, but you're a lazy and neurotic hooker as well.'

Never have truer words been spoken.

PART THREE

The Subtle Art of Carving

There will be lots of smiling faces, as the bird is now ready to be carved.

But first let's admire its beauty. Hopefully the skin has not been stuffed too tightly, so it has not burst. Even with the filling, you have 'made like' a taxidermist, so the bird still resembles its former self, before slaughtering. Now we can enjoy the chicken, in its glory and its best!

After removing from the oven, let the chicken rest to make it easier for slicing

Jesus, I'm exhausted. Have I eaten?

Oh, that's right, I've only got junk in here. And a frozen sausage pizza. I'm throwing that away. I can't eat meat anymore. I'm sort of a vegetarian now. I only eat fish. And chicken. Sometimes. I'm thinking of giving up chicken too. Have you read about the way they eat each other's poo? Or the way they store hundreds of chickens in one little cage before they kill them? It's disgusting.

Maybe I'll just fast! I'll only take in fluids. Too bad I'm running low on vodka. Maybe I should just stick to supplements. Oh, but here are those pills I've been looking for. Dexadrine, with a drop of Stolichnaya. That's the ticket.

I bought these diet tablets a few months ago. I wanted to lose this flab around my waist line. I guess putting on a bit of weight so late in life has taken its toll, because, one night, I was hitting on some little faggot in some bar, and he said to me, 'Should you be wearing that T-shirt?'

I wasn't sure what he meant. I thought I'd broken some dress code or something. Or maybe there was blood on my shirt again, from having shaved around my nipples. Guys appreciate that. No one wants hair in their teeth.

But when I looked down to check my shirt out, I didn't see

a stain. And other people were wearing T-shirts, so I asked him, 'What do you mean?'

'Well, it's a bit weird around the belly, don't you think?'

I guess he was diplomatically letting me know he wasn't interested in someone with a gut. Instead, he hurt me even more. If he'd said, 'Listen, cunt, you're not my type so fuck off,' I could've handled that. But to poke fun at my belly. Well, that's just not right.

So I peed on him. He didn't even notice at first. We were standing near sliding glass doors and there was a light drizzle that evening. When he saw what I was doing, he called for security. Pussy.

As I was being yanked out of the place, I think I yelled out, 'What's good enough for cousin Pat is good enough for you, you little piece of shit!'

I don't think I'll be welcome again in that bar. Wish I could remember which bar it was.

Anyway, the tablets helped. I dropped a couple of pounds, but really, the only way to lose weight is the old tried and true way. The three-finger exercise program. Fuck pills, I needed an eating disorder. Barfing is the best, and the funnest, way to lose flab. I mean, look at teenage girls in the suburbs. Rich, white teenage bitches look fabulous. They can wear anything! They are so fucking skinny, and why? Because they barf up everything they put down their mouths. And I mean, everything. Breakfast, lunch, snacks, semen. It all goes. They just close their eyes, pull back their hair, and bam! The calories fly right down the toilet.

I got into it, too. It was fun not eating all day. The buzz was like a drug. I only ate at night, in the dark, like a good little bulimic. And after I ate, it felt so good to barf it up and start all over again the next day. I felt like I was keeping up with the kids. I mean, at first I didn't want to get as skinny as those teenage girls. I'd been skinny, and I hadn't felt confident. But once you start, you just cannot stop. The challenge took over, and I wondered if I could get skinnier than the chick who sells men's underwear at Macy's? You can see her hip bones through her trousers. Now that's making a statement. I thought, I'll never be muscly, so why not go the other way?

I started eating popsicles, made of water and food coloring. I drank chocolate shakes, made with chocolate Maalox. What I didn't barf, I shat. But, after a few weeks of feeling great, I passed out backstage at the Improv. When I woke up, they had an IV in my arm. They were feeding me through a tube, without my fucking consent! I almost sued them. But then, once I started eating, I couldn't stop, and by the time I checked out of the hospital, I'd gained most of the weight back. And my parole officer made me promise I wouldn't diet again.

I swear to Christ, once you break the law, you really lose all your freedom as an individual.

I'm pooped. My eyes could actually use some rest too. And a lift. Just a tuck around the edges. Some of the comics I see on stage are half my age. They're embryos with a couple of punchlines. It's daunting. A lot of headliners I know give the new comics a hard time. They say these upstarts are only thinking about getting on TV, they don't appreciate hard work, they never really learn the craft of stand-up. It's all bullshit. The truth is that the older guys are jealous. For fuck's sake, a lot of us wrote our best jokes years ago, when we were young, and we're still doing them. Nope. All these angry peers of mine are just afraid of turning into Carol Channing.

Taylor, are you old enough to know who Carol Channing is? She's kind of a show business icon. She's been a Broadway star for eons, mostly playing only one character. She was and still is the star of *Hello Dolly*. You're way too young to know about this, unless you're a huge musical theatre queen, like Mark is.

You're probably not. And why should you be? Broadway is no fun anymore. Straight people go there. With their kids. The mayor of New York – that harelip, what's-his-name, the Wop – has turned New York into Disneyland. All the trashiness and whorishness is gone. Why go? Especially to Broadway, which used to be so seedy and flashy and everything new started there. That's why fags loved it. Fags love pop culture. Fags create pop culture, only now it's all done out of LA. New York is too docile. And expensive.

But when New York was nasty, Carol Channing was big. That was in the '60s. And she's still dragging her tired old ass in a sequin gown across the boards, singing that same old shitty score, and that's what all the comics I know never want to become. Can you see me in forty years?

'So I had my dick in her mouth . . .'

Nobody wants to see that. I don't. And I especially don't want to watch Carol sing 'Before the Parade Passes By' for the billionth time. But a lot of people do. Especially the Japanese. They love Carol. They are so camp, the Japanese. And so gullible. They'll spend big money to see anything truly American.

Carol is doing *Hello Dolly* in Tokyo right now. 'Well, hello fellas, this is Dolly, fellas . . . Oh, sorry front row, can I have my teeth back? Thank you so much. And can you hand me my eyeglasses? And while you're at it, can you hand me my eye. Oh, and don't mind my farts, that happens sometimes . . . This is Dolly, fellas . . .'

What do the Japanese actually think they're watching? *Jurassic Park: The Musical*?

'Oh,' the Japs must say, when they leave the theatre, 'we ruv Steven Spielberg. He genius! He make dinosaur sing! How he do that, we never know.'

You know, I know from an actor friend of mine that she's

incontinent. Carol, I mean. This guy, he played one of the supporting cast members during that dreadful run in New York a couple of years ago, and he told me that she has to wear a diaper while on stage. Maybe he was putting me on, but I thought, well sometimes, because she's so old and forgetful, she probably neglects to wear her diaper, and since she's on stage for two hours, she must have to go at some point, and well, that's what scenery is for, I guess. She probably has to run behind a flat, lift her skirts and poo and piss all over the stage!

Then she doubtless yells, 'Sawdust, please', and some poor Equity member has to come out and sprinkle sawdust all over the floor so that no one does the splits unintentionally.

'Well, hello, fellas, this is Dolly, fellas . . . Phewww . . . Oops, sorry front row, I don't remember eating cream corn . . .'

Isn't showbiz glamorous?

I'm one parade away from calling for the sawdust man.

My friends try to fend off that aging process in any way they can. Some of them are going straight to their dermatologist for botulism treatments. Have you heard about this? People are now having botulism shot into their face. Some dermo has come up with this stuff called botox, which freezes the skin and rids you of any wrinkles in that area. The dopey side effect is that you can no longer use that part of your face anymore. So forget expressing excitement. Or joy. Or talent. But if success in this business was measured by talent, I wouldn't be here talking to you right now. I'd be in LA, winning awards and going to my dermo every two months for a botox shot. And everyone would love me. Maybe even you.

But what I'll probably be, much sooner than I like to believe, is some tired old queen sitting in some tired old bar, wearing all black, because it's slimming. I'm moussed and glossed and dyed and scented and flossed and pulled up and lifted back and tortured into a purely submissive type of aging Ken Doll beauty. And there I rule, owning my own stool, while my white poodle naps in my white Mercedes. A frosted martini glass rests in one hand, and a white cigarette holder rests in the other, as my third eye peruses the room.

'That bartender is so gorgeous, if he has a brain there is no God. Fill me up! Whose dick do I have to suck to get an olive around here?! You're young and fresh. What's your name? Ever take a ride in a Mercedes before? What? Fuck off! I'm still big, it's the comedy clubs that got small. Phewww! Sawdust, please! Sorry, that happens sometimes. Now, tilt your head for me, I need your blood.'

Maybe I've thought a bit too much about this, but wouldn't it be better if we aged backward? Everything would be easier if we were born senior citizens. Well, hard on the mothers, to pass an old pile of bones in a jogging suit, but better for the 'baby'. Because, as we aged, we'd get younger. Then, when we're our oldest and our wisest, we're also our best looking. We'd all commute to work on a skateboard, retiring eventually so we could take up surfing. Then, when we were annoying, helpless little screeching infants, we would be dropped by our children down a well. Splash! And that's our memorial service! Great, don't you think? Taylor? Are you asleep? You never age. Well, you won't anymore. Think of how lucky you are! No more worries, no more appearance alterations. No more lying.

CHAPTER TWO

Garnish the heated platter with parsley

I'm gonna need some more sleep soon. Especially if I'm driving later. The six hours I had, whenever that was, wasn't enough. I'm still feeling very lethargic. That handful of Dexedrine has hardly affected me, and now my head hurts. That's it. I'm giving up chicken byproducts too. No more McNuggets. I wonder what I can take to stop the dreaming. Because I had the scariest dreams last night. The first dream was so real. I dreamed that you arrived at my house wearing a dog collar. And in the dream, you told me you wanted to perform S and M sex. You said that you and your boyfriend do it a lot, and then you laid down splayed on my living room floor and explained to me that our code word would be 'yellow'. Whenever I heard that word, I was supposed to stop 'abusing' you.

'So,' I said, 'When you say "Hello", I should untie you?'

'No, Tom, "yellow"! When I say "yellow", then you untie me.'

'Sorry. Yellow. That's awesome!'

Then somehow you held me captive. You were the victim, but I was trapped. I couldn't get free, and I couldn't stop hurting you. Then you were gone. Your spirit floated away, and I thought I could finally rest.

I put my head back down, and I was quiet for a moment.

I thought all the bad times were over, but then you came back to me. You flew at me, and you held a gun to my head for a long time, while other people were in the room, and they were yelling, 'Do it! Just do it!' And you shot me, and I was still alive after I hit the ground. Well, sort of alive, and I saw my forehead where you'd pointed the gun and there was a little round shadow, sort of like a hole in my head might look if I were someone who'd been shot in some old black and white gangster film.

I woke up really frightened, as if I was still asleep. I suppose it was the medication I took to feign my suicide last night. I was barely able to walk, or think clearly. A half bottle of sleeping pills will do that to a dreamer. My pupils still look kind of miniscule. Maybe I'm not Sanpaku after all! Maybe I'm just overdrugged. Is there such a thing? Isn't overdrugged really just 'overdosed'?

Maybe I'm dead. But if I were dead my beard wouldn't be growing.

God, I should shave before we leave. If I get stopped by the police, they'll be totally suspicious. Where did these circles under my eyes come from? I have the face of a terrorist. I know I shouldn't trust my reflection in a toaster, but I thought I was better looking than this.

I wish you could speak, and tell me exactly what happened last night. Actually, maybe it's better I can't hear your voice, because I'm a bit irritable right now, and you're just a bit too grating sometimes. Has anyone ever commented on how high your voice seems to be? I kind of liked that about you when we first met. It made you seem more boyish, and I enjoyed the surprise of being fucked like a truck by a guy with a voice like an opera buff. But it's one of those things about someone that, when things start going wrong, can get really irritating.

And your voice gets higher when you get emotional. High

and squeaky. Not femmy, but girlie. Sort of like a bird. Like a little fragile bird. And all tied up, like last night, in my first dream, whimpering and writhing, you were my little bird in a cage.

I wanted to crawl into that cage. That lamp. That God. I wanted to close the birdcage door, and turn out the light bulb, and just hold you, spoon style.

But when I moved toward you, you wouldn't let me soften the blow. All I wanted was to kiss you, but you screeched, 'What are you doing?'

'You look upset.'

'No, Tom. I'm fine. Keep going for fuck's sake. Don't stop until I say that color identifier!'

That was when you started molting.

Now, Virginia would've held your head under water, but I'm not that cruel. Not even in my dreams, when I could be, if I wanted. Actually, I did hold your head down, so I could continue fucking it, but your sing-song voice was getting on my nerves.

'Just remember, don't come in my mouth.'

Did that mean I was supposed to come in your mouth? Isn't that unsafe? Maybe that's why you liked it.

That wasn't what I wanted from you. I didn't want to hurt anyone. Why wouldn't you let me kiss you? But everytime I tried, you bit my lip, hard. That's why I put that thick plumber's tape over your mouth. Then after I rolled you on to your back, I tightened the ropes, and I spread your legs. I could tell you wanted to say something. The veins in your neck were bulging, and you looked scared. You started thrashing about and, for a bound-up little bird, you looked pretty strong and intimidating. Maybe it was 'yeah' or 'yel-low' or 'help'. Wouldn't have mattered. Birds don't talk. They only chirp.

I fucked you. So it must have been a dream. I fucked you and fucked you and fucked you.

I fucked you so hard and for so long that you bled all over my new floor covering I'd just bought at a Macy's White Flower Day Sale.

Don't worry. It's not your fault.

Now looking back on last night, I can't remember if I was wearing a condom. All that pushing and pulling, it might have slipped off. Oh well, it doesn't matter. We're both white, and I take Vitamin C.

When I finished, I untaped your mouth, and you started yelling, 'Are you fucking nuts?'

I taped your mouth again. You just laid there and glared at me. You tried to remove the restraints, but I made sure you weren't going anywhere. I turned up the music on the stereo. I didn't want the neighbors to hear you. You were hysterical after all.

I untaped.

'I'm not staying here. I'm getting out of here.'

I retaped. I didn't want to let you go. I was afraid you'd kill me.

Had I gone too far?

I untaped.

'When I get out of here, my boyfriend is gonna kick your ass.'

I retaped.

When you tried to get up, I saw what had happened to your back. You tried to stumble to your feet, but of course you collapsed. You laid on your stomach, and by then your shirt was gone, and I saw red welts across your shoulders. And big brown bruises with teeth marks covered the middle part of your back. Did I do those? I didn't know.

You looked exhausted, so I brought you a glass of water

and, when I untaped, you started blathering on and on about calling the police about me.

I retaped.

That's when I was scared. I mean, I'm sort of a public figure. You had the power to get me into trouble. Rape was the last thing I needed the *Tonight Show* people to read about in the paper. And that's what you would've told the cops, isn't it? That I raped you? Isn't that what you would've said? Or that I'd kidnapped you, and held you against your will? You know that isn't true, but what would the fag-hating press have printed?

And what about all those PC women who run the gay press? They can't fucking deal with the fact that 'no' doesn't always mean 'no'.

And what about Trish. She's my best friend, but she is also a feminist, after all. Who would she side with?

And my family? They'd cut me off completely.

That's when I gave you a sedative. Of course I have sedatives around the house. I'm a fucking minor celebrity after all. I just needed time to think, so I turned on the television to soothe you as you passed out, and that's when that story about the cult came on. The one in San Diego. They follow that comet. Well, some other crazy motherfucker just joined them, he killed himself. Maybe it was Jay Sky. Better late than never if you ask me, but that's when I got the idea to make it all look like a suicide pact. Me with my failed career. You with HIV. I'm not sure if you are an HIVIP. You didn't look griddled. But I added it to your suicide note anyway. They won't do a blood test once you're dead. Or will they? I wonder if I can stop them.

Anyway, I dragged your body across my apartment, and laid your head in my gas oven. I turned on the gas, updated one of my old suicide notes, and then I took enough medication to make it look like I was *trying* to kill myself. Of course, I know what dosage would have killed me, and this one wouldn't.

CHAPTER THREE

To carve, start nearest the neck, and slice thinly across the grain

B ut when I woke up six hours later, I smelled something strangely sweet. My first thought was, 'Hmm, sticky buns.'

Of course, that's often my first thought in the morning. But then I remembered there were no buns in the oven. By the time I got to the kitchen, I realized everything had gone horribly wrong. My first dream wasn't a dream. It wasn't even a nightmare. It was worse. It was real. I'd done all those things to you. I'd tortured you, and drugged you, and turned the oven on to 250, so I didn't gas myself. But I forgot to turn out the pilot light. And while I slept your head baked. Really slow. From the shoulders up, you looked like a big casserole. Actually, your brains had ballooned through your skull. You looked more like a soufflé. When I tapped your head with a fork, it rolled over, and that's when I saw all the grill marks on your face.

The tape had slid off, and all sorts of things were coming out of your mouth, and that's when I couldn't remember if you'd said 'yellow'. Maybe the whole thing was a game. Maybe you were still playing when you said that stuff about the police. And then I panicked.

Have you ever taken apart a roasted chicken? You know how the wing just sort of slips off when you tug on it? The smaller bones are so cooked, they just sort of separate? Well, that neck bone of yours was pretty skinny.

And now you're in there. Well, just your beautiful head, I mean. In a greasy paper bag. I can see you through the holes I cut into the bag, and you don't look very happy. Maybe I shouldn't have put you in there, but you were slipping around the counter while I was mixing drinks. I think you would've wanted to be in the bag.

I hope your fingers aren't getting in your way. Those are what are making the crunchy sounds. They're near your throat. I had to slice them off. They weren't cooked, but I removed them anyway. Now you can't be identified. Or can you? That's what I need to know. Do you know? Do you know a good lawyer? Do you know OJ?

And what am I gonna do with you? What would OJ have done? Just leave the scene of the crime. But the scene of the crime is my apartment. That's not a good strategy. Maybe I should roll you down the freeway. But that seems undignified. I could take you to a dump, let the seagulls eat you up. But where is there a dump in San Francisco? Don't we just dump all the trash into the sea? I could throw you into the sea. That seems more ceremonial.

Maybe I should call Oprah. She'll know what to do.

PART FOUR

Afterlife

Don't throw away those bones. That chicken still has more to give. In time, you'll realize that this meal has fed you many more times than you ever thought possible.

So eat up, but don't waste one bit. Because, believe it or not, this feast has just begun!

CHAPTER ONE

Let's stir up some soup

A nd today, doctor, Virginia is tormenting two great-grandchildren. The guest list known as my family just gets longer and longer.

I got another letter from her. She wrote that she and my mom were cleaning out my apartment. The police finally let them go in there. She said in the letter that she was shocked to find dirty magazines under my sink. A decapitated body, no big deal, but pictures of naked men. Now that is just too much!

My mother wanted to get my things. But why? I can't wear anything other than this smock in here, can I, Doc? And the books, and the other junk, why would Mom care about that stuff? Maybe she wanted my birth certificate. For old time's sake.

Virginia probably strolled from room to room, looking for images of herself. She's a ghoul. I'm sure she got a date out of the visit. She probably rubbed up against one of the cops.

See, Ama helped me find the place, when I moved back to San Francisco from LA. Now she's ashamed that I was such a poor tenant, especially since the landlady is a friend of hers.

I wish I could read you the letter she wrote me about going there, but they've got me all tied up. No chance of loosening these, huh? It's okay, Doctor. We've never dated, so you're safe. Still, no? That's all right, I've had it read to me so often, I've memorized it.

She said: 'You were such a clean little boy. You always lined up your little plastic cars all in a row. A very careful, symmetrical row of cars. And you wouldn't let anyone near them once they were in place. They belonged to you, just the way they were, and nobody could even move one without you crying like a banshee. I thought then that you'd grow up to be a very neat man, someone I could trust. Someone I could rely on to be responsible with an apartment. Now I see I was sadly mistaken. And of course you've ruined the chances for your siblings ever renting from Mrs Hauttes. She won't even return my calls of apology. I mean, really, Tom. Newspaper print stains all over the hardwood floors? Those floors might have to be replaced. And all that blood got in between the tiles on the kitchen counter. Your mother is still scrubbing, right now, as I write this, with a toothbrush she dug out of her purse. The police are trying to stop her, but she insists. Since when is your mother cleaner than you?'

Ama visited her father's grave on his birthday. At least, she *claims* that it's her father's grave. God only knows. It's probably some stranger's grave, with a tombstone made of marble that matches Virginia's eyes. Red marble.

Actually, now that the police have given her car back to her, she goes to his grave a lot. I think it's because she likes to drive, but has nowhere to go. I mean, she liked her father, but she loves that car. She takes such good care of it. Watches it like it's her only child. She must have reported it stolen about five minutes after I drove off with it. If she would've just given me a couple of hours, I could've made it to the Golden Gate Bridge, to drop something off. And then on to Nevada.

And then, what? That's what she says. 'And then what, honey? Murder is illegal there too, you dope.'

Most of the letters she sends contains paragraph after paragraph about her family. I think she enjoys having me here, with nothing to do. She knows I'll read them, and that makes writing them all the more interesting. Finally she can tell her version of her life to a captive audience.

And it is fascinating, all the little facts I'm learning about the Pettidoigts. I have Benny, the guard, read them to me, over and over. He does that for me, in exchange for a favor or two. And maybe it's because I've heard them so often, seven, eight, nine times a day, that I've noticed the facts in Ama's letters keep changing. Relations that have been dead for years seem to mutate.

For example, Ama's father has become more courageous, more loving. Her mother has become more God-fearing. Her sister-in-law has become more handicapped – from a limp to practically limbless – and just recently she's visited me here, and she told me that all of her brothers have, at one time or another, hit on her. And she considered that a compliment, since they were all good dancers.

I used to dance pretty well myself, which made me eligible as a suitor for my grandmother. Come closer, Doctor. I'd get up, but these restraints won't let me. I really don't want Benny to hear this.

Problem was, Virginia knew that I enjoyed sucking cock. And that, she didn't like. Couldn't stand the competition I guess.

Why are you fidgeting, Doc?